Preface

When the first practical large-scale computers became available in the 1950s and 1960s, there was a great deal of concern about the social and economic impact that they would have on our way of life. An "automation revolution" was envisioned (and feared) by many to be just around the corner. The prospect of giant computers running whole factories without the aid of humans seemed inevitable to most people. When years passed, and the revolution did not come as quickly as first thought, the vision began to fade. When the revolution did begin, few noticed, as it was led not by "giants" but by "midgets."

Although these "midgets," or microprocessors, have been commonly available since the early 1970s, the full scope of their power and usefulness has only begun to be realized in the industrial and consumer marketplaces. The 6502 family must be counted among the microprocessor families that have been proven to have excellent technical and economic merit. The availability of 6502-based products, such as the AIM 65, Apple, PET 2001, and several single-board computers, makes the 6502 an excellent choice for a wide variety of control applications.

Before the 6502 can be of any use in control applications, it must be properly programmed and interfaced to the system it is to control. Although there are many interface boards available for the 6502 and other microcomputers, there is (and will remain) a strong need for people who know how to effectively interface these computers to "the outside world." It is the purpose of this book to provide the designer with some guidelines that he can use in this task.

Since this is an advanced book, it would be best for the newcomer to refer to *Programming and Interfacing the 6502*, by

Marvin L. De Jong. Additional information on programming can be found in 6502 *Software Design*, by Leo J. Scanlon.

JOHN M. HOLLAND

Acknowledgments

I wish to extend my deepest personal thanks to the many people whose comments have contributed to this book. Most especially, I wish to thank my technical editor, Dr. Christopher A. Titus of The Blacksburg Group, Inc. His long-suffering efforts over my manuscript have provided both the work and myself with many fresh ideas.

I would also like to thank my technician, Mr. William Grady Spiegel, for his excellent help in the checking and editing of this work. Additional thanks must also go to Mr. Robert "Bob" Morris, formerly of Beacon Inc., for his help in obtaining Rockwell literature and sample parts.

J.M.H.

This book is dedicated to the scientists, engineers, technicians, and hobbyists who have the "spark." On the tireless work of these men and women, mankind is finding its destiny in the stars.

Contents

CHAPTER 4

CHAPTER 5

CHAPTER 6

CHAPER 7

CHAPTER 8

APPENDIX A

APPENDIX B

APPENDIX C

1

System Architecture

The 6500 family of microprocessors is made up of third-generation microprocessor devices that incorporate an 8-bit bidirectional data bus and a unidirectional address bus consisting of from 12 to 16 address lines. All of the 6500 family microprocessors, except the 6500/1, contain the same silicon chip. The 6502 and 6512 are housed in 40-pin DIP packages, while the 6503, 6504, 6505, 6513, 6514, and 6515 are housed in 28-pin DIP packages.

The 6512 offers a data bus enable (DBE) signal not found on the more popular 6502. The reason that the 6512 chip is not often used is that systems complex enough to require direct memory access (DMA), which is made possible by the DBE signal, almost invariably have external data bus buffering. Bus access in such systems is accomplished at the buffers. The other processors previously mentioned are offered in the less expensive 28-pin package by simply eliminating certain control and bus signals. In production designs, the savings in component cost derived from using these smaller devices is approximately 10%, and the savings in board area is approximately 0.6 square inch. The instruction sets are identical for all devices.

The 6500/1 is a stand-alone single-chip microcomputer that contains four 8-bit I/O ports, two internal timers, ROM, and R/W memory. The instruction set includes the full 6502 set, plus several special instructions associated with its internal timers and ports. Since this device contains its own I/O ports, and is not normally associated with complex interface problems, it is not discussed in depth in this book.

The architecture of the 6500 family is very similar to that of the Motorola 6800 family, the most noticeable difference being the absence of the 6800 valid memory address (VMA) signal. This similarity means that both families can be considered as a resource pool in designing interfaces for either microprocessor family. This combination represents a very substantial level of support. Most of the interface circuits presented in this book can be used with the MC6800 family microprocessors, provided that the designer simply ANDs VMA with $\phi2$ and uses this signal where the $\phi2$ signal is used (mostly in address decoder circuits).

MEMORY VERSUS REGISTERS

The 6500 (and 6800) microprocessors are designed around a memory-oriented concept as opposed to the register-oriented concept found in processors such as the 8080 and Z80. Both concepts have their strong and weak points, and it is important that the designer recognize and utilize the positive features. Under the memory-oriented concept, interfaces to the outside world are treated exactly as if they were memory locations. There are no special input or output instructions in the instruction set. Any instruction that can be used with memory can also be used to communicate with peripheral devices.

Since one of the advantages of the memory-oriented concept is the ability of the microprocessor to do numerous logic and mathematical operations directly on memory (without first transferring data or data pointers to registers), this same power can be applied to the interface devices.

PAGE ZERO AND INDIRECT ADDRESSING

Page zero (Z-page) has special significance in the 6502. Besides the absolute mode (that can access any memory location), there are two additional modes of addressing that are associated with page zero. These two modes are called Z-*page* and *indirect addressing.*

When the microprocessor uses Z-page addressing to access memory in page zero, it must generate a 16-bit address just as in the absolute addressing mode, but only two bytes are required in the program. The microprocessor recognizes the op code as implying not only the operation (LDA, STA, EOR, etc.), but also the high-address byte. The microprocessor will always generate a high byte of the address that is zero. The lower eight bits of address are specified in the byte that follows the op code.

In indirect addressing, page zero can be used to store up to 128 16-bit addresses or pointers. When the microprocessor encounters an indirect op code in the program, it will do two read operations in page zero. The first read will be at the Z-page location addressed by the byte that follows the op code, and the second will be at the next higher Z-page location. The two bytes read during these fetches will form the low and high bytes, respectively, of the memory location at which the op code will be executed. Thus, at times, these memory locations will act as if they were actually registers in the CPU chip. While it is not within the scope of this book to go deeply into programming the 6500 microprocessor family, it is essential that the interface designer understand the power of the indirect addressing technique for him to efficiently interface to these processors.

Some designers incorporate I/O interfaces into the Z-page memory space to take advantage of the abbreviated instructions mentioned earlier. This use of Z-page *is not recommended* unless the scope of the system is very limited. There are two reasons for this: first, the interfaces use up memory locations which could be used more effectively to store pointers, and, second, portions of a program that are not concerned with the I/O operations may attempt to use this address space as memory, and thus cause strange and unexpected operation of peripherals. In any system that is running a diversity of software, page zero can become a very crowded and busy place.

PAGE ONE AND THE STACK

In the 6500 family microprocessors, page one of memory ($0100 to $01FF) contains the stack. While the location of the stack may be manipulated within this page, the high-order address byte of all stack operations remains #01. Because of this, addressing interfaces within this page is not advisable.

PAGE $FF AND THE VECTORS

Page $FF, the highest address page, contains the NMI (nonmaskable interrupt), RES (reset), and IRQ (interrupt request) vectors. In a dedicated control system these vectors are usually in ROM (read-only memory), while in most general purpose systems they are contained in a small block of R/W (read/write) memory. Systems that contain these vectors in R/W memory usually utilize a technique known as *ROM first RAM* or *bootstrapping*, where a ROM device occupies this portion of the microprocessor's address space when the power-on reset is activated. This ROM contains a reset vector or address that causes the microprocessor to jump to the beginning of the initialization program. This program, by communicating with an I/O port, causes the ROM to be disabled, and a block of R/W memory to be enabled, whenever an address that contains $FF in the high byte is on the address bus. The software then causes the appropriate vectors to be written into the R/W memory.

The locations of these vectors, or address pointers, are as follows:

NMI	low address byte	FFFA
NMI	high address byte	FFFB
RESET	low address byte	FFFC
RESET	high address byte	FFFD
IRQ	low address byte	FFFE
IRQ	high address byte	FFFF

Before using page $FF for I/O operations, the designer must ascertain that no conflict exists between the memory address used in the interface, and the R/W memory or ROM.

THE SYSTEM CLOCK

The 6500 processors are dynamic devices, meaning that they cannot be halted without the loss of information stored in the registers. While the clock speed may be varied over a reasonable range, most applications utilize either the 1-MHz or 2-MHz version of the CPU chips, and operate the clock at that speed. In actuality, the 2-MHz parts are simply derived from sorting the CPU chips, and are otherwise identical to the slower parts. Running either device below 500 kHz is generally inadvisable. While the 6500 processors are advertised as containing a built-in clock oscillator circuit, they contain only an MOS inverter which can serve as a simple oscillator.

Many of the early clock oscillator circuits recommended by the manufacturers were not reliable when used with a variety of crystals. One factor that affected this was the rise time of the system power. Occasionally, the oscillator would start at either a subharmonic or harmonic of the desired frequency, and occasionally the oscillation would be in the parallel mode for series crystals and vice versa. In most cases, if a crystal is operating in the wrong mode it tends to have an error in frequency of from 1% to 20%.

The oscillator circuit shown in Fig. 1-1 has been widely published in applications literature. Resistor R1 is used to balance the duty cycle of the oscillator (make it closer to 50%). While the circuit is very reliable with high values of R1, it becomes

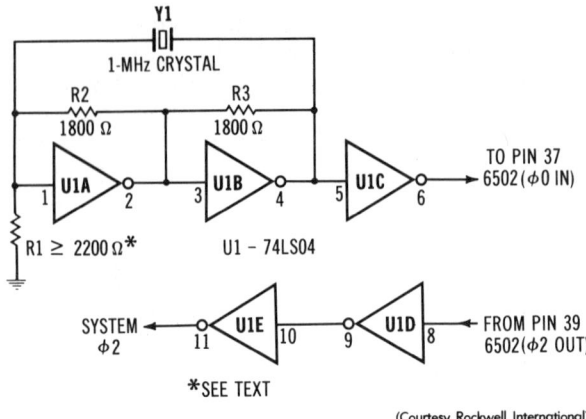

(Courtesy Rockwell International)

Fig. 1-1. Factory recommended clock circuit for the 6500 series microprocessors.

less reliable as R1 approaches 2200 ohms. Sometimes it is not possible to obtain a 50% duty cycle without losing reliability.

A slightly modified version of the oscillator is shown in Fig. 1-2 and is recommended here for oscillators that are running at the system clock rate (and, therefore, require a 50% duty cycle). The interstage coupling capacitor (C1) in the second version reduces the dc loop gain, and thus causes a 50% duty cycle to be obtained.

In some cases, it is economically beneficial to use a crystal at twice or four times the system clock frequency. These crystals are smaller and often less expensive than their lower frequency counterparts. The use of a divider after the oscillator eliminates the problem associated with obtaining a 50% duty cycle.

In operation, the clock determines the system timing. In conjunction with the read/write line, the clock controls the flow of data on the data bus. The two half cycles of the clock are referred to as $\phi 1$, and $\phi 2$. During $\phi 1$, the processor puts the address of the next memory operation on the address bus. During some cycles this is meaningless, as the processor has not yet fully constructed the address desired. On the next half cycle ($\phi 2$), data will be transferred to or from the addressed device.

THE READ/WRITE LINE AND PIPELINING

The 6500 microprocessors utilize a technique known as *pipelining* to increase the throughput on the chips. Pipelining means that the CPU may still be processing previously received data while reading new data. The read/write line determines

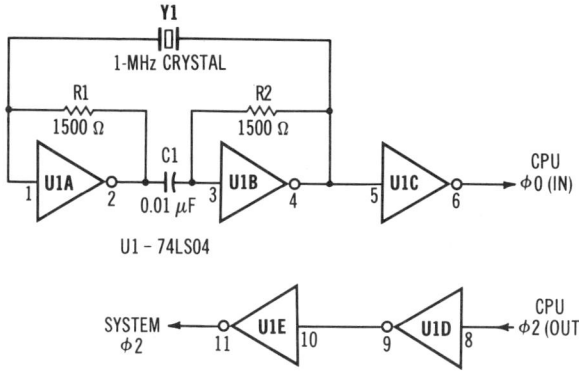

Fig. 1-2. Modified version of the circuit shown in Fig. 1-1. This clock circuit uses capacitive coupling to obtain duty cycle balancing.

the direction of data flow on the data bus when $\phi2$ is active. This line will be high (logic true or near +5 volts) if data is to be read from the addressed memory location or interface device, and it will be low (near ground) if the transfer is to be from the processor to the device (write).

A special word of caution is in order at this point. Since the 6500 processors do not generate a VMA or valid memory address signal as do the 6800 processors, an interesting bug can arise. It was mentioned earlier that during some cycles when the full desired address had not yet been calculated, an incorrect intermediate address is output on the address bus. Normally, this address is the base address of an impending indexed address operation. For example, if the processor were calculating the memory address to be used for LDA ($1000),Y, it would go through one cycle in which the incorrect address of ($1000) was read from memory. This value would then be discarded by the processor, and the correct value of the address ($1000+Y) would be read. Since these incorrect addresses always force the read/write line to a read state (logic one), the effect of the fetch of the incorrect memory address is that some data value is placed on the data bus, but it is ignored. This is not true in fetches from interface devices. Since some LSI interface chips contain up to 16 register addresses, indexed addressing is often used to initialize or reinitialize groups of registers. The problem arises when a port of the device is operating in the *handshaking* (see Chapter 2) mode and inadvertently receives a false read operation as described above. This may cause an undesired reset of the data-ready flag in the status register of the LSI chip,

13

and can be extremely difficult to debug. This bug occurs frequently in the 6522, since the register that occupies the relative address of zero is a handshaking port, and since the 6522 contains a large number of other registers. For this reason, it is important that the designer understand the pipelining concept and realize that problems can occur as a result of this technique.

THE READY (RDY) SIGNAL

This input is similar to the halt input found in some static processors. However, the RDY signal is often used with slow memory and direct memory access (DMA) devices. A negative transition on this input during or in coincidence with the $\phi 1$ clock will halt the processor, provided that it is doing a read operation. The address being output on the address bus will remain valid through the next $\phi 2$ clock interval in which the line is held low. If the ready line is taken low during a write operation, it will take effect at the beginning of the next read operation. The ready signal was originally intended for use with early, slow ultraviolet erasable PROMs (EPROMs or UV EPROMs), which had access times greater than 500 ns. The feature still finds some use with slow memories and certain direct memory access (DMA) schemes, and in single-step circuits (see SYNC).

SYNCHRONIZATION (SYNC)

The sync output signal is available primarily for debug purposes, and goes to an active (high) state at the beginning ($\phi 1$) of an op code fetch cycle. While it is very useful in implementing real-time hardware trace logic, it has a second function when used in combination with the ready input. If the ready line is taken to a slow state during the $\phi 1$ clock cycle in which the sync line went high, the processor will stop in its current state (it actually goes into an internally generated loop condition), until the ready line returns to the high state. A simple circuit can be used to single-step the processor for debugging purposes. This type of single-step operation is useful, however, only if the processor has some type of display attached to the address and data buses.

The AIM 65 uses the sync line in a different manner (Fig. 1-3) to accomplish single stepping. The $\phi 2$ clock and sync signals are ANDed with a third signal (monitor ROM enable), and used to generate an NMI signal. When an op code of the user's program is fetched, the processor receives an interrupt. The NMI

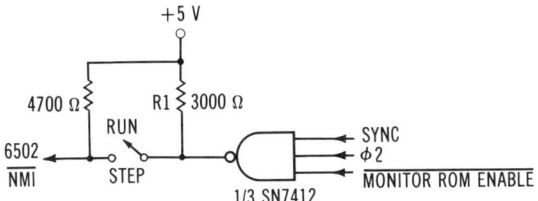

Fig. 1-3. Simplified circuit of the AIM 65 single-step logic.

vector is set up to point into a special area of the system monitor. In this area, the program causes the registers, program counter, and stack pointer to be listed out for the operator. The monitor ROM enable signal inhibits additional interrupts while the processor is executing the monitor routines (this would be most confusing, and would cause a continuous looping condition). This signal is a logic zero when the monitor is being executed, thus no interrupts can occur.

SET OVERFLOW FLAG

Little has ever been said about this rather novel input, although it does bear some resemblance to the SID line of the 8085 microprocessor. A negative transition of this input sets the overflow flag in the status register of the processor. The signal must be externally synchronized, and is sampled on the trailing edge of the $\phi 1$ clock. Apparently this input was provided for use with anticipated expansion devices which were never released. Although some suggestion has been made to the effect that this line could serve as a 1-bit input interface, this could lead to some strange mathematical results if care was not taken in its use. This author prefers to respect the obscurity of its usefulness.

RESET

The reset input is used to start the processor when power is first applied. This signal has been specified in a number of ways since the processor was first released. Fundamentally, the line is held low (logic zero) for a minimum number of cycles after the application of power, to allow the internal logic of the microprocessor to reach a cleared condition. Early applications circuits showed a capacitor connected from this input to ground, with a pull-up resistor to the positive supply. More recent literature has reflected the fact that a fast rising edge (in the neighborhood of 20 ns) is essential on this input in order to obtain a reliable reset. Once the +5 volts is applied to the CPU chip, a minimum of six clock cycles should be applied to the chip before a positive transition occurs on the reset pin. Most popular reset circuits consist of a one-shot timer that provides reset of at least a few thousand cycles duration.

When the reset is taken high, the processor will execute a six-cycle initialization sequence, set the IRQ mask, and fetch the reset vector located at memory locations $FFFC and $FFFD. The processor will then load this address into the program counter and begin program execution at this location. The processor may be reset to stop a particular program from being executed, if the system has "gone off into the woodwork" because of encountering an improper program code.

Another word of caution is in order regarding this signal: the reset signal should never be used to hold the processor in an inactive state for more than a few hundred milliseconds! While this problem is not commonly known, the processor has a definite tendency to become unsynchronized if the reset input is used in this manner. The problem varies with different individual parts, and is a function of temperature and the length of time that the line is held low with power applied. It is most probably a topological heating phenomenon, but can easily be avoided by placing the processor in a software loop to generate the required delay. When used as recommended above, the reset signal should be quite reliable.

The circuit of Fig. 1-4 is from the AIM 65, and uses an NE555 timer to generate the appropriate signal. While this circuit is adequate for most applications, the circuit shown in Fig. 1-5 should be used if the manual reset input switch is to be located out of the immediate area of the circuit, especially when the system is to be used in a noisy environment. This circuit uses one of the two timers in the NE556 in the same manner as the circuit in Fig. 1-4, generating a pulse of approximately 70 ms in response to a power-on transition, or when the remote reset switch is activated. The other half of the device is used as a Schmitt trigger input stage, giving a single and clean pulse for each activation of the switch. Resistor R1 is added simply to protect the 5-volt power supply in event of accidental shorting of the reset switch line to ground.

INTERRUPT REQUEST (IRQ)

The IRQ input is used to cause the microprocessor to execute an interrupt program in response to an external event or system

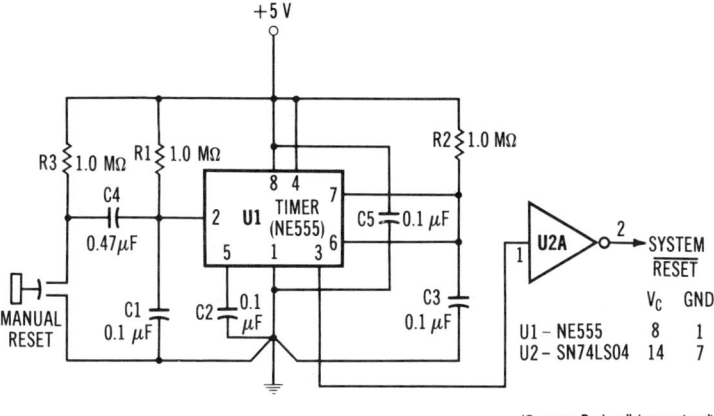

Fig. 1-4. Reset circuit for the 6500 microprocessors used in the AIM 65.

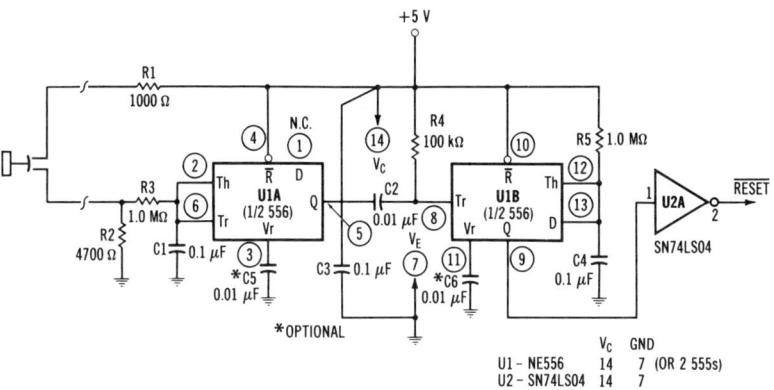

Fig. 1-5. Reset circuit with high noise immunity and manual input.

timer. This input is similar to the NMI input, except that the IRQ signal can be selectively ignored by the processor, depending on the state of the mask bit in the status register of the microprocessor. The signal should be synchronized to the leading edge of the system $\phi2$ clock when generated by nonstandard (non-6500 family) interface devices. When the IRQ input is driven to a low state, the processor will recognize the interrupt request on the next op-code fetch, provided that the mask bit is not set (true or a logic one). The program counter and process status register will then be pushed on the stack, and the IRQ vector located at $FFFE and $FFFF will be loaded into the program counter, thus transferring control to the interrupt service subroutine. The use of this signal is covered in depth in later chapters. Both the IRQ and NMI signals are tested by the processor during $\phi2$ and action is taken in the next $\phi1$ cycle (after completion of the current instruction).

NONMASKABLE INTERRUPT (NMI)

The NMI input is essentially the same as the IRQ input, except that its effect cannot be masked or ignored by the microprocessor. The vector for this input is at addresses $FFFA and $FFFB. The NMI signal is also tested during $\phi2$ and action is taken in the next $\phi1$ cycle.

ADDRESS DECODING

The first element in any interface design is to develop a signal that will serve to alert the interface that the processor wishes to write data into it, or to read data from it. Since the microprocessor always places a 16-bit address on the address bus when it is accessing memory (or in this case an I/O interface), this address is often decoded to generate the required signal. In the 6500 family, this logic is usually very simple. Essentially, the address decoder simply looks for a combination of address and control signals corresponding to the assigned address of the interface element. The designer is the one that assigns an address or a group of addresses to a particular interface. Fig. 1-6 contains a simple address decoder. Notice that the appropriate combination of address signals and inverted address signals are ANDed together with the $\phi2$ clock signal to generate a negative-going pulse whenever the address $1000 is present

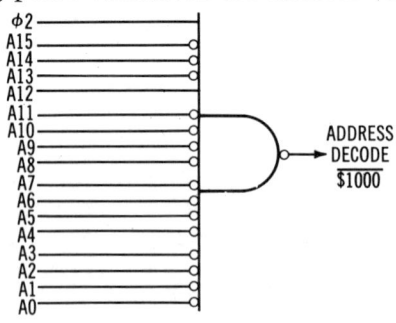

Fig. 1-6. Logical simplification of an address decoder.

on the address bus. The read/write line could have been applied to the input of the NAND gate as well, if the pulse were desired only for read (or conversely write) operations. The inclusion of the $\phi 2$ clock signal ensures that the interface will not receive glitches while the address lines are changing during $\phi 1$ of the cycle.

Often, the interface will occupy more than one memory location. In this case, the lower address lines are not included in the decoding logic. Thus, the address decode signal becomes valid for a group of contiguous addresses. This is often done, even when only one address is required, in order to reduce the com-

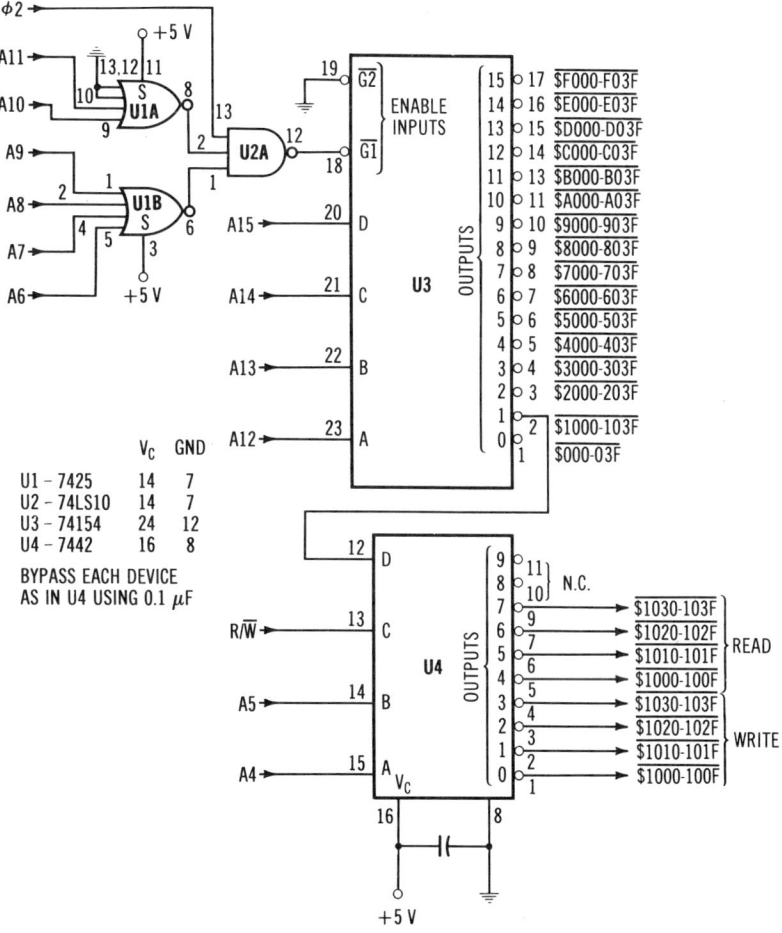

Fig. 1-7. Practical address decoder circuits.

plexity and expense of the decoding logic. The effect of this incomplete decoding is to cause *images* of the interface within the block of addresses generated by the decoder. Fig. 1-7 contains a practical address decoder that generates eight decode signals. Each signal is valid for a block of 16 addresses, and the first four signals are write signals, while the second four are read signals that correspond to the same address blocks as the first four.

A decoder that will generate 16 single address strobes, each of which is valid for either read or write operations, is shown in Fig. 1-8. Notice that in Fig. 1-7, high-order address selection is

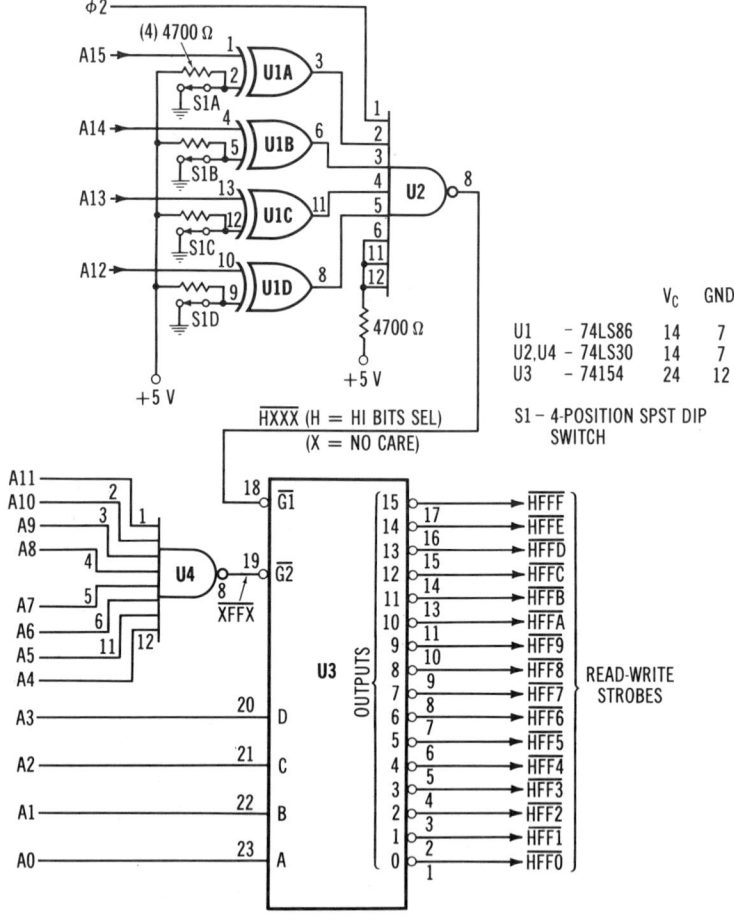

Fig. 1-8. Address decoder circuits using Exclusive-OR gates.

done by selecting one of the outputs on the SN74154, while the decoder of Fig. 1-8 utilizes Exclusive-OR gates to program the high-address values.

There are as many ways to implement address decoding as there are designers. In fact, a high-speed (40 ns) Schottky PROM can even be used as an address decoder (Fig. 1-9). The advantage of this circuit is that the various outputs can each have widely different block sizes, since the correlation between inputs and outputs is totally programmable by the user.

Programmable logic arrays (PLAs) also may be used with the result being a single-chip decoder. Unfortunately, the special programmers required for these devices and PROMs usually tend to discourage their use in anything but very high-volume applications. The use of EPROMs is not suggested because of the relatively slow speed of these devices.

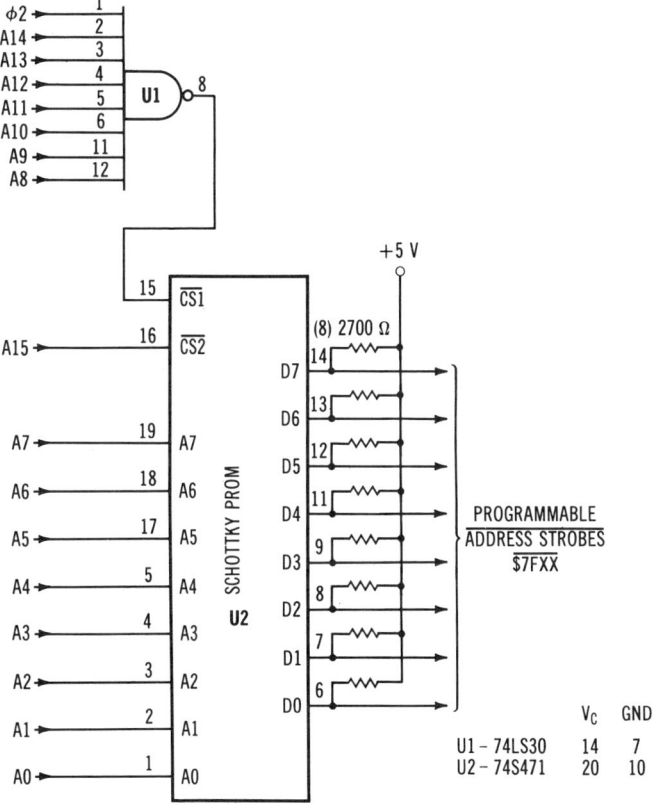

Fig. 1-9. Address decoder using a high-speed PROM.

The addressing method that the 6500 family uses to address memory and peripherals is extremely straightforward, and decoding can be easily implemented, provided that the above guidelines are followed. Circuits should be constructed with either TTL or low-power Schottky TTL devices. The use of CMOS (even buffered CMOS) is not recommended, even though the specifications may lead one to believe that it is sufficiently fast.

REFERENCE

1. Scanlon, L.J. *6502 Software Design*. Indianapolis: Howard W. Sams & Co., Inc., 1980.

2

Input Port Design

Before discussing the family of 6500 and 6800 series chips that were designed for interfacing, it will be beneficial to examine the fundamentals of all input/output (I/O) ports. Inexperienced designers often utilize relatively expensive and complicated interface devices, where less expensive latches and tristate buffers are sufficient. The reason for this is that they are afraid that they do not fully understand the requirements of the interface circuitry. Once the principles of reading, latching, handshaking, and control registers are understood, the designer may avoid the unnecessary use of large-scale integration (LSI) chips, and do a better job of selecting among them when they must be used. Furthermore, the ability to custom-design an interface from standard logic elements will allow the user to better fit the hardware to the software, in a way that will solve problems that cannot be solved by standard LSI devices. Many production designs require such techniques in order to establish a competitive position in the marketplace.

Fundamentally, an 8-bit (byte) wide input port may be used to interface a single 8-bit word, eight separate 1-bit words, or a combination of words of various lengths. The input port of Fig. 2-1 consists of nothing more than eight tristate buffers whose inputs are wired to external (peripheral) signals, and whose outputs are wired to the data bus of the microprocessor. The tristate control input(s) are wired together and connected to a read-strobe signal which is generated by the address decode logic. The pulse generated by the address decoder logic will be a logic zero for one half of a clock cycle, corresponding to the positive phase of the $\phi2$ clock. This pulse will occur as a result of the microprocessor generating the address which the decoder

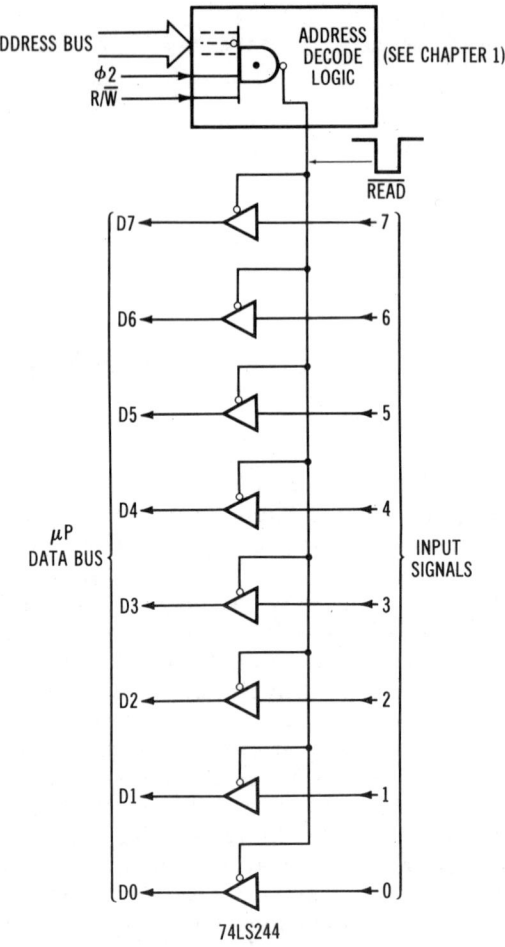

Fig. 2-1. A simple input port.

is set to recognize, and at the same time generating a logic one (read) on the read/write (R/W) line. Several of the 6500 instructions will cause this strobe signal to be generated, including the LDA, AND, ORA, EOR, BIT, LDX, LDY, ASL, ROL, LSR, ROR, INC, DEC, ADC, and SBC instructions.

LOAD AND LOGIC INSTRUCTIONS

While the LDA instruction loads the value of the input port directly into the accumulator, the AND and ORA logic instructions can be used to mask (set or reset) any combination of the input bits within the 8-bit word. This is done by first loading the accumulator with the mask word, and then either ANDing or ORing the accumulator with the content of the input port. A conditional branch instruction such as BNE is often executed after the logic instruction in order that the processor can make a decision based on the input port value. *A word of caution is in order for the programmer who has a background in other processors* (especially the 8080 and Z80): a large percentage of the 6500 family instruction set affects the flags of the processor. This is especially true of the N and Z flags. All load instructions affect these flags.

THE BIT INSTRUCTION

The BIT instruction allows the testing of bits 6 and 7 of an 8-bit value, without changing the contents of the accumulator or the X or Y registers. Bit 6 is placed in the overflow (V) flag bit of the condition code register, and bit 7 is placed in the negative (N) or minus flag of this register. The BIT instruction also compares the content of the accumulator to the content of the input port and sets the zero (Z) flag if they are equal, although this feature is not often used. If one or two single-bit signals require frequent testing, and the assignment of these signals to either bit 6 or 7 of their respective ports may ease the programmer's job and speed execution of the program.

OTHER USEFUL INSTRUCTIONS

The shift and rotate instructions may be used in such applications as driving the windings of stepping motors, with the result being a saving of program instructions. While many of the instructions listed above may seem unrelated to I/O operations and interfacing, the innovative designer eventually will find applications where they can be used beneficially. Indeed, the ability to apply such instructions to I/O operations is a very important feature of the 6500 and 6800 processors.

An excellent application of the interface shown in Fig. 2-1 is to use it to interface to signals that seldom change, such as "personality" DIP switches. In this application, the input port based on the SN74LS244 is much less expensive than the equivalent LSI input port design. On the other hand, if the input port is to be used with signals that change frequently, or which when they do change require immediate service from the processor, this simple design may place an unacceptable burden on the processor. The limiting factor here is that the processor must read the input port frequently enough to ensure that it detects any change in a signal (or combination of signals), and detects it soon enough to take the required action(s). Obviously, it would be desirable if the interface could signal the processor only when data must be input from it, or, in the case of an output port, only when data must be output to it.

The act of reading data from, or writing data to, a port is called *servicing* the port. A paper-tape reader makes a good example. The format of a typical eight-level ASCII paper tape is shown in Fig. 2-2. Most modern paper-tape readers contain eight light sources and eight light detectors spaced 0.1-inch apart, so that the information (holes or no holes) may be detected as the tape passes between the detectors and the sources. If no tape is in the reader, light will be transmitted from the light sources to the detectors. As the tape passes through the reader, light may or may not strike the detector(s), depending on whether or not there is a hole between it and the light source. Using the input port shown in Fig. 2-1, it would be extremely difficult to read the information from the tape, simply because we would have no way of determining whether a no-hole condition was due to the fact that no hole was punched in the tape, or whether the tape was between two data words.

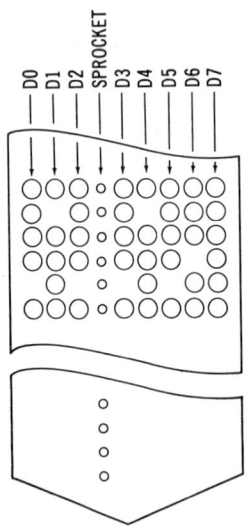

Fig. 2-2. Eight-level paper-tape format.

To simplify interfacing requirements, almost all paper-tape readers contain an additional light source and detector which is used to detect the sprocket hole in the tape. As a matter of accuracy, many tape readers also contain a stepper motor to accurately position the paper tape with the holes directly under the detectors at the end of each step.

In any event, the sprocket detector will significantly reduce the software required for the paper-tape reader's interface. Since bit 7 (the most significant bit) of most ASCII paper tapes can be ignored, it would be simple to wire the output of the sprocket hole detector directly to this bit of the input port. If all eight bits of the tape must be read, an additional input port could be used to input the signal from the sprocket hole detector. If a single 8-bit port was used, this signal would best be connected to bit 6 or bit 7, so that the BIT instruction could be used to determine when the paper tape was properly positioned. This, in turn, would simplify the software.

With either of these two approaches, the processor would simply poll the sprocket bit until it indicated that the 8-bit word was properly aligned in between the light sources and detectors (the true state). The program would then input the data and adjust it as required (inverting it with an EOR instruction if necessary and then masking it with #$7F if bit 7 was used for the sprocket detector). The value probably would then be stored in memory. After digesting the word, the processor would enter a loop during which it would wait for the sprocket hole detector to go to the false state, before repeating the process. This may be an acceptable solution to the problem, but it requires a large amount of software overhead time, especially if the processor has other concurrent tasks to perform.

A SINGLE INTERRUPT

The circuit of Fig. 2-3 contains both the input port of Fig. 2-1 and an interface to the interrupt (IRQ, or NMI) input of the processor. In this case, we will assume that both the data and sprocket signals are inverted (a logic zero represents a hole, and a logic one represents no hole); thus, an inverting tristate buffer is used in the interface, to avoid the necessity of having to invert the data in software.

The interrupt interface consists of two flip-flops and either an open-collector IC or discrete transistor. The flip-flop (SN74LS74) on the right-hand side of Fig. 2-3 is edge-triggered by the sprocket hole detector signal, and the Q output of this flip-flop is synchronized to the system $\phi 2$ clock by the flip-flop on the left-hand side of the figure. Since the IRQ and NMI signals may have to be wired to a number of other circuits, an

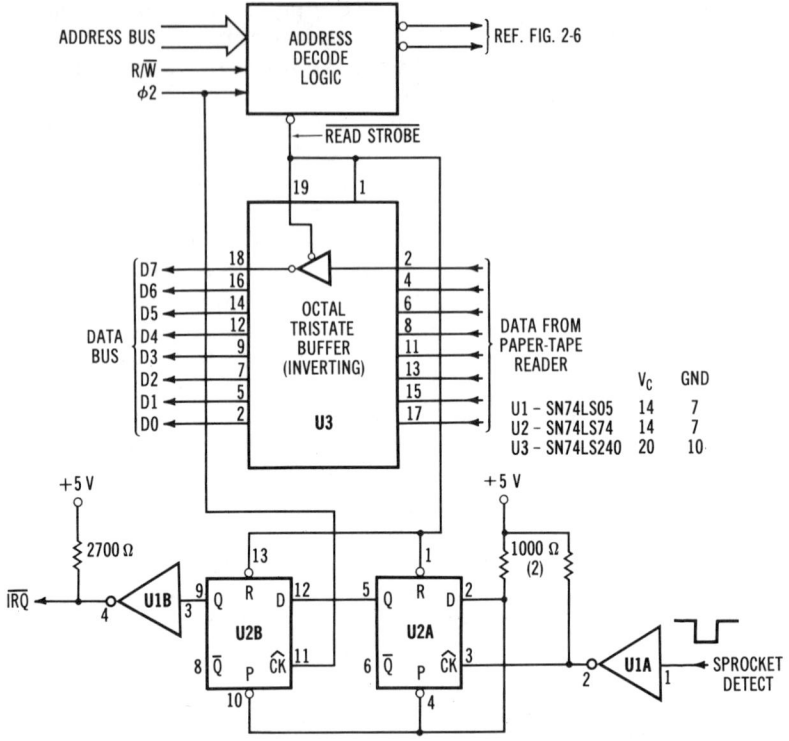

Fig. 2-3.   Paper-tape interface circuit with interrupt.

open-collector IC or a transistor is used to interface the Q output of this flip-flop to the IRQ input of the processor. If no other devices were expected to require use of this interrupt, the inverted output of the flip-flop could have been connected directly to the IRQ (or NMI) input.

Using this input port design, a minimum amount of software is required to input data from the reader. This means that the processor spends a minimum amount of time servicing the paper-tape reader. Notice that the output of the address decoder is connected to the reset inputs of the flip-flops, so that each interrupt causes data to be read, which, in turn, resets the interrupt. If some means of resetting an interrupt signal is not incorporated, the processor will immediately reenter the interrupt loop as soon as it has executed an RTI (return from interrupt) instruction.

Since there are many different formats for paper tape, there would be little benefit to going into detail about the software required. In very general terms, Fig. 2-4 shows the structure of the routine that would service the reader. Before any information can be read from the paper-tape reader, the microprocessor has to enable the interrupt, set the vector for the IRQ input, and then possibly set up some memory pointers for the values that are to be read from the paper tape. Once these tasks are performed, the processor starts the motor in the reader, or pulses the stepper motor. The microprocessor can then perform any of a number of other tasks, because it will only be interrupted, and thus service the paper-tape reader, when a sprocket hole is detected.

When the interrupt occurs, the information will be read and processed, and then the microprocessor can return to the task it was executing when the interrupt occurred. At some point, the microprocessor will determine that no more data is to be read, and will turn off the reader's motor and disable the interrupt.

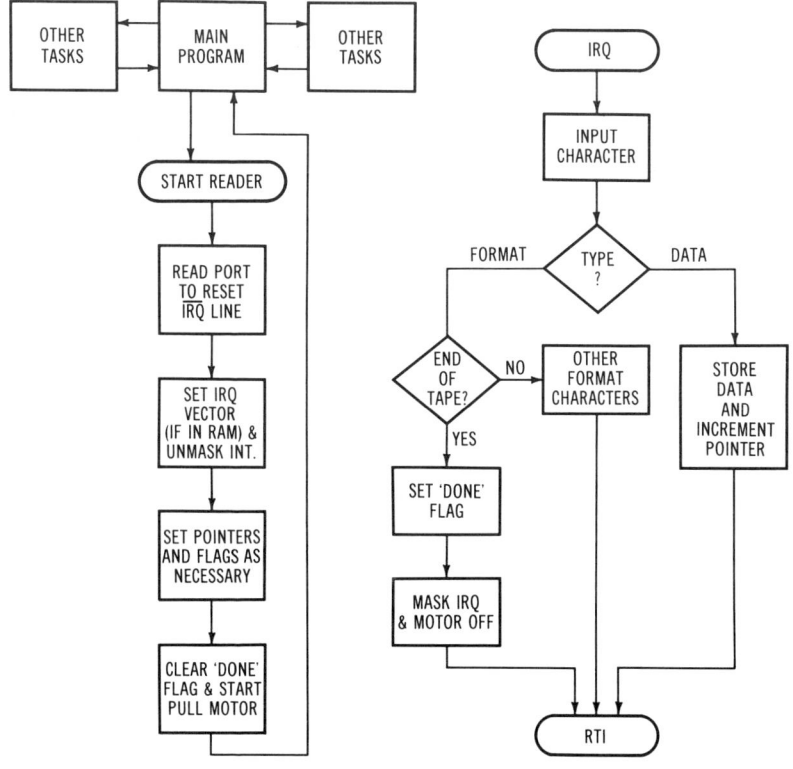

Fig. 2-4. Tape reader initialization and interrupt service routines.

MULTIPLE INTERRUPTS

In systems with multiple interrupts, the processor must be able to determine which peripheral caused the interrupt. The input port shown in Fig. 2-3 does not offer this "identity" capability, so it may be necessary to make an addition to the original input port design. The result is shown in Fig. 2-5. Another input port-like circuit has been added, but its inputs are the various latched interrupt signals that are generated by the other system peripherals. This type of quasi-input port is called an *interrupt register,* and the entire interrupt circuit is known as *input handshaking* logic.

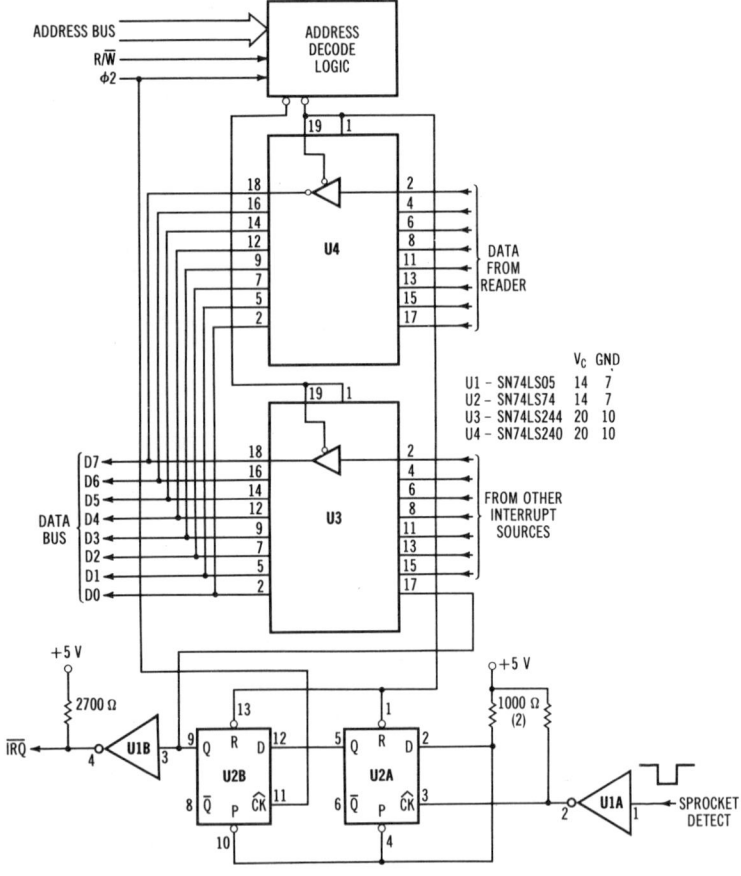

Fig. 2-5. Paper-tape reader interface with interrupt register.

Now let us assume that the system has many peripherals that generate interrupts, and that the reader must read tapes *very* quickly. In operation, we find occasionally there is too much of a delay between the time the sprocket signal occurs and the actual reading of the input port by the processor. This causes the holes in the tape to no longer be aligned with the detectors, and errors are occurring. Of course, this would be a problem only in a streaming-type paper-tape reader, and not one that is driven by a stepper motor.

To solve this problem, the circuit of Fig. 2-6 includes *input latching*. Notice that data from the paper-tape reader is latched into the SN74LS374, thus allowing more time for the processor to service the interface. In addition, the circuit would probably contain an interrupt circuit as shown in Figs. 2-3, 2-5, or 2-7.

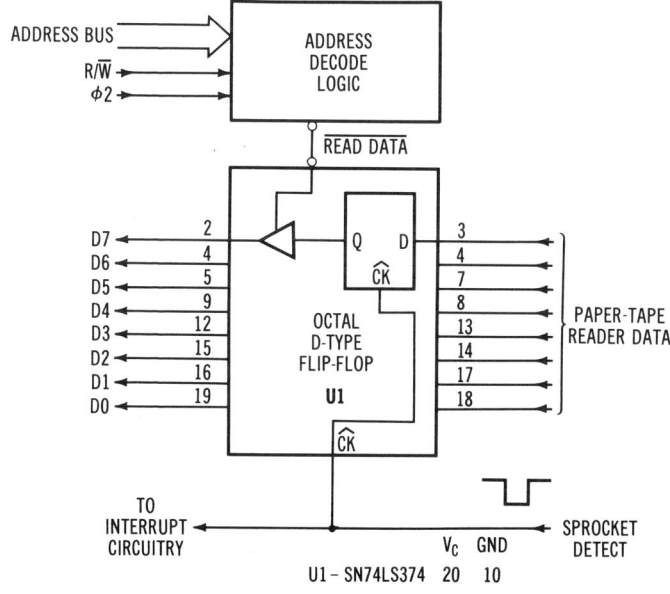

Fig. 2-6. An SN74LS374 used to latch the paper-tape reader data.

INTERRUPT MASK REGISTERS

The circuit of Fig. 2-7 contains an *interrupt mask* or *interrupt enable* register. Used in conjunction with the interface of Fig. 2-3, this register allows the processor to enable or disable any combination of interrupts (1 = enable, 0 = disable) at any time.

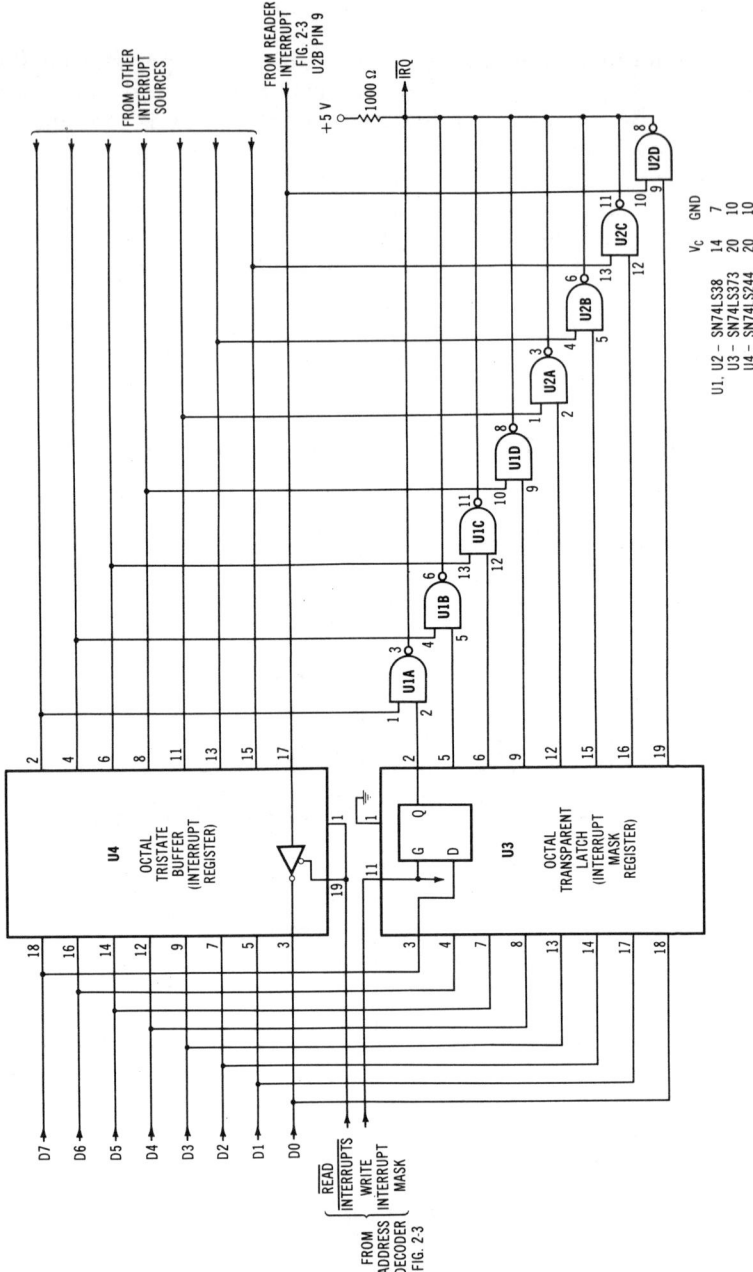

Fig. 2-7. An SN74LS373 used as an interrupt mask register. (This augments the circuit in Fig. 2-3.)

Such a register can reduce wasted CPU time, and simplify control of interfaces.

Unfortunately, these improvements have increased the parts count of the interface, and thus the manufacturing cost, to a rather uncomfortable level. Somewhere between the circuit of Fig. 2-1 and the circuit of Fig. 2-6, we should have considered the use of an LSI interface device with the appropriate characteristics. Often, one LSI device can be used to provide the "exotic" interface requirements of a system, and simple TTL devices can fill in elsewhere. In other chapters of this book we discuss the interrupt capabilities of the 6522 and other LSI port chips.

ADVANCED INPUT PORT DESIGN

There are a number of integrated circuits in the 7400 series of logic that have three-state (or tristate) outputs. These types of devices are used when peripherals or memory devices must send information to the CPU. By using one of these devices (Fig. 2-7), it is easy to poll up to eight peripheral lines.

BIT-MAPPED I/O

Recalling that earlier in the chapter we discussed the advantage of using the BIT instruction, and how it is used to test certain bits (6 and 7) of I/O ports without changing the content of the accumulator, the circuit in Fig. 2-7 can be used to test all eight of its inputs with the BIT instruction. The technique used here will be referred to as *bit-mapped* I/O, and its uses are much more extensive than one might at first imagine. The disadvantage of this technique is that in order to input a single bit of information, a single memory location is required. In previous designs, a single memory address was used to input eight bits of information. However, since many processors do not have 64K of memory, and since most designs do not fully decode all 16 address lines for the I/O ports, this disadvantage is usually small to nonexistent.

In order to understand the advantages of this input port design, let's first consider the case of an input port that interfaces eight unrelated signals. Further, we will assume that the programmer has reached a point in his program where he wishes to determine if a cooling fan is running. The accumulator contains a temperature measurement that will be needed by the software in the event that it is found that the fan is not running.

First, let us examine the software when a conventional

word-mapped input port as shown in Fig. 2-1 is used. In Example 2-1, we will assume that bit 4 represents the fan's status. In this example, the content of the accumulator is saved in memory, then the input port is read. The AND instruction masks out, or sets to zero, all bits in the accumulator *except* bit 4. If bit 4 is a logic one, the fan is running, so the processor branches to FANEXT. If the fan is not running, the accumulator will be zero, and the microprocessor will execute the instructions at FANOFF. At this point in the program, the temperature reading, which was in the accumulator at the beginning, is read back from memory into the accumulator, and is compared to a temperature limit value called TEMPL. If the content of the accumulator is less than the value of the limit, the processor will branch to FANEXT. In this case the temperature was not hot enough to warrant turning on the fan. If the temperature is equal to or greater than the value of TEMPL, then the processor will call the TURNON subroutine.

Example 2-1: Using an AND Instruction to Test a Single Bit of an 8-Bit Port

```
         STA ASAVE    ;Save the accumulator (temp).
         LDA PORTA    ;Get 8-bit word from port A.
         AND #$10     ;Mask out all bits but bit 4.
         BNE FANEXT   ;Fan is already on, so exit.
FANOFF   LDA ASAVE    ;Return temperature to accumulator.
         CMP TEMPL    ;Compare to temperature limit.
         BMI FANEXT   ;Temperature is low, leave fan off.
         JSR TURNON   ;Temperature is high, turn fan on.
FANEXT                ;Program continues.
```

By using a bit-mapped input port, as is shown in Fig. 2-8, the software can be simplified. The results are shown in Example 2-2. In this example the microprocessor tests the fan status by executing a BIT instruction. The label FAN would have previously been equated to the single address that corresponds to the desired one of the eight input lines of the port (the use of such easy-to-remember labels speeds the task of programming). The BMI instruction then tests the state of the N flag as set by the BIT instruction. If the fan is on, the branch to FANEXT is executed; otherwise, the CMP TEMPL instruction at FANOFF is executed. Of course, this compares the value of the accumulator to the temperature limit value stored in memory. Again, if the temperature is greater than the "set-point," the fan is turned on; otherwise, it is not. Notice that not only have three instructions been eliminated, but the execution time has been shortened as well.

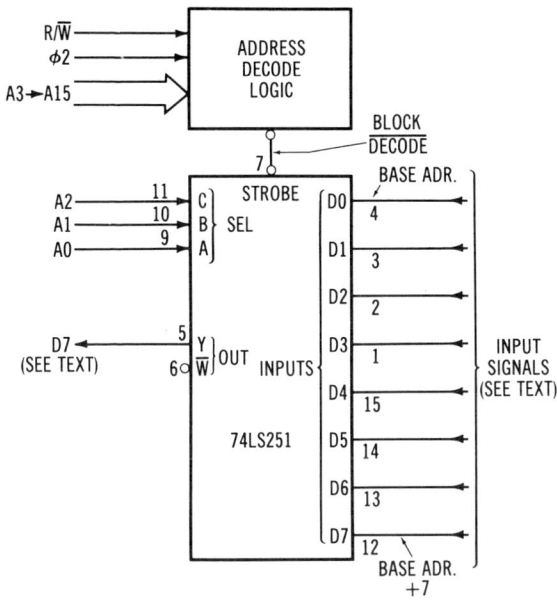

Fig. 2-8. A simple bit-mapped input port.

Example 2-2: Using the BIT Instruction to Test the Single Bit of a Bit-Mapped Port

```
         BIT FAN       ;Test the fan's status.
         BMI FANEXT    ;Fan is already on, so exit.
FANOFF   CMP TEMPL     ;Compare accum to temp limit.
         BMI FANEXT    ;Temperature is low, so exit.
         JSR TURNON    ;Temp is high, so turn fan on.
FANEXT                 ;Program continues.
```

In even a small system, the amount of memory saved can be exceptional (remember that 2049 bytes of program will not fit in in a single 2K × 8 PROM). Additionally, we avoid the use of troublesome mask words that often cause wasted debug time.

Another type of problem can be easily solved by the bit-mapped input interface. As an example, assume that the accumulator contains a number between 0 and 7. The input port is wired to eight switches. If the switch corresponding to the number in the accumulator is in the logic one state, a specific action will be performed. This action might involve unlocking a door or allowing some other action to occur. In this example, a match between the accumulator number and the switch bit will cause the detonation of a self-destruction device (say two sticks of dynamite for excitement). Example 2-3 contains the software that would be used with the word-mapped port of Fig. 2-1. While a subroutine could have been written to generate the mask (instead of using a table of mask words), the length of the program would have been about the same, and the execution of the program would have been slower.

**Example 2-3: Using an AND Instruction and a Mask Table
to Determine if a Switch Is On (Word-Mapped Port)**

```
        TAX             ;Move switch number to index X reg.
        LDA MSKTBL,X    ;Get the mask for the number.
        AND PORTA       ;Mask out undesired bits.
        BEQ NODEST      ;Don't self-destruct.
        JSR DESTR       ;Stack, memory, and room will be
                        ;cleared by this subroutine.
NODEST          .       ;Program continues.
                .
                .
MSKTBL  .BYTE $01,$02,$04,$08,$10,$20,$40,$80 ;Masks
```

Now consider the software required for the bit-mapped input port (Example 2-4). In this example, we cannot use the bit instruction because it cannot be used with indexed addressing. While one might be tempted to use the standard mask test for bit 7, and thus save only the mask table, a slightly shorter program is possible by using the ROL instruction.

**Example 2-4: Simplifying the Switch-Sensing Software
With Bit-Mapped I/O**

```
        TAX             ;Put switch number in X reg.
        ROL PORTA,X     ;Rotate bit 7 into carry.
        BCC NODEST      ;Don't self-destruct.
        JSR DESTR       ;OK self-destruct.
NODEST:         .           ;Program continues.
                .
                .
```

Notice that not only is the mask table eliminated, but also that an AND instruction is not required. Since the input port is "read only," the word, once it has been rotated and written back out to the interface, is not actually stored in the interface. However, the carry flag will be set when the CPU's arithmetic logic unit (ALU) does the actual rotate. The interface designer should understand that a 6500 ROL instruction causes the CPU to read a word, rotate it in the ALU, and write it back out to the memory location that it came from. Since the interface of Fig. 2-8 does not store the word that is written back out to it, the test described above cannot be repeated for data bus bits 6, 5, 4, 3, 2, or 1 if they are used in the port. Therefore, the software of

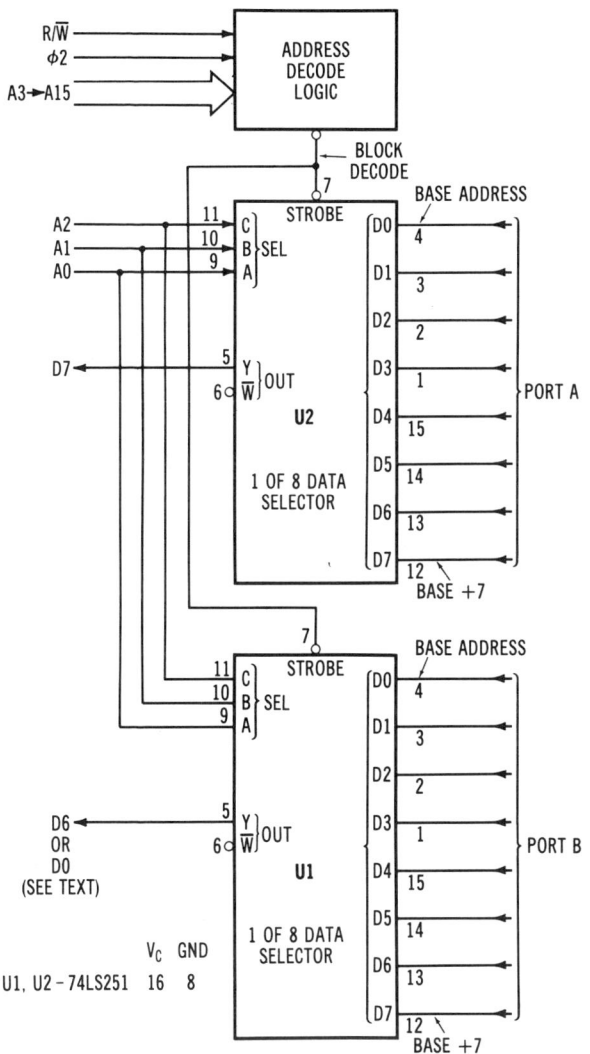

Fig. 2-9. Dual bit-mapped input port. (Note: A triple port can be made using D6 and D0.)

Example 2-4 must *not be used with the interface shown in Fig. 2-8* (except for testing bits 7 and 0).

A third and very important application for the bit-mapped input port is in connection with high-level languages such as PL/M, PL65, and Pascal. These languages often contain flag structures which use only one bit in a word. This structure allows statements such as "IF FAN$ON DO . . .". Here the language essentially bit-maps the flags; but, unfortunately, the I/O is usually still done in much the same manner as assembly language. If the designer can determine which bit is used in the flag operation of a particular language, it is possible to bit-map his I/O in such a way as to fit this structure and greatly improve I/O operations. Not only is readability improved, but execution speed is also greatly improved. This is especially true because many programmers will set up a time-consuming I/O procedure to simplify programming in the absence of a better technique. This simply transfers the burden of the sluggish hardware from the programmer to the processor. Output ports can also be bit-mapped as explained in the next chapter, and the advantages are equally as great.

Since one bit is used in each memory location, two or more ports may share a common address decoder signal as shown in Fig. 2-9. While bit 6 may be tested by the BIT instruction, bit 7 may be tested either by this instruction or by the ROL instruction, and bit 0 may be tested by the LSR instruction. All three bits might be used if the address space for peripherals is limited.

Besides the advantages discussed in this chapter, one additional benefit is derived from the use of TTL-type I/O ports, and that is that they do not require (as a rule) much initialization software when the microprocessor system is powered-up. These simple I/O ports are "born" knowing that they are input ports, and they also "know" just how to act. The I/O efficiency obtained by the use of these techniques, and those of the following chapters, often means that the software for some applications can be very short.

3

Output Port Design

In the 6500 and 6800 families, output devices are interfaced to the microcomputer using memory-mapped I/O techniques. The concept is simply to *latch* the data that appears on the data bus at the time that (1) the interface address appears on the address bus, (2) the read/write line is low, and (3) the $\phi2$ clock is high. As discussed in Chapter 1, the address decoder is the same as would be used for an input interface, except that the read/write line must be in the logic zero (write) state for the strobe output to be generated.

As in the case of input interface circuits, it is extremely important that the designer understand the fundamental concepts behind the output interface before making component selection. Fig. 3-1 shows a simple parallel output. The eight lines may represent eight separate signals (such as lamp driver controls), one 8-bit byte, (such as information to be punched on paper tape), or any combination of single and group signals.

A SIMPLE OUTPUT PORT

The SN74LS373 octal latch shown in Fig. 3-1 is one of several simple transparent-type TTL latches that can be used with this circuit. A transparent-type latch is one in which the data output follows the data input while the enable input is active. It is also possible to use clocked D-type flip-flops in these type circuits (by latching on the negative transition of the $\phi2$ clock). But, the transparent latches are more widely used because their timing more closely corresponds to that of the memory devices with which the microprocessor was designed to interface. The SN74LS373 also has the added feature of tristate outputs. This

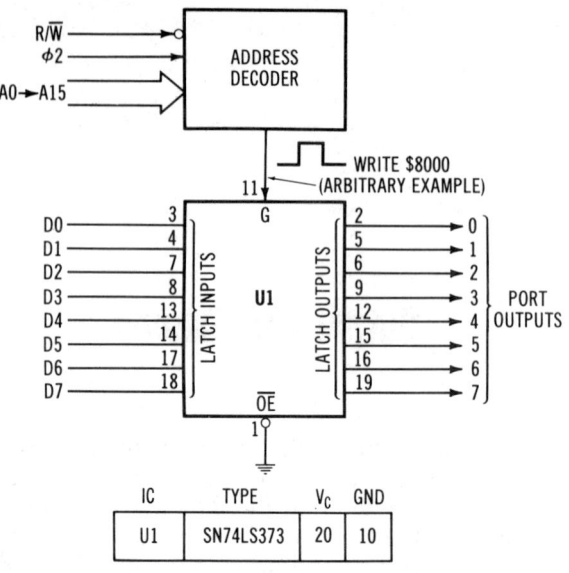

Fig. 3-1. Simple parallel output interface.

feature is not necessary for most applications, but can be very handy when needed. Because of this control input, the device could be used as a latching input interface, or as an interface between microprocessors. In Fig. 3-1 this pin is grounded so that the outputs are always enabled and never in the "third state." The latch enable pin is simply connected to the positive strobe pulse from the address decoder.

The most obvious way to write data to this device is simply to load the accumulator with the data to be output, and then execute a store (STA) instruction, using the address of the interface. This technique is quite adequate if the data to be output is a single 8-bit word, but difficulties will arise if the port represents two or more groups of independent information.

To understand this problem, consider the case in which the interface controls eight independent and unrelated lamp drivers. Now, assume that an event has been detected by the program which requires that lamp number 0 (numbering here is 0–7) be turned on. If we simply load the accumulator with #$01 (01 HEX) and write this to the interface, lamp number 0 will light, *but any other lamps that may have been on will be turned off.* We must assume that at the moment the processor decides to turn on lamp number 0, the state of the other lamps is not stored in memory. Each of these lamps may have been controlled by a different program segment. Since the port of Fig. 3-1 cannot be *read,* there is no way to tell which lamps are turned on, unless each program segment that controls a lamp also stores the resultant bit pattern in an R/W memory location. This means that there must be two write commands for each output operation. In some designs, hardware cost tradeoffs may actually dictate this type of solution. In other cases the circuit of either Fig. 3-2 or Fig. 3-3 is preferable.

THE CONCEPT OF READBACK

Both types of circuits shown in Figs. 3-2 and 3-3 appear in LSI interface devices (sometimes in the same device), and it is important to understand the difference between the two. The circuit in Fig. 3-2 combines a simple input interface (U2) with the output interface in Fig. 3-1 (see Chapter 2 for a functional explanation of the input interface). This combination allows for not only writing to the latch, but also reading the data present in the latch.

A noninverting buffer (U3) has also been added to the circuit. This buffer serves a dual function: it allows the port to drive heavier loads, and it isolates the input port (readback) data from he loaded output.

To understand the importance of this register type of read-back, consider the case in which we drive the base of an npn power transistor directly with the output port pin (with no base resistors). This is sometimes done when driving large LED or lamp displays, because of the large number of transistor drivers involved. When the port pin is set to a logic one, the voltage will rise to the transistor V_{BE} (approximately 0.6 volt or 1.2 volts for a Darlington). If the readback interface was connected to this pin directly (as in Fig. 3-3), it would still read a logic zero, even though the lamp was illuminated. It might seem, there-fore, that the configuration of Fig. 3-3 is incorrect. But, this configuration also has its uses, as will be seen later.

It should be mentioned that this direct base drive technique should be used with the following considerations: (1) the port *must* use passive pull-up devices either internally or externally, (2) calculations using the beta of the transistor and the value of the pull-up resistor must be made to assure that the transistor is always driven into saturation, and (3) the load currents passing through the transistor must not cause unacceptable ground noise on the port negative supply. Such nonisolated drivers should never be used with inductive loads.

SOFTWARE CONSIDERATIONS

Before proceeding to more complicated output port configurations, it will be helpful to consider the software implications of the readback capability we have added to the interface. To do this, consider again the case in which the processor has suddenly decided to turn on lamp 0. Example 3-1 contains an instruction sequence for turning on the lamp without affecting the other lamps.

Example 3-1: Turning On a Single Lamp

```
LDA    #$01    ;Turn on mask bit.
ORA    PORTA   ;Read in other bits from the interface.
STA    PORTA   ;Write result to interface.
```

Likewise, Example 3-2 shows the simple process of turning off a single lamp without affecting the other seven lamp drivers.

Example 3-2: Turning Off a Single Lamp

```
LDA    #$FE    ;All bits high except bit 0.
AND    PORTA   ;Read all other pins.
STA    PORTA   ;Output result.
```

In order to further demonstrate the power of being able to perform logic operations directly on the I/O device, Example 3-3 shows a simple method of alternating a single lamp's state without affecting the other lamps. This might be done in the case of a flashing lamp. Each time a timer times out, these instructions could be executed, with the result that the state of lamp 0 would be turned on and off (toggled).

Example 3-3: Toggling a Single Lamp

```
LDA    #$01    ;Lamp to toggle.
EOR    PORTA   ;Inverts only bit 0.
STA    PORTA   ;Output result.
```

While the shift and rotate instructions (ROL, ROR, ASL, and LSR) are occasionally used in output operations, they must be used with caution to assure that they do not erroneously affect other output bits. Their possible application includes such tasks as shifting the drive signals for the phases of a stepping motor. Using the rotate and shift instructions in combination with manipulating the carry (to set or clear bits 0 and 7) is not advisable with this type of interface because of the effect on the other bits of the interface. Such techniques can be quite useful with bit-mapped output ports, however, as will be seen later.

The increment and decrement instructions may also be useful

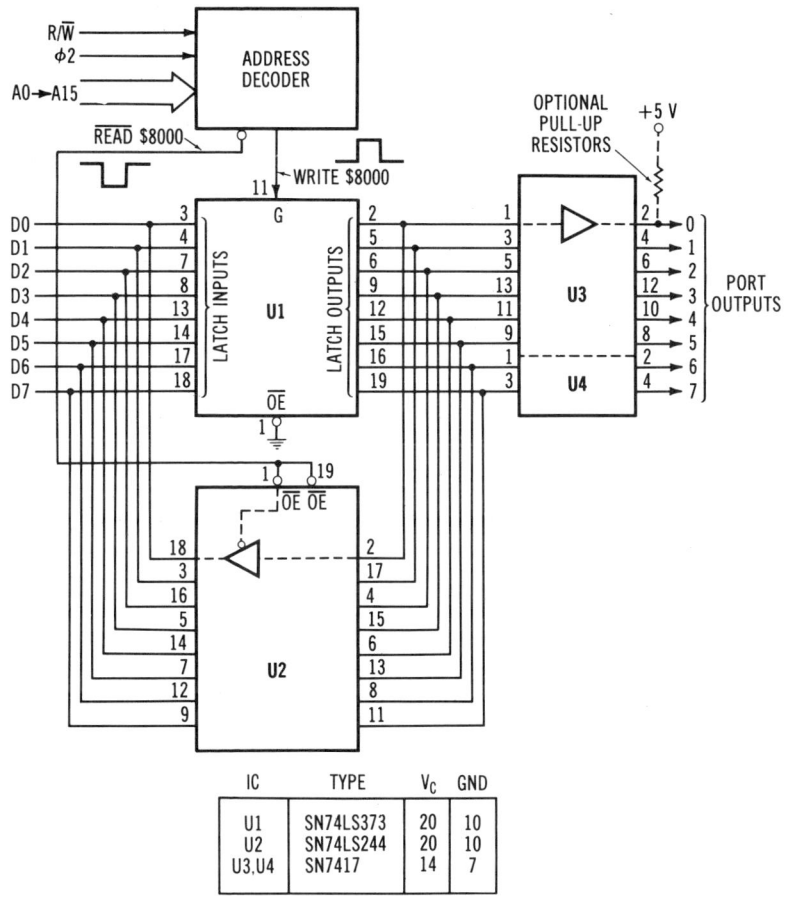

Fig. 3-2. An output interface with a register readback.

in some cases, but these instructions should also be used with caution to avoid undesirable side effects. This group of instructions is most likely to find application in such cases as interfaces to D/A converters when they are used as part of a closed-loop control circuit. Likewise, the add and subtract group will also find occasional application.

LARGE-SCALE OUTPUT INTERFACES

Fig. 3-4 shows an interesting expansion of the parallel interface. In this circuit it is assumed that the application requires a

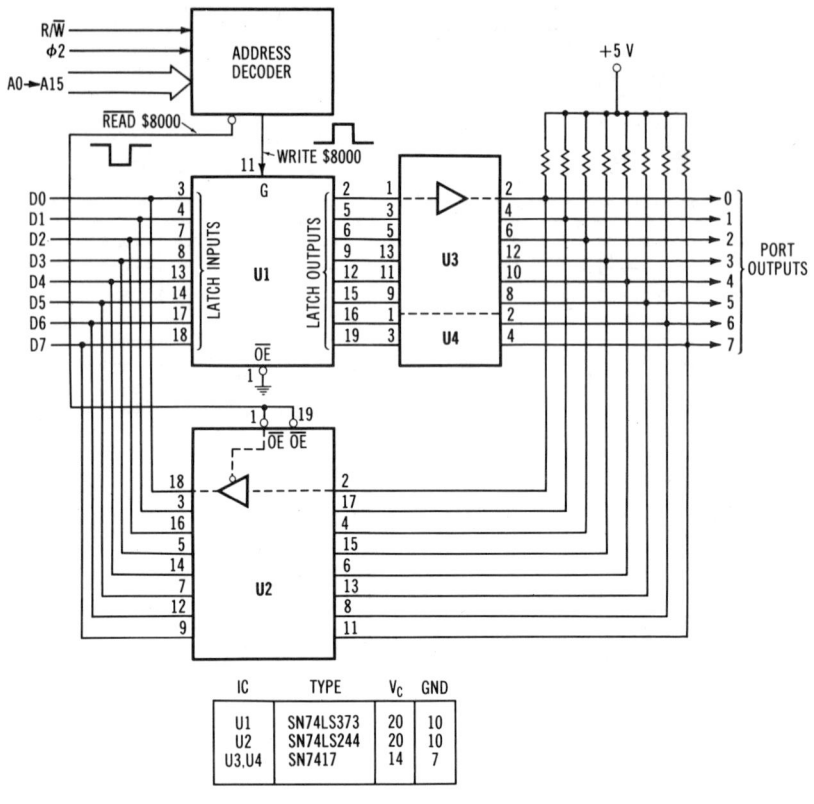

Fig. 3-3. An output interface with a pin-type readback.

large number of output ports with register-type readback. In order to eliminate the readback buffers, the ports are simply addressed on top of a block of read/write memory. When power is applied, there will be no correlation between the contents of a particular memory location and the latch with which it shares its address. This is quickly overcome by a start-up procedure that writes (usually zeros) to all port pins. After this is done, there will be a direct correlation between the ports and memory, and the ports will appear to have individual readback circuits. In some cases the cost savings can be very substantial.

EFFICIENT USE OF OUTPUT INTERFACES

An interesting application for the 6520 (an LSI port device) can be seen in Fig. 3-5. In this case, the port is equipped with

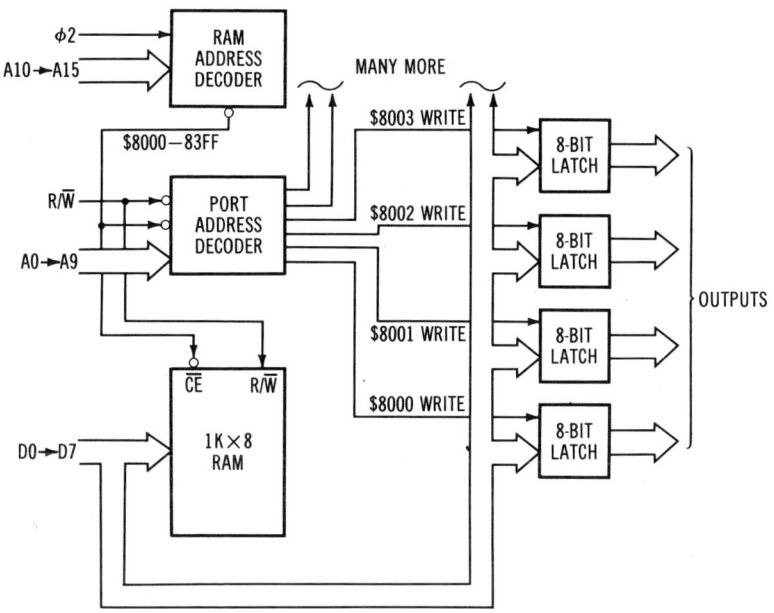

Fig. 3-4. A mass output interface with a pseudo-register readback.

passive pull-up outputs (PAO-PA7), and with readback of the type that actually reads the pin of the device. In this case, port A of a 6520 does the job nicely. It should be noted that port B is of the type shown in Fig. 3-2, and would, therefore, not work in the following scheme (unless repeatedly changed from an output to an input through the use of the control register).

What this rather novel circuit does is to take a number of simple momentary, normally open, illuminated push buttons, and make them operate as momentary, alternate action, or as banked selector-type switches. Not only are the switches made to appear to be more complex in operation than they are, they actually require only one port pin (which is used for both input and output) per switch. In addition to emulating their more complex (and expensive) cousins, they also allow for overriding features that would require elaborate solenoid-type switches if implemented in hardware.

The concept is actually very simple. Several times a second, each pin is set to a logic one for a very short interval. (If already in the logic one state, it is left in that state.) Since the duration of this state is only a few microseconds, the lamps will not flicker on if they are off. The output pin of the port is then read.

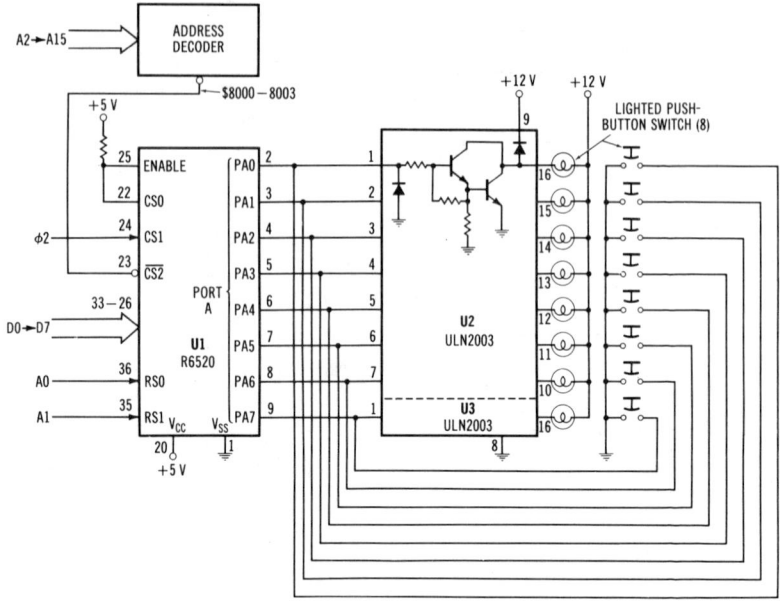

Fig. 3-5. Effective use of an LSI port.

If the corresponding push button is not pressed, the processor will read a logic one. And, of course, if the button is pressed a logic zero will be read. The processor then makes a decision on what state to set the pin to (and those pins with which it is functionally associated), based on what it found when it read the pin, and on the *personality program* for that pin. If the push button is programmed to act like a momentary push button, it will simply leave the pin in a logic one state and take the required action within the program. Notice that the lamp will have been illuminated while the button was *not* depressed, and would extinguish when the button was depressed, as a result of the input to the lamp driver being shorted to the logic ground. This is at least as sensible as having the lamp turn on only when the button is pressed (and the lamp is covered by someone's finger).

In the case of an *alternate action personality,* the processor would have stored the last state of the output in a separate memory location, and complemented the output of the interface in the event that the button were found to be pushed. Because of the action of the switch, the lamp will extinguish as soon as the button is pushed during an off cycle, but will not appear to be turned on until the button is released in an on cycle. This also happens in many mechanical switches.

Finally, if the personality is that of a bank selector switch, the lamp associated with the depressed button will be turned on (as soon as it is released), and all other lamps will be turned off. With proper software, a combination of all these personalities can exist on a single 8-bit interface. The lesson to be learned from this example is not simply how to control lighted push buttons, but rather the fact that by understanding the internal operation of the LSI interface element we have avoided the use of two 8-bit ports where one would suffice.

PRECAUTIONS

The programmer must always look out for two potential problems. The first is contact bounce. This can be overcome by using delay loops with the microprocessor verifying that the state of the switch is stable after the delay. The second problem is the curiosity some operators have for finding out what the computer will do when every conceivable combination of inputs is generated. If such an operator is supplied with a one-of-eight bank selector switch, he will use both hands (and a foot if necessary) to depress all the buttons at one time, his secret desire being to cause a malfunction which will demonstrate his superiority to the machine. The program must be written to consider such strange inputs in the safest and most benign way possible.

OUTPUT HANDSHAKING

When a parallel port is used to interface a computer with another device of an interactive nature (such as a printer, a terminal, or another computer), special problems arise. Using any of the output interface circuits shown so far, the computer would be forced to send (transfer out) data at a rate that was slow enough to assure that the receiving device had read one byte before another was sent. Many devices (such as printers) may be able to digest data very rapidly for a short time, but then they require time to take action. For example, a dot-matrix printer might fill an internal line buffer, and then print the whole line. If the transfer of each byte of data is slowed to the time required for the worst case, the throughput of the system will be penalized severely.

Fig. 3-6 shows a simple output port *handshaking* circuit added to the basic output port discussed earlier. In this example, register readback has been omitted.

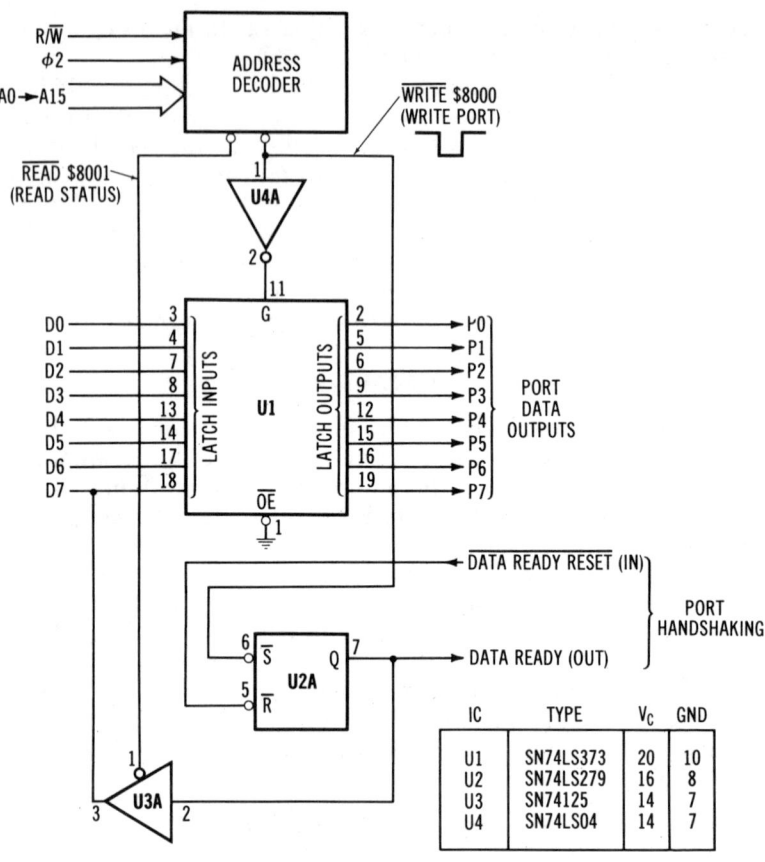

Fig. 3-6. A simple output port with handshaking.

An SR (set-reset) type flip-flop (U2) has been added, along with a tristate buffer. The buffer is connected so that the processor can read the state of the SR flip-flop (handshaking register). Whenever the output port is written to by the processor, the Q output of the handshaking register flip-flop is set. The receiving device can tell that a new byte of data is ready for transfer by testing the output of this register. In the interface to the outside world, this signal is normally called *data ready*. When the receiving device has read the data available at the port, it generates a negative strobe on an input line called *data taken or data-ready reset*. This resets the handshaking register to assure that the data is not read again, and to inform the sending computer that the data has been read.

When the microprocessor has additional data ready to be transferred, it will first test the handshaking register to see if the previous data has been accepted by the receiving device. If the old data has not been accepted, the processor will normally enter a wait loop. In the case of multitasking programs, the output task can be suspended, allowing other tasks to utilize the processor. Normally the task would be reactivated periodically to test the status of the register, or the executive might be capable of testing the flip-flop itself, and thus reactivate the task when the data has been read by the peripheral.

Normally, it is preferable to connect the tristate buffer output to either bit 6 or bit 7 of the data bus to allow the 6502 to test the status of the handshaking register (by using the BIT instruction). This prevents the necessity of masking out the other bits when testing the register.

INTERFACE LEVELS

Although quite a number of peripheral devices will accept the TTL signal levels generated by the circuit of Fig. 3-6, most require a signaling protocol referred to as RS-232. Under this standard, a bipolar signal is generated that alternates between $+12$ volts and -12 volts. The result of this type of signaling is that signal-to-noise ratio is improved, and longer transmission distances are possible. Several other standards exist, and include such techniques as balanced, dual-line differential transmission, and current transmission. Whatever the interface specification might be, the principles behind the exchange of data remain the same.

OUTPUT HANDSHAKING WITH INTERRUPTS

As was mentioned earlier, it is often desirable to allow the processor to take care of other business while it is waiting for the receiving device to accept a byte of data. Fig. 3-7 shows the handshaking circuit of the previous example with the addition of interrupt logic and an interrupt mask register (U2B).

The operation of this circuit is actually very straightforward. When the processor wishes to begin sending a string of bytes to the receiving device, it writes the first byte to the interface (thus setting the data-ready signal high), and then writes to $8003 (what it writes is not important) to set the interrupt mask register to enable interrupts. After this point, an interrupt will be generated any time that the handshaking register is reset by the receiving device. The interrupt service subroutine will cause

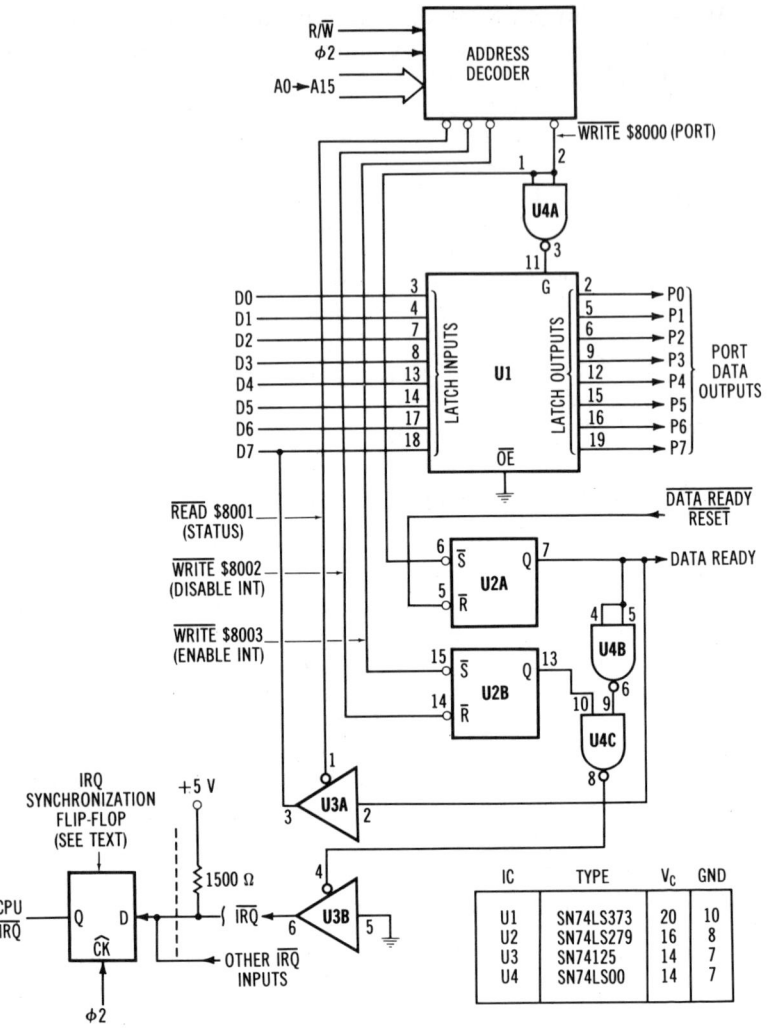

Fig. 3-7. Handshaking output port with interrupt capability.

the processor to service the output port by placing the next byte into output port latch. This write operation will, in turn, cause the data-ready signal to return high, thus eliminating the interrupt. This process will continue until, in the course of servicing the port, the microprocessor finds that the transfer is complete. At this point the microprocessor will write to $8004 to clear the interrupt mask register, and will then exit from the interrupt sequence. The technique is much the same when a multitasking program is involved.

It is good procedure to add a flip-flop somewhere between the various interrupt sources and the 6502. The interrupt signal should be applied to the D input, and the clock input should be connected to cause loading on the positive transition of the $\phi2$ clock. This is not always necessary, but is a good precaution if some interrupts are being generated by circuits other than 6502 family LSI devices.

When we have reached a complexity level as represented in Fig. 3-7, the use of LSI devices is definitely called for. If the reader has carefully considered the material in this and the previous chapter, he/she should have no trouble in understanding the specifications sheets of the various LSI interface circuits (as pertains to their input and output elements).

BIT-MAPPED OUTPUT INTERFACES

In Chapter 2 the concept of bit-mapped input interfaces was presented. Their counterpart, bit-mapped output ports, are at least as useful. As with the input interfaces, bit-mapped output interfaces may find special applications when adapted to take advantage of the flag structures of certain higher level languages. In assembly language programs they greatly simplify the software requirements, and improve the readability of the program.

Fig. 3-8 shows an addressable latch (SN74LS259) used as an output interface. Since the address lines A0 through A2 of the processor are connected to the latch-select inputs, each latched output has a unique memory address. While this configuration is not well-suited to signals composed of more than one bit, it is ideal for single-bit signaling. In this configuration, the data bus is not connected to the latch at all; instead, the data input pin of the latch is connected to the read/write line of the processor.

To clear a 1-bit latch to a logic zero, the processor only needs to perform a write operation to the address of that latch. Conversely, a read operation will cause the output to go to a logic one state.

While the circuit of Fig. 3-8 has the advantage of occupying only one memory location per bit, the circuit of Fig. 3-9 offers a more readable source code, and protection against false read operations that result during indirect addressing (see Chapter 1). This interface uses address line A0 as the data input to the latch and address lines A1 through A3 for latch selection. This results in each latch being represented by two consecutive ad-

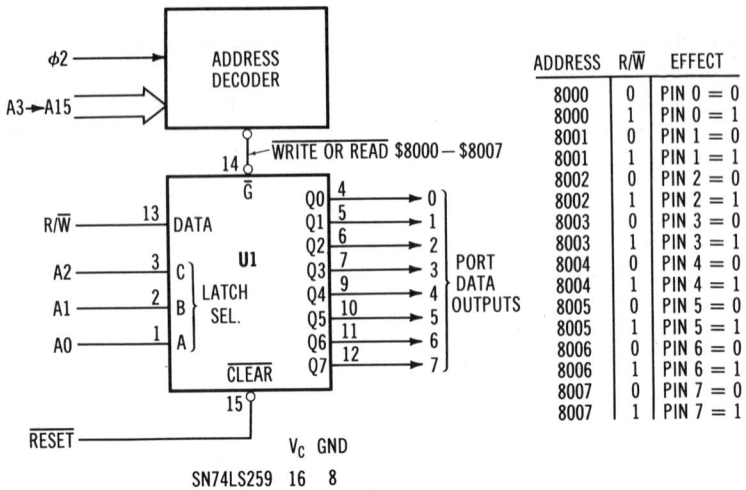

Fig. 3-8. Bit-mapped port with read-to-set and write-to-clear addresses.

dresses. Writing to the lower one of these two addresses causes a logic zero to be latched, and writing to the higher causes the latch to go high. Example 3-4 demonstrates the readability of source code for operating such a port.

Example 3-4: Software Operation of a Bit-Mapped Port

```
FAN$OFF    EQU $8000      ;Define off address.
FAN$ON     EQU $8001      ;Define on address.
           .
           .
           STA FAN$OFF    ;Turns off fan, contents of
                          ;accumulator not important.
           .
           .
           .
           STA FAN$ON     ;Turns on fan, contents of
                          ;accumulator not important.
           .
```

Notice that the software required for each operation is approximately one-third that required with a normal 8-bit, parallel output interface. And, as an added bonus, the accumulator contents are not affected. When the low cost of this circuit is considered, it is remarkable that it is not used more often.

There are numerous other ways to configure the addressable latch to serve as an output interface. For example, the latch-select inputs could be tied to the lower bits of the data bus, and the data input could be tied to A0. In this example it would be

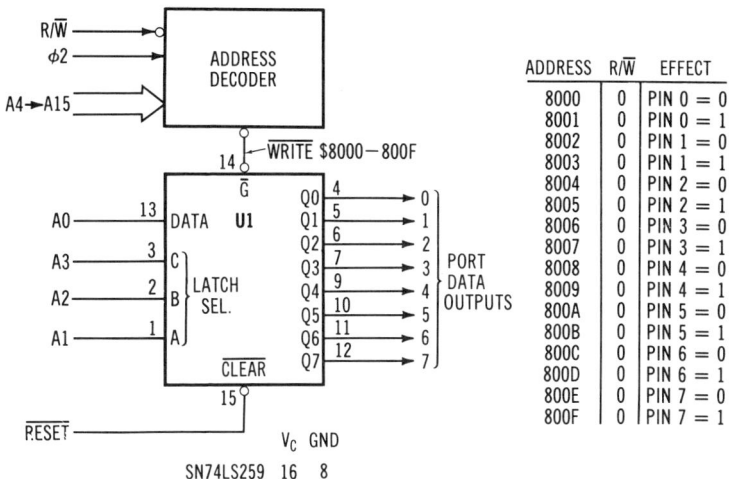

ADDRESS	R/W̄	EFFECT
8000	0	PIN 0 = 0
8001	0	PIN 0 = 1
8002	0	PIN 1 = 0
8003	0	PIN 1 = 1
8004	0	PIN 2 = 0
8005	0	PIN 2 = 1
8006	0	PIN 3 = 0
8007	0	PIN 3 = 1
8008	0	PIN 4 = 0
8009	0	PIN 4 = 1
800A	0	PIN 5 = 0
800B	0	PIN 5 = 1
800C	0	PIN 6 = 0
800D	0	PIN 6 = 1
800E	0	PIN 7 = 0
800F	0	PIN 7 = 1

Fig. 3-9. Bit-mapped port with separate set and clear addresses.

necessary for the address decoder to generate a strobe that was valid for two consecutive addresses. Writing a value of #$07 to the higher address would set latch number 7, while writing #$07 to the lower address would clear it.

4

Serial Communications

Much of the communications between microcomputers and peripherals and between different microcomputers is done by the use of *serial communications*. The reason for this, of course, is the fact that serial communications require only a single signal path. Thus, any digital communications link that must use radio, fiber optics, or telecommunications as a medium will almost invariably use some type of serial communications. There are literally hundreds of communications protocols that have been devised for this purpose. But, generally they divide into two fundamental concepts: synchronous and asynchronous communications.

SYNCHRONOUS COMMUNICATIONS

Synchronous communications is usually selected in systems where continuous data transmission/reception is required, and/or where the enhanced data recovery capability of this method is needed. The important distinction between synchronous and asynchronous communications is the fact that in synchronous communications, a clock signal that is in perfect synchronization with the received data is required at the receiving device. This may be accomplished either by transmitting the clock signal separately, or by extracting (recovering) the clock from the spectral information in the received data. Many different communications codes have been devised (Miller Code, Manchester Code, etc.) specifically to make clock recovery more reliable.

Because an LSI device for synchronous communications does not have to execute any internal operations beyond the data rate, these devices can usually operate on the order of 16 times faster than their asynchronous counterparts.

This type of communications is most useful in applications such as *continuous* remote control and guidance, and in bulk transfer of information between larger computers. Because it is not commonly used with smaller microprocessor systems, synchronous communications is not given detailed coverage here. The designer who has a requirement for this type of communications will find that the Motorola MC6852 SSDA (Synchronous Serial Data Adapter) offers communications rates up to 600K bps (bits per second) with several synchronization options.

ASYNCHRONOUS COMMUNICATIONS

Asynchronous communications is used extensively in microprocessor systems. The most commonly used data rates are 110, 300, 600, 1200, 2400, 4800, and 9600 bits per second. Devices are available to allow asynchronous communications at rates of up to 50K bps. The term *baud* is often used in regard to these data rates. This term originated from the word *Baudot,* which was an early, five-level, serial data code. It is used to indicate the transmitted bit rate. It should be noted that the actual rate of communication of *information* bits is less than the baud rate. The reason for this is that in addition to the information bits, an asynchronous data stream contains start bits, parity bits, and stop bits. It is more concise to use the term *bps* (bits per second) rather than baud, and it will be used in our discussion.

Fig. 4-1 shows a typical communications waveform for asynchronous communications. Data is transmitted in short "packets" of pulses, each of which corresponds to a 5- to 8-bit data word. For simplicity, the following discussion will assume an 8-bit data word. LSI devices used to send and receive these signals are often given acronyms such as UART (Universal Asynchronous Receiver Transmitter), USART (Universal Synchronous Asynchronous Receiver Transmitter), ACIA (Asynchronous Communications Interface Adapter), and so forth.

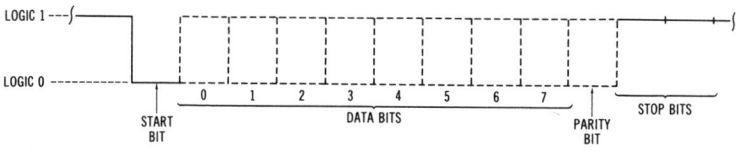

Fig. 4-1. A typical asynchronous data word.

When the asynchronous transmitter is in the idle state or between words, the serial output line remains in a logic one state. This is a carry-over from the days of current loop communications, when the continuous (idle) current assured the receiving terminal of the integrity of the line. At RS-232C levels, this causes a −12-volt signal, while at TTL levels the line will be in the high (3.5 to 5 volts) state.

THE ASYNCHRONOUS TRANSMITTER

An asynchronous transmitter is nothing more than a shift register with some additional logic (Fig. 4-2). The first bit of the register is the start bit and the last bit is usually the parity bit (although this is optional with some devices). The bits in between are the data bits, and they are transmitted in order, starting with the least-significant bit. With most LSI devices, a *transmitter data buffer* is provided. The buffer is loaded by the processor which can then go on to service other needs of the system. When the transmitter buffer is loaded, an internal flip-flop, called the *transmitter data buffer empty* flag, is cleared. This flag is sometimes wired into the status register of the device so that it can be read by the microprocessor, and is always available externally either as a logic signal or ORed into a composite interrupt signal. This allows the device to generate an interrupt and request service from the processor when the buffer becomes empty as a result of the data being transferred to the *transmitter register*.

Transfer of data to the transmitter register (the data area of the output shift register) occurs when the previous data has been shifted out. A flag flip-flop, called the *transmit register empty* flag, is set if both the transmitter and transmitter buffer registers are empty. This flag is useful at the end of a communication, and informs the microprocessor that the last data word has cleared the shift register, so that an appropriate action may be performed such as turning off the modem. During the transmission of the data bits, the parity flip-flop is usually toggled each time a logic one data bit is transmitted. Once all the data bits have been transmitted, this bit may or may not be transmitted, depending on how the user has wired the UART. This bit is described in more detail in the next section of this chapter.

After the transmitter becomes empty as a result of shifting out the data word and parity bit (optional), a pause is generated by the internal logic before the next start bit is transmitted. This pause is referred to as the stop bits interval, and is actually a timed period that is often programmable to either a 1-, 1.5-, or

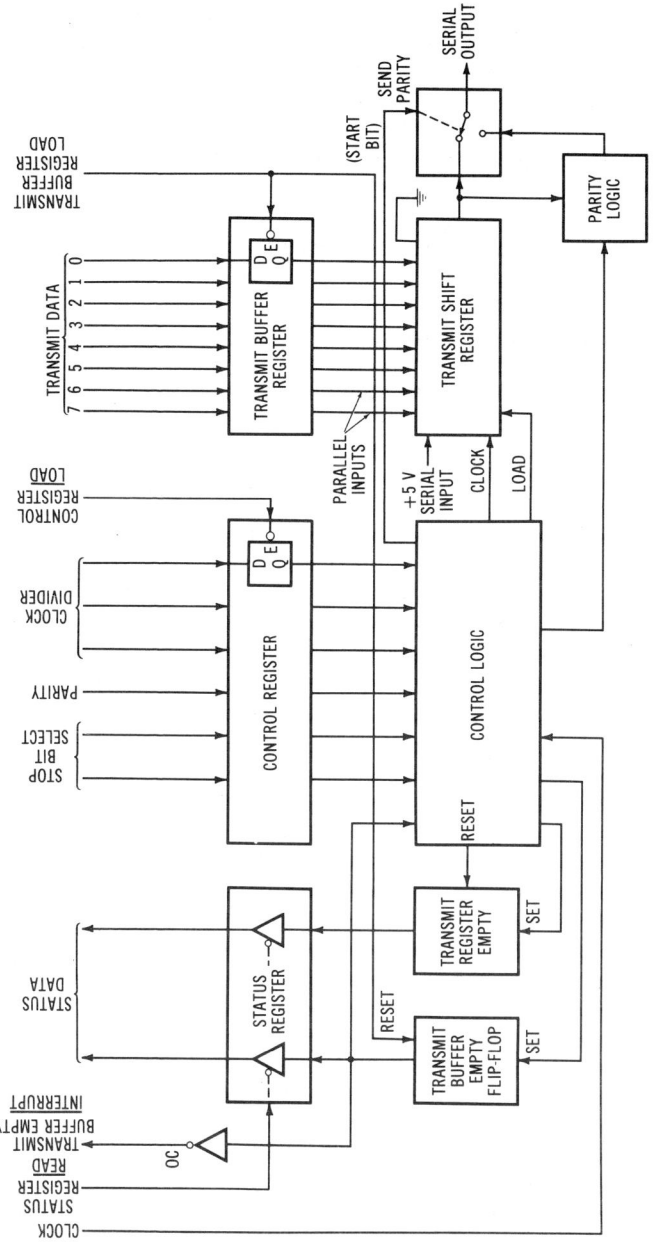

Fig. 4-2. A typical asynchronous transmitter block diagram.

2-bit interval. The output remains in the mark (logic one) condition during this time. The purpose of this interval is to allow the receiver to clear its logic. If the receiver becomes unsynchronized during reception, it may use data bits in the next word as the start bits. The longer the stop bit interval is, the sooner the receiver will get back in word synchronization with the transmitter. Unfortunately, the longer stop bit intervals reduce the communications data rate. The original purpose of this interval was to allow mechanical printers time to print the received character. With modern buffered printers, this requirement is disappearing.

With many LSI devices, the user can program the number of data bits, the presence of parity, odd or even parity, and the number of stop bits by wiring control pins or by software control.

THE ASYNCHRONOUS RECEIVER

The process of receiving an asynchnronous word is shown in the flowchart of Fig. 4-3, and the block diagram of a typical LSI asynchronous receiver is shown in Fig. 4-4. The first bit of a word is called the start bit, and is always present and always a logic zero. The start bit is used to synchronize the receiving device, and is not part of the 5- to 8-bit data word. When the leading edge of the start bit is detected, an internal divide-by-16 counter in the receiving device is preset. The input of this counter is clocked by a local oscillator at 16 times the bit rate. While this oscillator is not locked (synchronized) to the incoming data stream, it must be accurate enough to assure that after 10 bit clock intervals it is still within one-half cycle of the true communications clock (i.e., better than 5%). For this reason, this clock signal is usually derived from a crystal or ceramic resonator reference. Several chips are available to provide the frequencies required for standard data rates from a single crystal. Two such devices are the MC14411 (Motorola), and the HD4702 (Harris).

The clock counter is usually preset to eight on the leading edge of the start bit. If the start bit is present for the correct time period, the timer will count down to zero *at the center of the start bit*. If the start bit is not still present at this time, the internal logic will reset and look for another start bit. If the start bit is still present (logic zero), the clock counter at the receiving device will continue to rollover (count through zero) and clock data into the receive shift register at what should be the center of each bit.

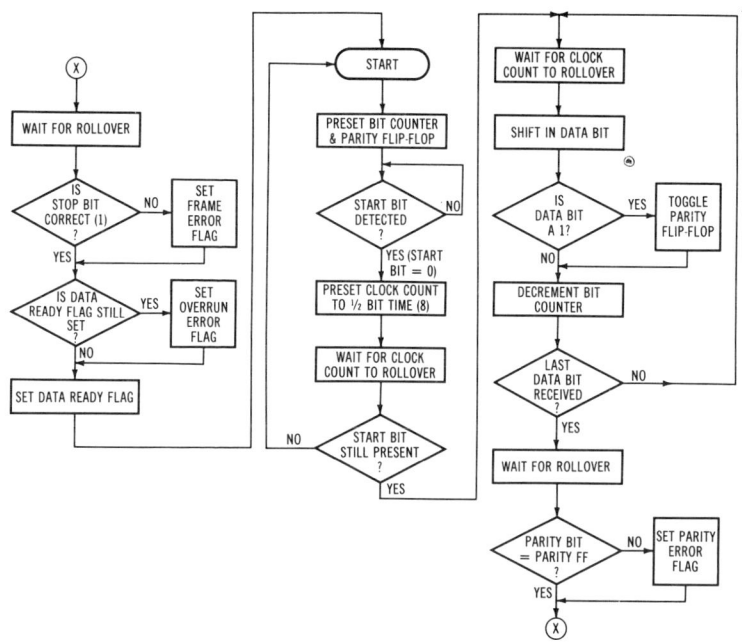

Fig. 4-3. A simplified flowchart showing the operation of a typical asynchronous receiver.

A bit counter is loaded at the beginning of each word with the programmed number of data bits to be transmitted or received. If the parity has been set by the user to be even, the parity flip-flop is set to a one; otherwise, it is cleared to zero. As each data bit is clocked into the receiver shift register, a bit counter is decremented and the parity flip-flop is toggled if the received bit is a one. The result of this sequence is that if the parity mode is even, the parity flip-flop will be in a logic one state at the end of a data word in which there are an even number of ones.

When the bit counter reaches zero, the next bit will be clocked into the parity bit of the receiver and shift register. If the received parity bit is not the same as the parity flip-flop, a parity error will be generated. In most LSI devices, this signal is available in the status register, but does not necessarily affect the operation of the receiver when an error occurs. In fact, the parity bit is sometimes used as an auxiliary (ninth) data bit in data acquisition systems, as is demonstrated later in this chapter.

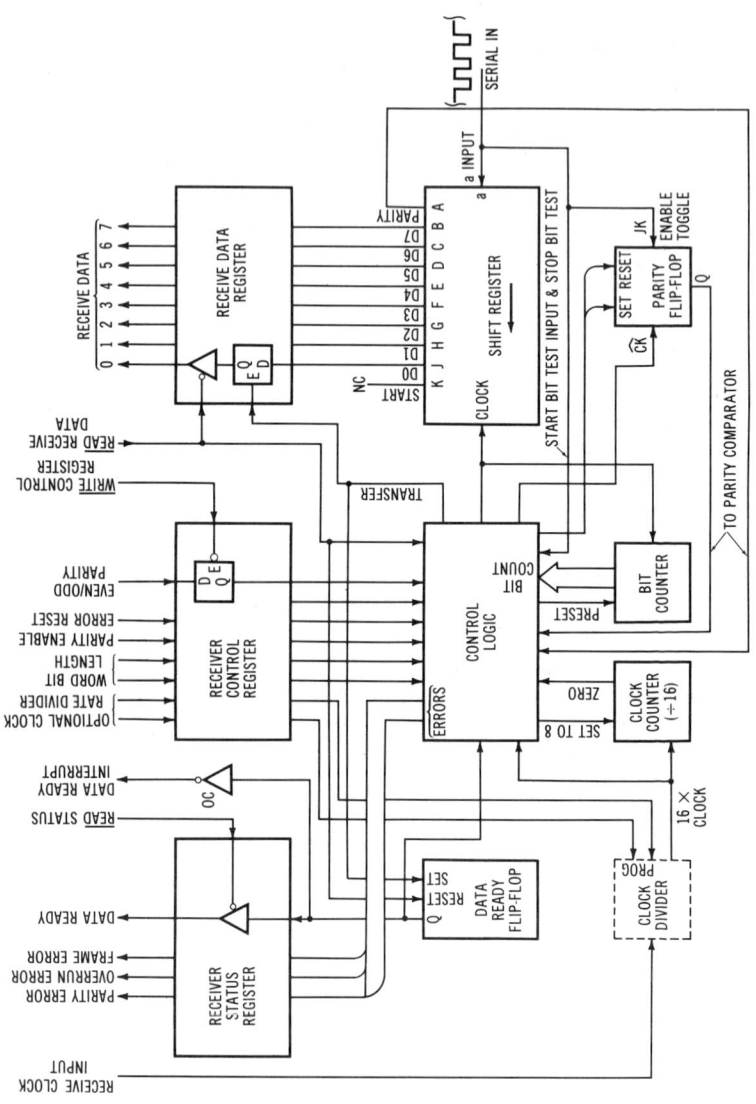

Fig. 4-4.   A typical asynchronous receiver block diagram.

After the parity bit is received, the data in the receive register is normally transferred to an 8-bit wide buffer. At this time the *data-ready* flag flip-flop will be set. This flag may be available as a bit in an internal status register and/or as an external (not tristate) signal. In some cases, it may be ORed with the *transmit buffer empty* signal into a single interrupt signal. The hard-wired output pin is useful for generating interrupts, whereas a tristate pin or an internally readable register signal is useful for software polling. If these signals are available only as external pins (not tristate) on an LSI device, they may be made available to the processor through an input port.

When the information in the data buffer register is read by the processor, some LSI devices will automatically reset the data-ready flag. Other devices have a *data-ready reset* input pin. This pin is usually an active low signal, and can be tied in most cases to the receive buffer tristate control pin, thus causing the data-ready flag to be reset when the information in the buffer is read.

In the event that a received word is transferred to the data buffer and the data-ready flag is still true, an overrun error occurs. This indicates that the processor did not service the receiver fast enough and has lost at least one received data word. Again, this signal does not necessarily affect operation of the receiver, unless the system software monitors this signal.

An error signal will also occur if the first start bit position following the parity bit is not a logic one. This error is called a *framing error* and is usually present in the status register. It indicates that the receiver has become unsynchronized, or that the clock frequency is wrong for the data being received. The microprocessor will normally take note of this signal, as it indicates that the received data is probably in error. In more sophisticated systems, the processor will automatically request a retransmission of the data from the transmitter when such errors are detected.

IMPLEMENTING THE ASYNCHRONOUS INTERFACE

There are several options open to the designer when implementing an asynchronous serial interface. In systems where the processor is heavily burdened with tasks, or where quick response to external events is required, it is usually advantageous to incorporate an LSI device in the interface. This device may be interrupt driven or it may be serviced through polling.

Table 4-1. A Comparison of Popular Asynchronous LSI Devices

Device	Type	Manufacturer	Max. Baud Rate (Asynchronous)	Package
P8251	USART	Intel/NEC	9600	28 Pin
P8251A				
HD6402	UART	Harris/Intersil	250,000	40 Pin
HD6402A				
AY31013	UART	General Instruments	30,000 (20–40,000)	40 Pin
AY31015				
MC6850	ACIA	Motorola	50,000 (500,000 with 1X Clock.*)	24 Pin
R6551(1MHz)	ACIA	Rockwell/Synertek	125,000 (External) ÷ 16	28 Pin
R6551(2MHz)			50–19,200 (Int)	
MC14469	AART	Motorola	4800	40 Pin

*In 1X clock mode, the receiver clock must be synchronized externally to the data being received.

Power Requirements (Typical)	Worst Reg Read/Write	Modem Signals	Clock Functions	Interrupt Masks	Notes
+5 V/225 mW	430 ns	4	*External: 1X, 16X, or 64X	None	
+5 V/270 mW	250 ns				
+5 V/10 mW	100 ns	None	External 16X	None	See Figs. 4-7, 4-8
+5 V→+12 V/10–25 mW	150 ns				
+5 V/70 mW to 105 mW	750 ns	None	External 16X	None	Pin Compatible with HD6402
+5 V/300 mW	500 ns	4	*External: 1X, 16X, or 64X	Yes (1)	
+5 V/350 mW	470 ns	5	External ÷ 16 or Internal Osc/Divider	Yes (1)	Built-in Baud Rate Divider and Special Echo Mode
	235 ns				
+5 V → 18 V/< 1 mW	N/A	16 Send 7 Receive	Built-in Oscillator	N/A	See Text & Fig. 4-10

THE SOFTWARE UART

At the other extreme, the system designer may elect to run the entire process by software. By using the functional description of the preceding section, a program can be written to cause the pin of a standard parallel port to act as either a serial input or a serial output port. Even the bit timing of the data transmission can be done by software loops. For example, the TIM (Teletype Interface Monitor) program does exactly this. Unfortunately, these programs slow system throughput, and preclude concurrent tasks from being executed. This is especially true when timing is done in software loops, as servicing any other task would cause a timing error.

An improvement can be made to the software UART by doing the timing with a hardware timer/counter as found in some LSI interface devices. Since the counter is wired directly to the system clock or some other clock source, timing errors will not occur as long as the processor returns to check the counter with sufficient frequency. The AIM 65 uses this technique to provide a serial interface. The unit contains two R6522 VIA (Versatile Interface Adapter) chips. One of these is reserved for the user's applications, and a timer and two port pins in the other VIA are used for asynchronous communications.

A further improvement can be made by using the timers with an interrupt. A completely interrupt-driven transmitter can be designed this way, with the only disadvantage being the fact that interrupts occur at the bit rate instead of at the word rate (as with an interrupt-driven LSI device), and the software is more complex. This concept can be used in the receiver section as well if an edge-sensitive input is used to cause an interrupt on the negative edge of the start bit. After this interrupt occurred, the timer would be programmed to interrupt the processor in the middle of each data bit (so the bit could be read into the processor) and the original edge-sensitive interrupt would be disabled. After the parity bit was clocked in, the software would enable the edge-sensitive interrupt for the next start bit.

One additional option is available in the R6522 VIA, and that is the use of the built-in 8-bit shift register to receive and transmit the data bits. This device would be better suited if it were 10 or 12 bits in length, but it can be used anyway if the designer is imaginative in its application.

The selection of one of these options will depend on the cost/performance tradeoffs of the system being designed. In all but the most cost-sensitive designs, the LSI device is usually a good investment. Table 4-1 contains a list of most of the asynchronous communications devices that are easily interfaced to the 6500/6800 families, along with some of their specifications and features.

ASYNCHRONOUS LSI DEVICE SELECTION

There are two fundamental types of LSI asynchronous interface devices: (1) chips that were designed solely for use by μPs (USARTs and ACIAs), and (2) chips that can be used with a μP or in standard interface designs (UARTs). The R6551 and MC6850 devices are typical devices in the first category. These two chips are not interchangeable, but they are comparable in function. These devices are referred to as ACIAs (Asynchronous Communications Interface Adapters). The distinct feature of this group of devices is that they have a minimum of external connections, and thus are housed in the smaller 24- and 28-pin packages. This smaller size is a result of the fact that the parts contain an internal data bus. Thus, instead of having separate pins for the transmitter data register, the status register, and the receiver data register, they have only one set of eight bidirectional data pins. The flow of data to and from the internal registers is controlled by the register select line(s), the chip select line(s), the read/write line, and the $\phi 2$ input (on the R6551).

ACIAs

The smaller size and internal bus of these parts makes them ideal for interfacing to microprocessors, but almost useless in circuits that do not contain a microprocessor. Fortunately, the UART-type devices of the second group mentioned earlier are very satisfactory for nonmicroprocessor-based applications. They will be discussed shortly.

Both ACIAs and UARTs contain the fundamental elements discussed earlier. In addition, the ACIAs contain some auxiliary input and output pins that can be used to control modems. These signals are more or less standardized through most of the industry. But, different modems may use them or not use them in accordance with their operation and switch settings. They are described here briefly, but for more specific information on these modem control signals, refer to the manufacturer's literature on the device you will be using.

Note: In the following explanations it should be remembered that a logic one is represented by a high (3.5 to 5 volts) signal at the TTL interface to the device, but as a negative (-12 volts) signal at the RS-232 interface. Conversely, a logic zero is represented by a low (0 to 0.7 volt) signal at the TTL interface, but as a high ($+12$ volts) signal at the RS-232 interface. References to low and high signals should be taken to mean those signals as seen at the TTL interface.

Data Carrier Detect (DCD)—This input signal goes to a logic zero to indicate that a tone carrier is being received back from the far terminal. In the MC6850 this signal can cause an interrupt when it goes high, which is particularly useful in preventing hanging of an interrupt-driven program when communications fail. In the R6551 it is readable in the status register.

Data Set Ready (DSR)—This auxiliary signal is not always used, and goes low to indicate that the modem is ready. It is not present on the MC6850, and is readable in the status register of the R6551. If needed with the MC6850, the signal could be brought through a standard port pin, or it could be logically ANDed with the DCD signal (using a device such as an SN74LS32).

Clear To Send (CTS)—This active low input from the modem is used to hold back transmission under the control of the modem. In the MC6850, this input simply inhibits the transmit data register empty flag. In the R6551, the shifting in the transmitter is inhibited until the line returns high.

Request To Send (RTS)—This active low signal is used to control the modem. In some systems the RTS output enables the modem, which then verifies that it is ready by pulling the DTR line to the low state. In both the MC6850 and the R6551, this pin is simply an auxiliary output pin that can be written much the same as any output port pin. It does not affect operation of the ACIA, except by the effect that it causes in the modem.

Data Terminal Ready (DTR)—This output is also an active low signal. Like RTS, it has no direct effect on the ACIA. It is used to signal the modem that the ACIA is ready. The DTR signal is absent on the MC6850, but the RTS pin can be used for this function in some cases.

Obviously, these signals depend on the modem being used, the software communications package, and the protocol in the particular system. It is not uncommon for a system to have these input signals wired to an enabled condition, and the output signals left unconnected.

The R6551 is a newer device, and contains more features than the MC6850. But, both devices have their place in certain system designs. The most important addition to the R6551 is a programmable baud rate generator. This circuit is actually a programmable divider with a built-in crystal oscillator. The circuit is capable of producing clock signals for all standard data rates between 110 and 19,200 bps, from a single 1.8432-MHz crystal. The MC6850 has a simple programmable divider that can divide the clock input by 1, 16, or 64.

UARTs, UARs, and UATs

In the earlier stages of LSI development, a variety of devices containing only receivers (UAR or Universal Asynchronous Receiver), and only transmitters (UAT or Universal Asynchronous Transmitter) were available. These were developed as a result of the economic considerations of yield and chip density that prevailed at the time. These devices typically required multiple supply voltages, and were relatively expensive.

As technology improved, these functions were consolidated into a single device called a UART, and the UART pinouts were standardized by the various manufacturers. Single supply, 5-volt units also became available, and costs were reduced. Since all the signals of these devices are available on separate pins, and since most outputs are tristate, the devices are well suited for both intelligent and nonintelligent environments. UARTs do not contain the modem control interfaces found in ACIAs. The internal organization of the UART is essentially the combination of the receiver and transmitter block diagrams shown and discussed at the beginning of this chapter. The result of this combination is shown in Fig. 4-5.

Representative of these devices are the Harris (and Intersil) HD6402. These chips are CMOS and offer both low power consumption (10 mW) and high speed. The internal registers can even be accessed by a 6502 running at 2.0 MHz, and the devices can transmit and receive at speeds of 250K bps. While this may seem like overkill in light of the currently used data rates in communications systems, the possibilities in data acquisition and remote control are excellent.

When one thinks of the application of a UART, there is a natural tendency to think in terms of ASCII communications, but the usefulness of these devices is far wider. A simple remote operator's console is shown in Fig. 4-6. In this circuit, the data inputs of the transmitter are connected to switches. These may be momentary- or toggle-type switches, as long as the transmitter sends the states of the switches at frequent enough intervals to assure that no activation is missed. The number of times each second the switch information is transmitted is controlled by one timer of an NE556 dual timer. The other half of this timer is used as an RS-232 receiver. This device is actually well suited for this application, since the threshold/trigger input has built-in hysteresis. When combined with a low-pass RC filter, this de-

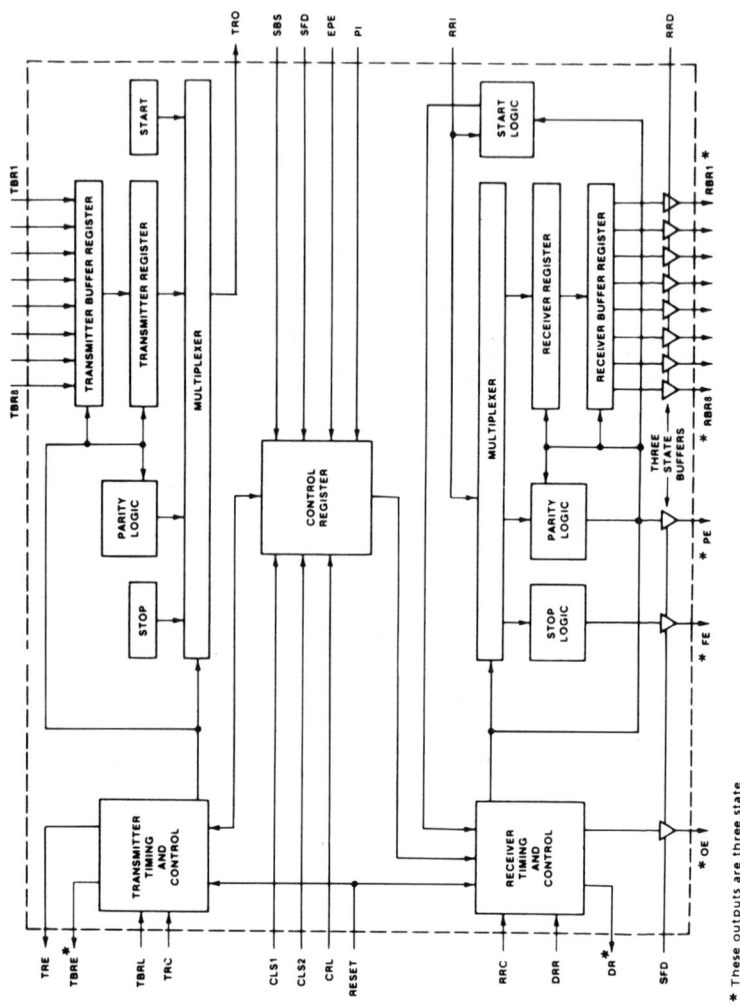

(Courtesy Harris Semiconductor)

Fig. 4-5. Functional diagram of a UART.

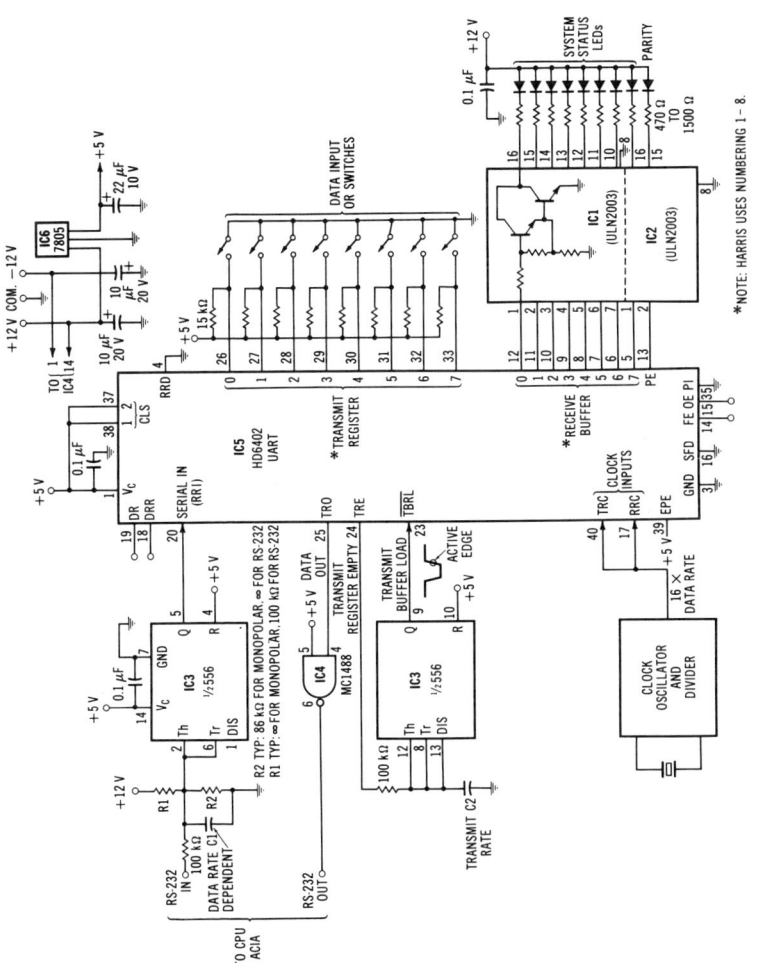

Fig. 4-6.   Diagram of a remote control panel using a UART.

vice has excellent noise immunity. The transmitter uses a standard RS-232C driver chip to develop the high-level transmission required for noise immunity.

The receiver data bits in this simple example are simply connected to a bank of LED status indicators, through integrated Darlington driver chips. Thus, the computer can indicate eight conditions to the operator, and receive eight commands from him/her.

Many variations of this simple circuit are possible. For example, if more switch inputs were required, the inputs of the transmitter could have been passed through two-to-one multiplexers, and the select signal for the multiplexer could be derived from toggling a flip-flop after each transmission. Such a circuit is shown in Fig. 4-7. Notice that the receiver at the microprocessor would not know which bank of eight switches was being received, except that the select flip-flop signal is connected to the EPE (Even Parity Enable) input of the transmitter. Thus, the receiving terminal could know that every other transmission should show a parity error. If a parity error *did not* occur on every other cycle, the receiver would know that an error did in fact occur!

Notice that in both these UART circuits, control pins such as the CRL (Control Register Load) and RRD (Receive Register Disable) are permanently wired to the enabled state. If the device were connected to a microprocessor, these pins would be wired to address decoder outputs, and the receiver, transmitter, control, and status buffer pins would all have been bussed together onto the data bus.

MONOPOLAR SIGNALING

Because of the requirement for ±12-volt supplies for the RS-232C driver, designers often abandon RS-232C when designing data acquisition systems that do not use long (greater than 100 feet) communications links. One popular alternative is the use of a monopolar 12-volt signal level, where +12 volts is a logic 0 and a voltage near ground is logic 1. This scheme means that the remote data acquisition modules need only a single positive supply that is used to produce both the +12- and +5-volt supplies. A typical output stage consists of nothing more than an npn transistor and a pull-up resistor. A typical circuit of this type is shown in Fig. 4-8.

When using a monopolar signal, the designer must remember to modify the receiving circuits appropriately. A simple, single supply comparator may be used for this purpose as shown in

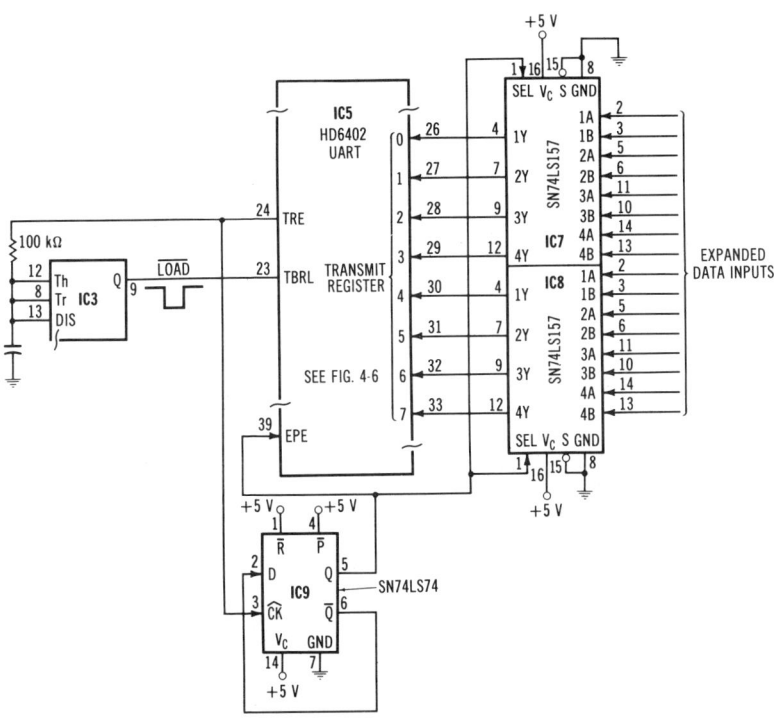

Fig. 4-7. The use of parity to expand the number of data inputs (addition to Fig. 4-6).

Fig. 4-8. Also shown in this figure is the use of the standard RS-232C receiver (DS1489) for monopolar interfaces. The *response* resistor, which controls both hysteresis and the switching point, is connected to a negative supply voltage to cause the switch point to be at 5 to 7 volts. The value of this resistor will depend on the version of the chip used, and the manufacturer. Some manufacturers offer different internal resistors, as indicated by different part numbers. Because of the fact that a negative supply is required, this circuit is useful only at the CPU end of the data acquisition links, where multiple supplies are typically available. On the data end of such links, a comparator or NE555-type circuit can be used. If the NE555/ NE556-type circuit in Fig. 4-6 is used for monopolar signaling, resistor R1 should be omitted to move the threshold back into the positive range.

When monopolar signaling is used, the noise immunity of the link will be reduced, unless the single supply is increased to

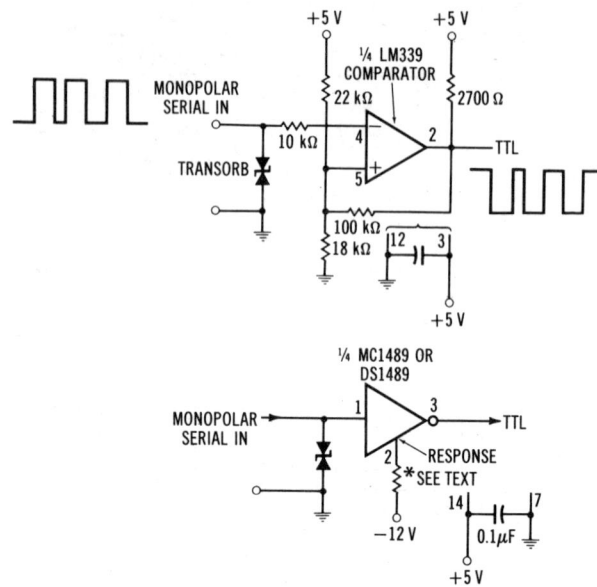

Fig. 4-8. Schematics of two monopolar receivers.

+24 volts (which is often undesirable). While this is not often a problem in short links (less than 100 feet), the proximity of lines carrying high current or inductive spikes must be considered. It may also be advantageous to connect transient suppressors across each line at both the acquisition and CPU ends of the line to prevent damage from power supply voltage spikes. In systems where human safety is involved, this should be done routinely.

THE AART

The Motorola MC14469 AART (Addressable Asynchronous Receiver Transmitter) is a component that has not been widely publicized to date. This clever CMOS LSI chip contains a transmitter, receiver, clock oscillator/divider, and a monopolar line receiver. The device also contains a transmitter multiplexer as shown in Fig. 4-7, and a receive data comparator that is capable of recognizing a preprogrammed address word. These features combined with a very low power consumption make it ideal for data acquisition.

The receiver section of this device uses one bit (bit 7) to serve as a flag. If bit 7 of a received word is a logic 1, the other seven

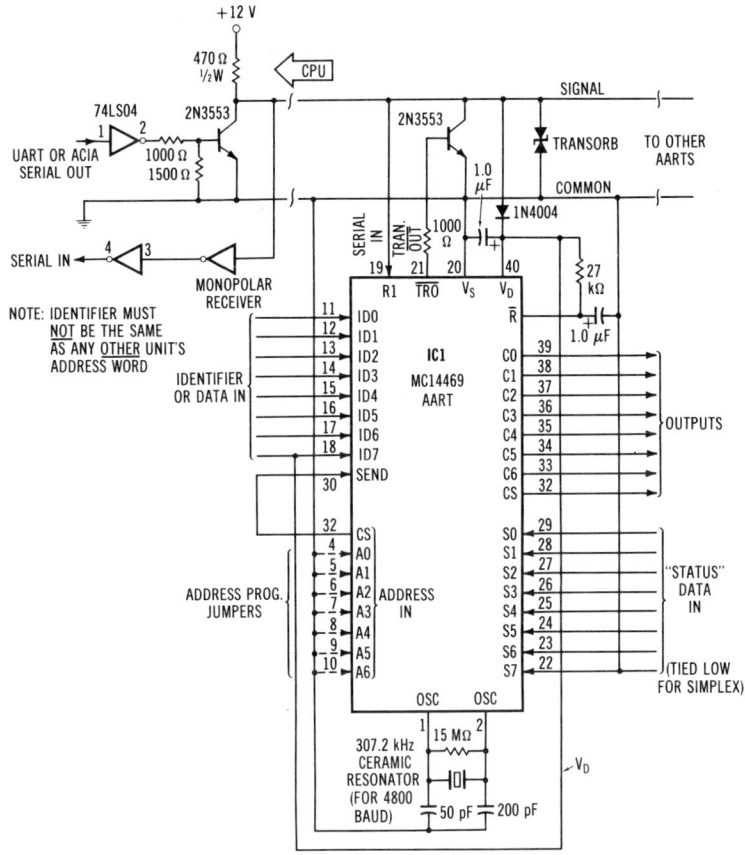

Fig. 4-9. Schematic of a line-powered AART acquisition network.

bits are compared to the address pins. A match between the address word and the preprogrammed address word will cause the receiver to capture the low seven command bits of the next received word (providing that the address flag bit is a logic 0 on the next word received). These seven bits are available for control of the acquisition circuitry, or for remote control or status indicators. Depending on the connection of the control pins, the AART can be made to transmit back two 8-bit words in response to having received the correct address and/or command words.

The low power consumption of the MC14469 permits the design of a very clever power supply. The power for the AART can be derived from the single full duplex data line. A small network (a diode, capacitor, and TRANSORB) using this scheme is shown in Fig. 4-9. Notice that when no information is being transmitted on this data link, +12 volts is present. This is the same as the TTL communications links described earlier. The reason for this is obvious when one considers powering the device from the serial line, since the line will be in the +12-volt state most of the time. One of the few disadvantages of the AART is the limited data rate (4800 bps). But, this is adequate in most applications.

This chapter has not been intended as a complete reference on serial communications! The subject could (and does) easily fill many volumes. The intention here has been to stimulate the designer to think in more general terms about the fantastic possibilities offered by the modern LSI serial interface devices that are available.

5

Timers and Timing

The control of many processes requires that the controlling device be able to measure time. This is true not only when time is directly involved in the calculation being done by the controller, but also when closed-loop control is being performed. The proper damping of such systems requires that a correction factor be applied to the output command proportional to the characteristics of the error sensed at the feedback point, and that this correction be applied at carefully controlled intervals.

Other requirements for the measurement of time involve applications such as the software UART described in Chapter 4. In this instance the time duration of a bit cell must be within a few percent of the timing at the other end of the communications link. The acceleration of a stepper motor may also require careful time measurement, as may a myriad of other functions.

THE SOFTWARE TIMER

The most obvious technique for causing the microprocessor to delay operations for a short period of time is to include a delay loop in the program. If only one delay is required, this may be included directly into the program. If several delays are required, a subroutine may be called as in Example 5-1.

Example 5-1: A Simple Nested Loop Time Delay

```
          .
          .           ;MAIN PROGRAM
          LDX TIME    ;N = 2, TIME is the delay (0 − #$FF)
          JSR DELAY   ;N = 6
          .
          .
DELAY:    PHA         ;N = 3, Save A on stack.
```

```
        TYA         ;N = 2, Save Y register in A.
        LDY #00     ;N = 2, Zero Y for counting.
LOOP:   DEY         ;N = TIME (2 * 256), Decrement low counter.
        BNE LOOP    ;N = TIME((3 * 256) − 1), Loop until Y = 00.
        DEX         ;N = TIME * 2, Decrement high counter.
        BNE LOOP    ;N = (TIME * 3) − 1, Loop until X = 00.
        TAY         ;N = 2, Restore Y.
        PLA         ;N = 3, Restore A from stack.
        RTS         ;N = 6
```

This simple time-delay subroutine is frequently used in systems that do not require concurrent tasks and do not have interrupts. *The programmer must be extremely careful in its use!* This is especially true when a high degree of accuracy is required.

The first problem with this type of time delay will become clear as we calculate the timing of it. Each line of the example contains a comment that starts with the number of clock cycles required to execute the instruction in the line. In a system with a 1-MHz clock, this number will be the number of microseconds spent executing each of the instructions. The number of clock cycles per instruction (usually two to six) is taken from the R6502 instruction set summary card supplied by Rockwell. The total time delay for a line is calculated by multiplying this value by the number of times that the line will be executed.

Care must be exercised when calculating the delay caused by the branch instructions. Notice that the timing for the BNE instructions is:

$$N = TIME ((3 * 256) − 1)$$

where TIME is the number of times that the time-delay loop is to be executed. The timing for a BNE instruction is three cycles *if the branch is taken*, but only two cycles if it is not. Thus, 255 times around the loop, the delay is three cycles, and once it is two cycles (thus the −1 term above). While this is a rather small error, the value of two shows in the summary card with an obscure subscript note. The programmer who misses this fact will have a significant error.

Additionally, the programmer may find that after calculating the total delay as is done below, there is an unexpected error:

$$DELAY = 2 + 6 + 3 + 2 + 2 + TIME ((5 * 256) − 1) + (TIME * 3)$$
$$− 1 + 2 + 3 + 6$$

or

$$DELAY = 25 + (1282 * TIME)$$

The actual delay is, in fact, in error by a factor of TIME * 256 or by TIME * 257. Either of these errors could be very troublesome. To add to the confusion, the error might well disappear on a subsequent reassembly of the source program. This is because the BNE instruction requires an additional cycle to be executed if the branch crosses a page boundary. It is often awkward to "reorg" a program to assure that such loops do not straddle a page boundary. It may be advisable to locate such loops at the beginning of the program, where such crossings are not likely to crop up as the program is edited and rearranged.

A final error can occur if the programmer allows interrupts to occur during this type of time delay. Since the processor cannot allow for the fact that it was off servicing the interrupt during the loop, the delay will be increased by the amount of time spent servicing the interrupt. If such delays are used in interrupt-driven programs, the programmer must either mask interrupts, or use this software time-delay loop only at the highest priority interrupt level.

Finally, the delay will not be any more accurate than the system clock. If this clock signal is generated by a temperature-sensitive circuit such as an RC oscillator, the delays will be inaccurate. In some applications, such as key debounce timing, these problems are not important; but, it is very important that the programmer be aware of their existence.

SIMPLE ANALOG TIMERS

A simple, practical, analog timer is shown in Fig. 5-1. While this timer does not offer the accuracy and reproducibility of the digital timers (discussed later on in this chapter), it offers the unique feature of being adjustable by a potentiometer (R2). This feature is particularly useful in applications that require the operator to routinely adjust time delays during system operation.

The circuit is controlled by three negative-going signals from an address decoder (see Chapter 1). The first of these is a START signal. This signal is buffered by applying it to the clock input of flip-flop IC1A. Buffering is done here because of the marginal timing requirement of the trigger input of the timer IC. When this signal causes the trigger input of IC2 to go low, the output of IC2 will go high, and the discharge pin of IC2 will go inactive, allowing capacitor C1 to begin charging through resistors R1 and R2. The logic 1 on the Q output of IC2 will also reset the trigger buffer flip-flop through inverter IC3A. When the voltage across C1 has reached 66% of the 5-volt supply

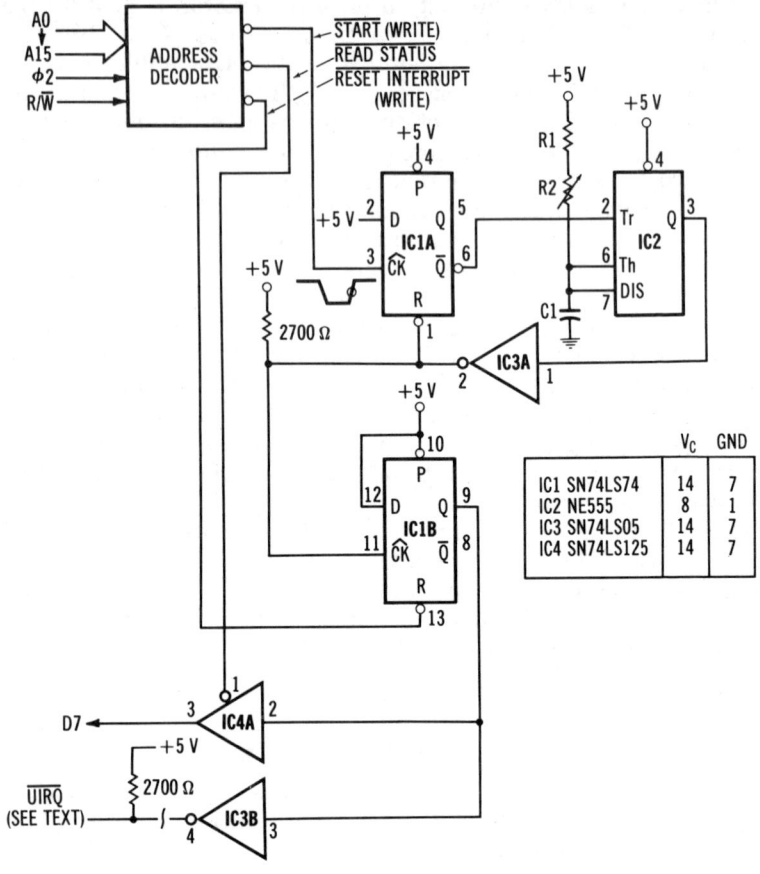

Fig. 5-1. Schematic of a simple analog timer.

level, the Q output of IC2 will return to the low state. This change causes a positive edge on the output of inverter IC3A, setting the interrupt flip-flop IC1B. The discharge pin of IC2 will then discharge capacitor C1, preparing the timer for the next cycle.

The output of the interrupt flip-flop drives the *unsynchronized system IRQ line (UIRQ)*. As explained in earlier chapters, this signal should be synchronized to the system ϕ2 clock. Since this synchronization is required only in one place in the system, it will not be included in each interface circuit. In most digital timers, the clock source will be the system clock, and additional synchronization may not be required.

In most systems there will be several interrupting signals, and the processor must poll the various circuits to determine the source of the current interrupt (assuming that no interrupt priority encoder is available in the system). In the analog timer being discussed here, this capability is provided by the second address decoder signal. This signal is called READ STATUS, and it activates the tristate output of IC4A. This signal is read on bit 7 of the data bus, and is thus testable with the BIT instruction of the 6502. Notice that reading the status does not affect the timer in any way. If the programmer wishes to reset the interrupt, writing to the address of the third output of the address decoder (RESET INTERRUPT) will accomplish this. Also notice that both the START and the RESET INTERRUPT write operations are data bus independent. This means that the programmer does not have to load the accumulator with any particular value before doing the write operation.

While address space could be saved by using one address and using one bit of the data bus to differentiate between the start and reset functions, this is not usually a true savings. The reason for this is the fact that the extra program instructions required to load the accumulator before the write operation will use much more memory space than the single address required to separate the signals. The logic is also simpler when the signals are derived from separate addresses.

A SIMPLE 8-BIT DIGITAL TIMER

As in earlier chapters, the policy here will be to explain the operation of discrete timer circuits before attempting to evaluate the LSI devices that are available. By doing this, you will develop a better appreciation for the design tradeoffs that govern these circuits. To this end, Fig. 5-2 shows an extremely simple digital timer.

There is a strong similarity between this circuit and the analog timer circuit in Fig. 5-1. This circuit is also controlled by three signals (pulses) from an address decoder. As in the previous example, these lines start the timer, read the timer status, and reset the timer interrupt flip-flop.

Writing to the START address causes the two counter ICs to be loaded with the 8 bits on the data bus. If a prescaler is present, it should be reset by the start signal. Thus, writing #$FF to the start (or load) address will cause a full count to be loaded into the counters. The counters will then begin counting down at a rate determined by the system clock and the optional clock divider circuit. This divider is necessary when longer time inter-

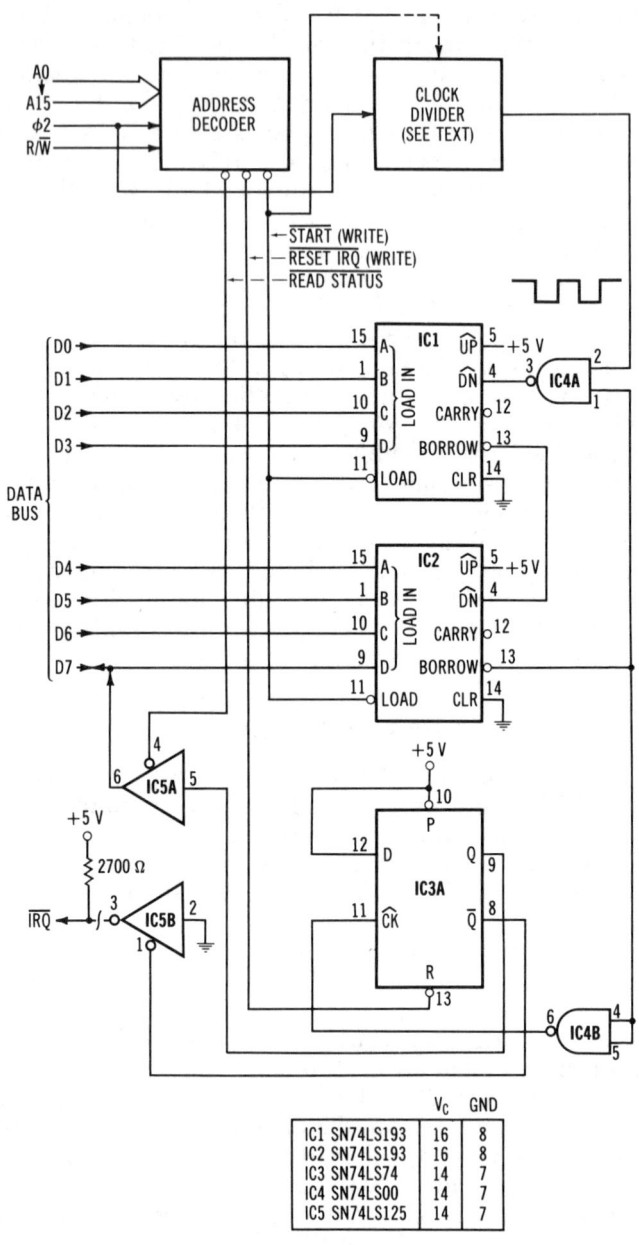

Fig. 5-2. Schematic of a simple 8-bit digital timer.

vals are required. An improvement of this circuit might include a divider circuit that could be software programmable (to change the time scaling without any hardware change). In fact, many of the LSI timer chips do offer this feature, as will be seen later.

When the count in the timers reaches zero, an active low borrow signal will be generated by IC2. This borrow signal will stop further clocking of the counters by inhibiting the clock signal at IC4A. The borrow will also set interrupt flip-flop IC3A. As with the analog timer, the state of this flip-flop can be read by performing a read operation at the READ STATUS address, through the use of IC5A. The interrupt flip-flop also causes an interrupt by activating the tristate input of IC5B. This variation in the use of a tristate buffer is helpful in reducing the design parts count. In the analog timer, an open collector device was used for this function. Unfortunately, the use of such a device will leave the designer with the option of either using pull-up resistors on the other inverters of the package, or of not using them at all. It should be mentioned that when large value pull-up resistors are used on open-collector devices, the gate speed and noise immunity are reduced. When lower values are used, the system power consumption is increased. Selecting the proper parts for implementing an efficient design can often be a considerable task, on top of the functional design considerations.

In some applications, the designer may wish to operate the timer without interrupting the 6502. Most LSI devices allow for inhibiting the interrupt output under software control. The danger of this is that the processor can only *test* the fact that the prescribed time has elapsed, not how long it has been since it elapsed. Thus, if the program did not test the status of the timer very frequently, there could be a considerable variation in the time delay generated from one operation to the next.

Even in systems that are interrupt-driven, this type of error can occur. For example, the program might have the interrupt mask set at the time that the timer counts down to zero. This would be the case if the processor was already servicing an interrupt of a higher priority. It would also be true if the processor was executing a subroutine that was called by both the main part of the program and the interrupt service subroutine, but that was not reentrant. In either of these cases, the processor would not be able to adjust for the reaction time that it had exhibited. In most cases, this is not a serious problem, provided that the programmer is prudent with his use of the interrupt mask. In some applications, however, it is serious because of the cumulative effect over many operations.

A common example of this problem is the real-time clock. In such an application, the processor would count fractions of seconds, seconds, minutes, hours, days, etc. Upon being interrupted, the processor would immediately reset the timer (start it again), and then execute the timekeeping program. Unfortunately, the reaction time of the processor is variable and is cumulative. Thus, a slow but steady error will creep into the time calculation. If the system is heavily interrupt-driven, the error might even develop rather rapidly.

There are two common solutions to this problem. The first of these is for the timer to continue to count down after rollover counting through zero (rollover). The counter outputs could then be read by the use of an octal, tristate buffer as in the simple input ports described earlier. Thus, if the processor found that the count was #$E8 at the time of entering the timer interrupt service subroutine, it could simply subtact #$18 from the next counter value before reloading the counter. Obviously, the correction count must be less than the target count to be loaded (before adjustment) or correction could not be made. Provided that the range of counting is kept within the bounds discussed above, the overrun count can simply be added to the target count, since it is a negative binary number. If the result of this addition does not generate a carry, a counting boundary error has occurred. Unfortunately, the cumulative error problem is often sensitive to even fractional count errors. For this reason, the early and simple LSI counters used a modified rollover count scheme. Under this modified scheme, the counter would continue to count down after rollover, not at the divided rate of the clock divider output, but at the full system clock rate. While this scheme makes accurate time correction possible, it certainly does not make it fun. The correction algorithm was usually complex and time-consuming (both for the programmer and the computer). The R6530 and R6532 contain just such circuits. These parts contain a simple 8-bit counter with a programmable prescaler and some interrupt logic, while the R6522, R6531, R6534, and MC6840 contain more advanced timers.

Another weakness of our simple 8-bit timer (Fig. 5-2) is the lack of counting range. The programmer can change only the time interval over a range of 1 to 256 clock pulses (either from the system clock or the clock divider). While additional range is gained by changing the prescaler, this is usually done *only* during initialization. This is because the controlling algorithm must be somewhat complex to allow for the changed scale factor.

A SIMPLE 16-BIT TIMER

A better alternative to solving the time interval problem is shown in Fig. 5-3. This 16-bit timer is merely an extension of the 8-bit timer of Fig. 5-2. Since the timer contains 16 binary divider stages, it has a counting range of 1 to 65,536 clock pulses. Unfortunately, it cannot be loaded in a single write operation from the 8-bit data bus. For this reason, a latch is provided (in this example it is wired to the low 8 bits of the timer). The latch can be loaded with the first 8 bits of the count without triggering the counter. The other 8 bits of the count can be loaded directly into the second counter (in this case the higher 8 bits). Directly loading this second counter also causes the first

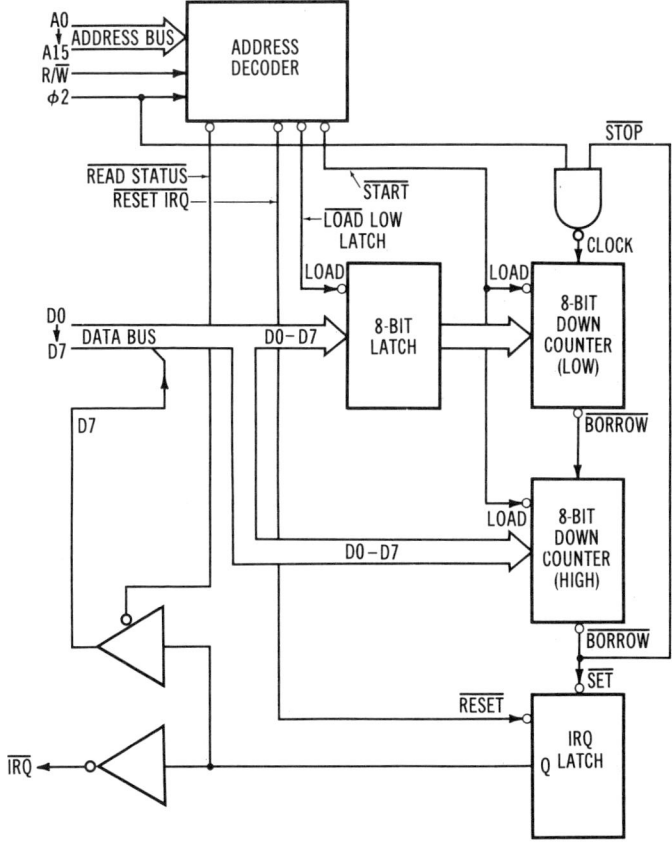

Fig. 5-3. Diagram of a basic 16-bit counter/timer.

counter to be loaded from the latch and triggers the counting operation. A prescaler could also be added to this circuit to further increase the range of the timer. While this circuit has an improved range, it does not offer any improvement in the area of cumulative error.

ADVANCED COUNTERS AND TIMERS

As the reader will recall, there are two common methods for correcting the problem of cumulative timing error. In Fig. 5-4 the 16-bit timer has been improved by adding an additional latch for the high byte of the counter. The two latches allow for the possibility of having the processor write the desired count to the timer during initialization only. The control logic of the circuit would then cause the counters *to be reloaded from the latches at each interrupt*, without the necessity (and delay) of having the processor load them. This scheme completely eliminates the cumulative error problem associated with the processor reaction time.

Fig. 5-4 also includes some additional features. The addition of the control latch (register) and control logic allows the clocking source to be determined under software control. For example, in a real-time clock application, the system designer may wish to use the 60-Hz line frequency for timing. Some LSI counter/ timer chips allow for clock source selection in just this way.

Another feature that is shown in the block diagram of Fig. 5-4 is the capability of gating the counter clock source from an external signal. This feature might be useful in an application such as measuring the time between two events. Since the reaction time of the processor is eliminated from the time calculation, relatively short delays between events can be measured quite accurately.

A further improvement could be made to the counter if the count could be read by the processor. It would also be helpful if the counters could be switched to count up as well as down. By doing this, the counter could provide a running total of the number of counting events that occurred since it was last reset. This could relieve the processor from performing complex *overhead* software, allowing it to perform more suitable tasks. All of these features are found in various combinations in LSI timer/counter circuits.

The cost of LSI devices is usually determined more by the size of the package than by the functional density (within limits). Since the total number of pinouts that are required for even

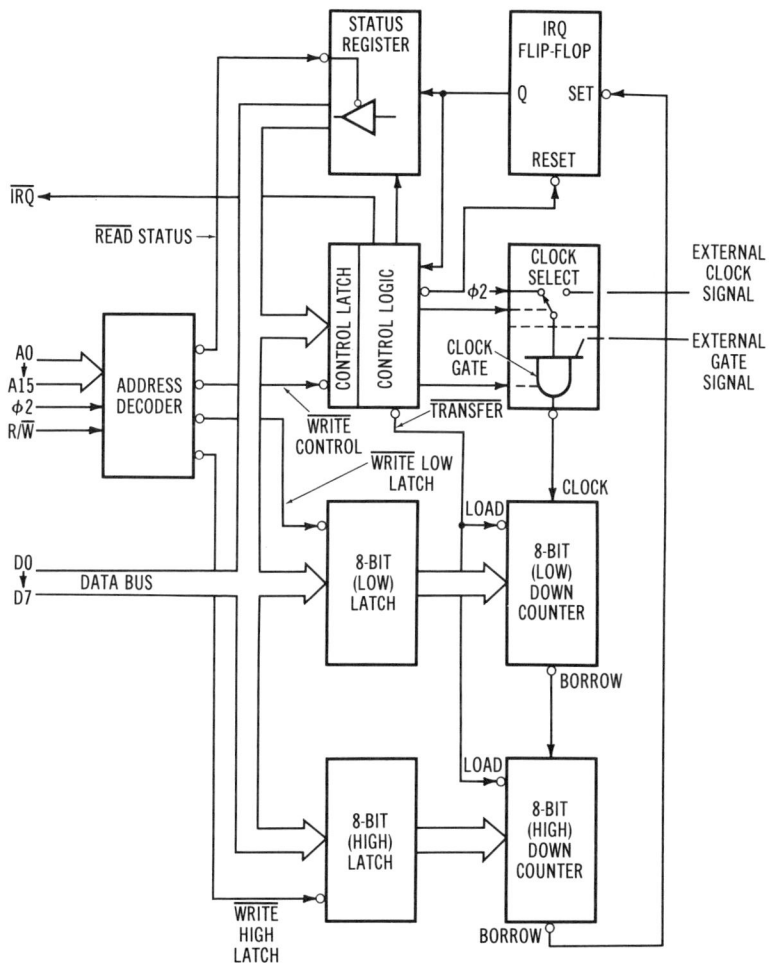

Fig. 5-4. A multimode 16-bit counter/timer.

a relatively complex counter is small, and since most of these are the bus signals, these circuits are usually included in LSI packages with other functional devices. In the case of the MC6840, three relatively advanced timer/counters are in one package. In the 6500 family of devices, the counters are included in packages containing various combinations of ROM, RAM, and I/O. Table 5-1 is intended to provide the reader with an overview of the available LSI timer/counter chips that will

Table 5-1. Characteristics of Clock/Timer Devices

Part No.	Timers/Pkg	Bits	Latched	Auto Reload	Prescaler	External Clocking	External Gating/ Trigger	Other Functions
R6530	1	8	No	No	÷1,8,64,1024	No	No	1024 Bytes ROM 64 Bytes RAM 16 I/O Lines
R6531 R6531Q*	1	16	Yes	Yes	No	Yes	Yes	2048 Bytes ROM 128 Bytes RAM Shift Register 15 I/O Lines or (Q version) * 27 I/O Lines
R6532	1	8	No	No	÷1,8,64,1024	No	No	128 Bytes RAM 16 I/O Lines
R6534 R6534Q*	1	16	Yes	Yes	No	No *Yes	No *Yes	4096 Bytes ROM Shift Register 14 I/O Lines * 26 I/O Lines
R6522	2	16	Yes	Yes	No	Yes	No	20 I/O Lines Shift Register
MC6840	3	16	Yes	Yes (with Jumper)	No	Yes	Yes	
MC6846	1	16	Yes	Yes	÷8 or ÷1	Yes	Yes	2048 Bytes ROM 10 I/O Lines

readily interface to the 6500 family of microprocessors. When the designer is choosing components for a production system, the tradeoff between desirable counter features and other I/O requirements is often very complex.

A REAL-TIME CLOCK

Many systems require that the time of day and date be available to the microprocessor and operator. If this function is accomplished with one of the timers just discussed and a software counting program, the clock will have to be reset each time the power is removed and reapplied. The real-time clock interface in Fig. 5-5 will not only eliminate this problem, but also will provide several additional advantages.

The MM58167 is a CMOS, real-time clock chip designed to be interfaced to the 8080 and Z80 family of microprocessors. When the chip is interfaced to these devices, it can be wired

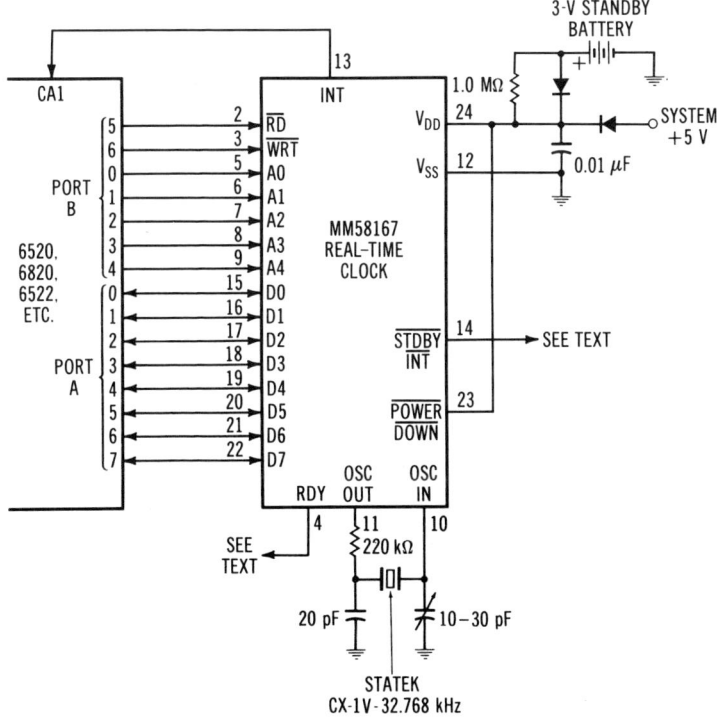

Fig. 5-5. Schematic of a real-time clock interface.

directly to the address and data buses, but interface to the 6500 family requires that a bidirectional port be used to buffer these signals. The reason for this is that the read and write times of the MM58167 are slightly over 1 μs. When the part is used with the 8080/Z80 family CPU chips, it causes the processor to wait for the required time by using the RDY (ready) line. Since the 6502 cannot use any wait states during a write operation, the bus signals must be latched and held for the required time. The RDY output of the MM58167 could be tested through an input port of the 6500 system. But, since the time it is a logic 0 (not ready) is so short, it would always test true (ready) by the time the processor could interrogate it, and thus there would be no purpose in adding the circuit for this.

The clock chip has internal registers that can be addressed by the microprocessor. The counter registers from 0.1 ms to months can be read from, and written to, at the interface. This device also contains an interrupt control structure that allows interrupts to be generated from between 0.1 s and 1 month. These interrupts occur on the INT pin of the MM58167. They are synchronized to the 6500 system by applying them to a handshaking control pin of a port. This handshaking port pin should be programmed to generate interrupts on the *positive-going edge* of the INT output.

Additionally, the MM58167 also contains a set of latches. These latches are compared to the time counters, and can generate an interrupt when they match. The latches can also be used with a power-down feature to turn the system back on at a preprogrammed time. To keep this interface simple, the power-down and standby interrupt features will not be used. A portion of the manufacturer's data sheet is available in Appendix A for your reference. Only the problem of interfacing it is discussed here.

At first, it might seem that the process of manipulating the I/O ports during read and write operations would be very messy. This can be avoided by the use of a *software interface* or *driver* module. This module would simply contain two subroutines (not including interrupt service software). The first of these subroutines would be called with the desired clock register number in the X index register, and would read the clock and return the contents of that clock register in the accumulator. The second subroutine would be entered with the desired clock register number in the X index register, and the data to be written to that clock register in the accumulator. No value would be returned, but the desired data would be written to the specified clock register. Examples 5-2 and 5-3 contain these subroutines.

These examples assume a 6522 is used, and that port B was initialized to be an output port when the system was initialized.

Example 5-2: Real-Time Clock Read Module

```
READCLK   LDA #$00      ;Set port A for reading.
          STA DDRA      ;Store in data direction reg.
          TXA           ;Register to accumulator.
          ORA #$60      ;Mask control bits high for safety.
          AND #$DF      ;Read strobe (bit 5) low.
          STA PORTB
          NOP           ;Time delay.
          LDA PORTA     ;Read register data.
          PHA           ;Save data.
          LDA #$60
          ORA PORTB     ;Don't affect other bits.
          STA PORTB     ;Turn off read strobe.
          PLA           ;Restore data.
          RTS
```

Example 5-3: Real-Time Clock Write Interface Module

```
WRTCLK    PHA           ;Save data to be written.
          TXA           ;Register to accumulator.
          ORA #$60      ;Read and write off.
          STA PORTB     ;Set up address.
          LDA #$FF      ;Make port A an output port.
          STA DDRA
          PLA           ;Recover data to be written.
          STA PORTA     ;Present it to clock data bus.
          LDA PORTB     ;Get ready to cause write.
          AND #$BF      ;Write strobe low.
          STA PORTB
          NOP           ;Timing delay.
          ORA #$60      ;Turn off write strobe.
          STA PORTB
          RTS
```

At this time, several manufacturers are working on real-time clock chips that will be directly compatible with the 6500 bus. While much of the specific data presented here will soon be obsolete, the fundamental approaches to solving these problems will not be. The key to a clean system design is meticulous organization and forethought. For example, it might be noticed that in both the above modules, the register number in the X index register is preserved. From experience, a designer will realize ahead of time that he will likely use some sort of loop in the process of writing and reading these registers. By preserving the X register it may be simpler to do this. Most of this discipline is developed with practice, but we will attempt to get a head start by pointing out a few examples from time to time.

Analog-to-Digital Conversion and Data Acquisition

The requirement to accurately measure analog phenomena is perhaps the most common, and certainly one of the most demanding, of the interface design tasks. The variety of transducers for measuring any one given phenomenon may be extensive, and the input circuitry used to interface a particular transducer must be carefully matched to the characteristics of the device. The relatively simple task of interfacing high-level (5 volts full scale or more) signals to a microprocessor is discussed first, and the more difficult interface problems are covered later in this chapter.

A SIMPLE SINGLE-SLOPE 5-CHANNEL A/D CONVERTER

The A/D converter circuit shown in Fig. 6-1 is intended primarily as an educational circuit, and as a platform for explaining the circuits that follow. Although the circuit can be built and operated, the disadvantages will become clear later in this explanation.

A repetitive voltage ramp signal is generated by the NE555 relaxation oscillator circuit in combination with a constant-current circuit and a buffer amplifier. The internal thresholds of the NE555 are set to cause the ramp to start at a voltage of one-third the supply voltage (between pins 1 and 8), and to peak at a voltage of two-thirds of the supply voltage. The reason for this choice of thresholds is related to the fact that the NE555 is normally used with an RC-type charging circuit, which generates

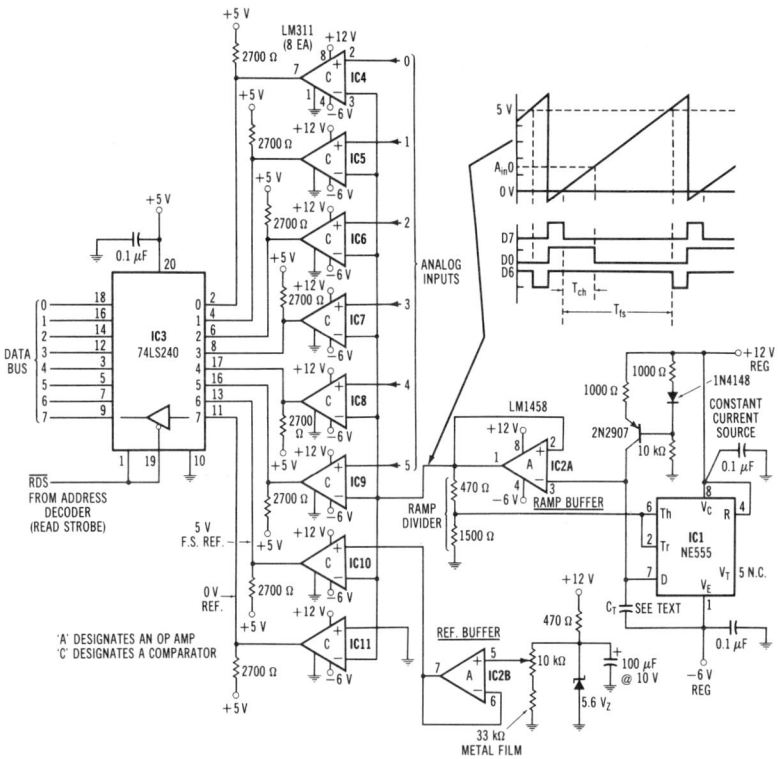

Fig. 6-1.   Schematic of a single-slope, monopolar A/D converter with references.

an exponential ramp. Our circuit uses a constant-current source, which generates a flat ramp. This improvement is necessary for accurate measurements, and also allows the expansion of the ramp thresholds without a deterioration of timing stability. The threshold expansion is accomplished by dividing the ramp feedback signal to the threshold and trigger inputs of the NE555. Thus, a ramp signal is generated that extends slightly below ground (0 volts), and slightly above 5 volts.

The ramp signal is wired to the inverting input of eight comparators. The LM311 was selected for this application because the output is TTL-compatible, while the inputs can operate over a ±15-volt range. The outputs of these comparators are interfaced to the computer data bus through a simple tristate buffer as discussed in the chapter on input ports.

Bits 6 and 7 of the interface are wired to provide calibration references for the converter. When the computer needs to read one or more of the analog inputs, it must first wait for bit 7 to go true, indicating that the ramp voltage is more negative than ground. Bit 7 was chosen because it can be conveniently tested by the BIT instruction of the 6502. When bit 7 returns to logic 0, the computer must start a timing operation. This timing could be done with a software loop. But, best accuracy will be obtained if a hardware counter is used as described in the preceding chapter.

The microprocessor must record the time at which each input comparator (whose channel value is to be read) goes to a zero state. The time at which the bit 6 reference comparator goes to zero (also testable with the BIT instruction) is then recorded and used as a calibration (full-scale) reference. The input voltage of each channel may then be calculated as:

$$V_{in} = \frac{T_{ch} \times V_{ref}}{T_{fs}}$$

where,

T_{ch} is the time that the channel comparator went to a zero state,

T_{fs} is the time that bit 6 went to zero,

V_{ref} is the calibration reference voltage (5 volts).

The requirement to perform this mathematical operation is the most noticeable fault of the circuit. While adjustment of the peak ramp voltage (via pin 5 of the NE555) may allow the designer to correlate the reference voltage and ramp timing so as to scale the channel time directly to volts or other measurement units, the circuit will not be stable over time and temperature.

With the reference voltage used in the calculation of the channel value, accuracy is dependent primarily on the stability of the reference circuit and the linearity of the ramp. Minor accuracy errors will be contributed by the offsets of the comparators and the system sampling rate. A variable error factor will also be contributed by channel noise.

When the reference is not used in the calculation, accuracy becomes dependent on all of the above factors, plus the stability of the peak ramp voltage and the frequency of the ramp. Both of these factors will contribute significantly to the error, and the circuit will be unsatisfactory for any serious application.

It should be noticed that a metal-film resistor is used in series with the reference adjustment potentiometer. Although absolute accuracy is not required, these resistors are more stable over time and temperature than carbon-composition resistors.

This converter has one advantage over the converters mentioned next, and that is that several channels can be measured by simply adding comparators; no multiplexer is required.

AN INEXPENSIVE DUAL-SLOPE A/D CONVERTER

The dual-slope A/D converter shown in Fig. 6-2 is a practical circuit for the measurement of signals to an accuracy of as much as 12 bits. The circuit is shown in a simple one-channel unipolar configuration for clarity. The central component of the design is an operational amplifier used as an integrator (IC1A). The output of the integrator is compared to ground (0 volts) by the comparator, IC4, and the result is interfaced to the computer through a tristate buffer.

The source of the input to the integrator is selected by writing bit 0 of the data bus to latch IC6 (see the chapter on output ports). A dual comparator (IC2) was chosen as a level translator between the TTL output of the latch and the gates of the FETs.

The processor begins the reading sequence by testing the input address to assure that the ramp is at a value below ground. A BIT operation indicates that the comparator is in the zero state. If this is not the case, the processor must write #01 to the latch address. This write operation will cause the integrator to integrate in a negative direction at a rate determined by the reference voltage and the integrator resistor and capacitor.

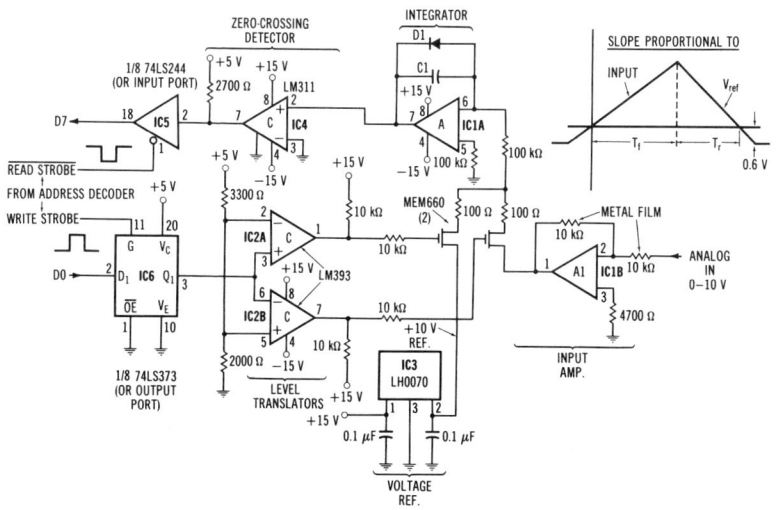

Fig. 6-2. Dual-slope unipolar A/D converter circuit.

When the comparator has been verified to be in the zero state, a value of 0 is written to the latch. This operation will cause the integrator to begin to integrate in a positive direction at a rate determined by the input voltage and the integrator RC. When the comparator goes to a high state, the processor must start a timer. This timer may be implemented in hardware or software, but hardware timers are generally preferable. The RC of the integrator must be selected so that when a full-scale input signal is present, the ramp will reach a value between half and full supply by the time the counter reaches a target (usually full) count. A design value of two-thirds of the positive supply is typical. It is essential that, over time and temperature, the ramp never reaches a peak value which would cause the comparator or integrator to operate in a faulty manner.

It should be noted that if the input signal is zero, the ramp will never integrate above zero volts. For this reason, the processor should execute a default timing loop while waiting for the comparator to go to a true state. This time will normally be somewhat longer than the full time count, and upon expiration of this time the program will consider the input to be zero. If this is not done, the program will hang up on zero input measurements. If accurate measurements near ground are required, this time will be longer. A low forward drop Schottky diode at D1 will minimize this time requirement.

When the counter has reached the full-scale count, a logic 1 is written out to the latch, and the counter is reset to zero. The integrator will now begin to integrate down at a rate determined by the reference voltage and the integrator RC network. When the comparator returns to a zero state, the computer will record the count. This count will be proportional to the input voltage, and can be scaled to directly correlate to any measurement unit desired. Diode D1 clamps the integrator a few tenths of a volt below ground to prevent a long wait on the beginning of the next reading cycle, and the converter will normally be left in this state between conversions.

A good quality nonpolarized capacitor should be used (e.g., polystyrene) in the circuit to avoid asymmetric charging effects. If this is done, the long-term stability and temperature coefficient of the integrator capacitor and resistor are not contributors to the accuracy of the circuit. This is the distinct advantage of this circuit over the single-slope circuit mentioned earlier. The main factor in determining accuracy is the voltage reference, with minor factors being contributed by offsets in the amplifiers and output comparator and by the matching of the on resistances of the two FETs. Small (100-ohm) series resistors were included in series with the switching FETs to prevent damage during switching, when both may be on for a short time. Because of the fact that these are small with respect to the main integrator resistor (100 kΩ), they should not contribute to inaccuracy substantially.

The accuracy of the input and feedback resistors on the input amplifier is critical to the accuracy of the converter, and the resistors should be appropriately rated metal-film types. The absolute accuracy may be trimmed by adding a small variable resistor in series with the feedback resistor on the input amplifier (and reducing the value of the feedback resistor by half the value of the variable resistor).

Ironically, the main drawback of the dual-slope type of A/D converter is also related to an advantage of it. The drawback is the fact that the integration cycle is relatively slow compared to the successive approximation technique covered next. There are two facets to the time consideration: the time that the processor wastes waiting for the conversion, and the restricted sampling rate of the input. If the sampling rate is not a problem in a particular design, the converter can be made to be interrupt-driven. This can be done by simply connecting the inverted comparator signal to the clock input of a D-type flip-flop (SN74LS74). The D input of this first flip-flop can be wired high, and the reset line can be made to clear the flip-flop when the comparator is read. The Q output of the first flip-flop should be connected to the D input of a synchronizing flip-flop. The clock input of this second flip-flop would be connected to the system clock. The output of this flip-flop would actually drive the IRQ line of the processor (as discussed in the chapter on input ports). This interrupt will signal the end of the negative ramp. Most hardware timers offer an interrupt capability, which can be used to signal the end of the positive ramp.

The advantage of having the converter integrate the input signal is that it makes the converter relatively immune to noise. Converters of this type rarely require filtering of the input signals.

The circuit of Fig. 6-2 could be made into a multichannel A/D interface by adding an analog multiplexer either in front of the input amplifier or in place of the FETs. If the multiplexer is used in place of the FETs, one input channel would be connected to the reference voltage, and other channels would be connected to the various input amplifiers. Having a separate input amplifier for each channel allows each input to be calibrated to the signal source to which it is connected.

The dual-slope converter can be made bipolar in several

ways. One technique is to allow the integrator to integrate in either direction according to the polarity of the input signal. In this configuration, diode D1 would be removed, and the comparator would be reset to zero volts output by turning on a FET across the integrator capacitor. The second ramp would then be driven by either a positive or negative reference voltage, according to the polarity of the integrator output after the first ramp time was completed. This would require that the reference voltage be inverted by an op-amp, and that an additional FET and control latch be provided for selecting this reference. By clamping the capacitor with a FET, this approach eliminates the delay problem on small signals discussed earlier, but it is more complex than other techniques.

An alternative approach would be to invert the input signal with an op-amp, and provide an additional comparator and input buffer element to allow the processor to determine the polarity of the input signal. This approach would also require a control latch and FET for selecting the inverted signal during negative polarity measurements.

A third approach would bias the input signal so that a 0-volt input would result in an output from the input amplifier of half the reference voltage. This technique will be somewhat less precise around zero than the earlier two approaches, but is simpler. The choice must finally be determined by the system requirements.

LSI dual- and quad-slope converter circuits are available that contain all of the functions mentioned above. These devices should be compared to the discrete approach to determine the most economical solution to a given problem. Notice that the circuit of Fig. 6-2 provides seven free input and seven free output pins, which can be used to fill other system I/O requirements. However, care must be taken if the output pins are used to: (1) assure that various program segments keep a current memory image of the port, and (2) do appropriate masking to avoid interfering with each other (see the section on readback of output ports).

SUCCESSIVE APPROXIMATION A/D CONVERTERS

The simplified diagrams of Figs. 6-3A and B show two variations of the successive approximation-type A/D converter. The principle is exactly as the name implies: the input signal is compared to a consecutive series of converging "guesses." Each consecutive guess is half the difference between the known limits.

The switches shown in Fig. 6-3 are normally implemented with FETs, and are used to select the approximation values. Fig. 6-3A uses a binary-weighted set of resistors to generate the approximation references. While this is the most obvious solution, it is more difficult to fabricate into LSI devices than the R-2R ladder shown in Fig. 6-3B. This ladder is also inherently more monotonic.

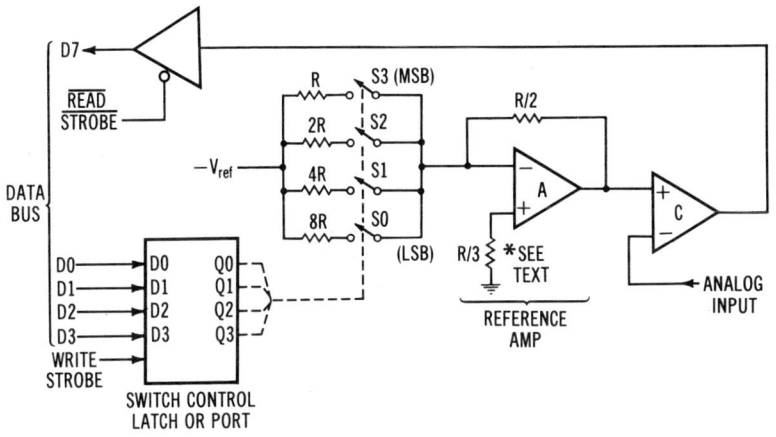

(A)   References generated by a binary-weighted set of resistors.

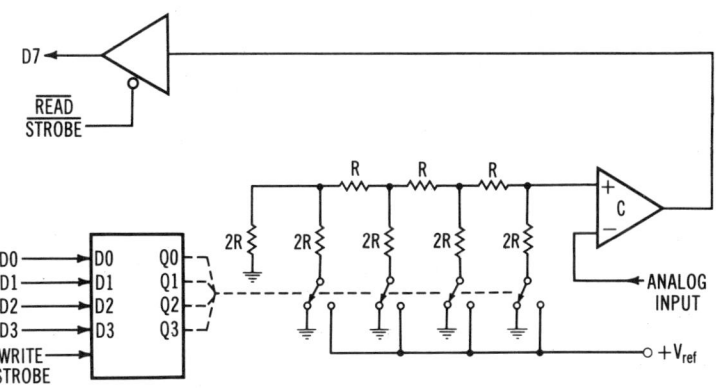

(B)   References generated by an R-2R ladder.

Fig. 6-3. Successive approximation A/D converter circuits.

The conversion process is extremely simple. The processor first closes the switch that corresponds to the most significant bit (one-half full scale). If the input is greater than this value, the processor leaves the switch closed; otherwise, the switch is reopened. The processor then closes the next most significant switch, and the process is repeated until all switches have been tested.

The successive approximation converter is very fast, but it is also very susceptible to input noise. It is important that the input signal to this type of converter be bandwidth-limited to a frequency whose period is considerably longer than the conversion time. Some of the LSI versions of these converters will actually add noise to an input signal if the driving impedance is not sufficiently low. This is due to coupling of the edges of the approximation staircase across the comparator inputs, and other stray noise.

A Simple 16-Channel Data Acquisition Interface

The National ADC0817 chip combines an 8-bit successive approximation converter with a 16-channel multiplexer. A typical application circuit for this device is shown in Fig. 6-4. The chip requires only a voltage-reference circuit and a clock source. The voltage reference was chosen to be 5.12 volts, as this provides a direct binary correlation to the input signal. The 500-kHz clock signal is generated by dividing the 1-MHz system clock.

Noise filtering can be provided on a channel-by-channel basis as shown on channel 0, or a single filter could be connected between pins 15 and 18. Any resistance in the filter must be chosen so as not to cause an uncompensable error. Some resistance is often required, as the driving circuit is often unable to tolerate a direct capacitive load. Most op-amps, for example, will become unstable if their output is loaded with a significant reactance. If a series resistance cannot be tolerated, it may be necessary to add an active filter between pins 15 and 18.

The conversion sequence is started by writing the channel number to the base address of the converter (write strobe 0). The actual conversion is then started by writing (anything) to the second address (write strobe 1).

The designer may elect to read the EOC (end of conversion) line with an input port, or to connect this line to the interrupt circuitry, or both. When the conversion is done, the processor simply reads the value at the base address (read strobe). Where accuracy better than 8 bits is not required, the ADC0817 can be used in an extremely simple analog interface.

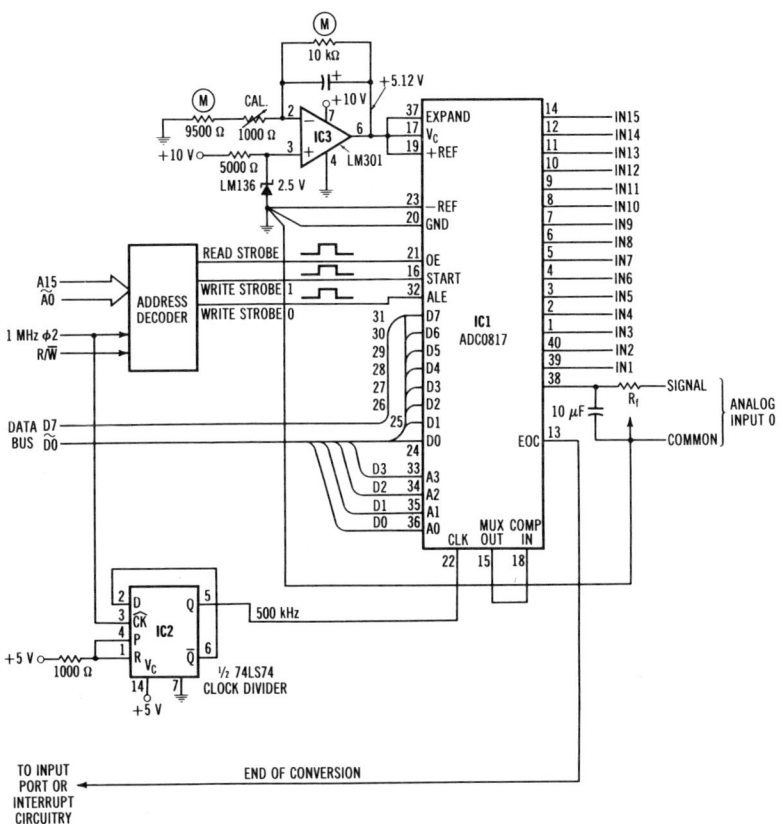

Fig. 6-4. Schematic of a 16-channel interface.

A Precision 16-Channel Data Acquisition System

When an application requires precision measurement at high speed, a circuit such as that shown in Fig. 6-5 may be required. The heart of this interface is the Analog Devices AD574, 12-bit, successive approximation, A/D converter. This A/D converter features an excellent built-in voltage reference, and a digital multiplexer for easy interfacing to 8-bit systems.

The mode 12/8 input configures the data bus multiplexer for 8-bit or 12-bit bus structures. In the 8-bit mode (MODE = 0), address input A0 defines the data that will be placed on the data bus. When A0 is low, the upper 8 bits are placed on the bus; when A0 is high, the lower 4 bits are placed on the bus. Care

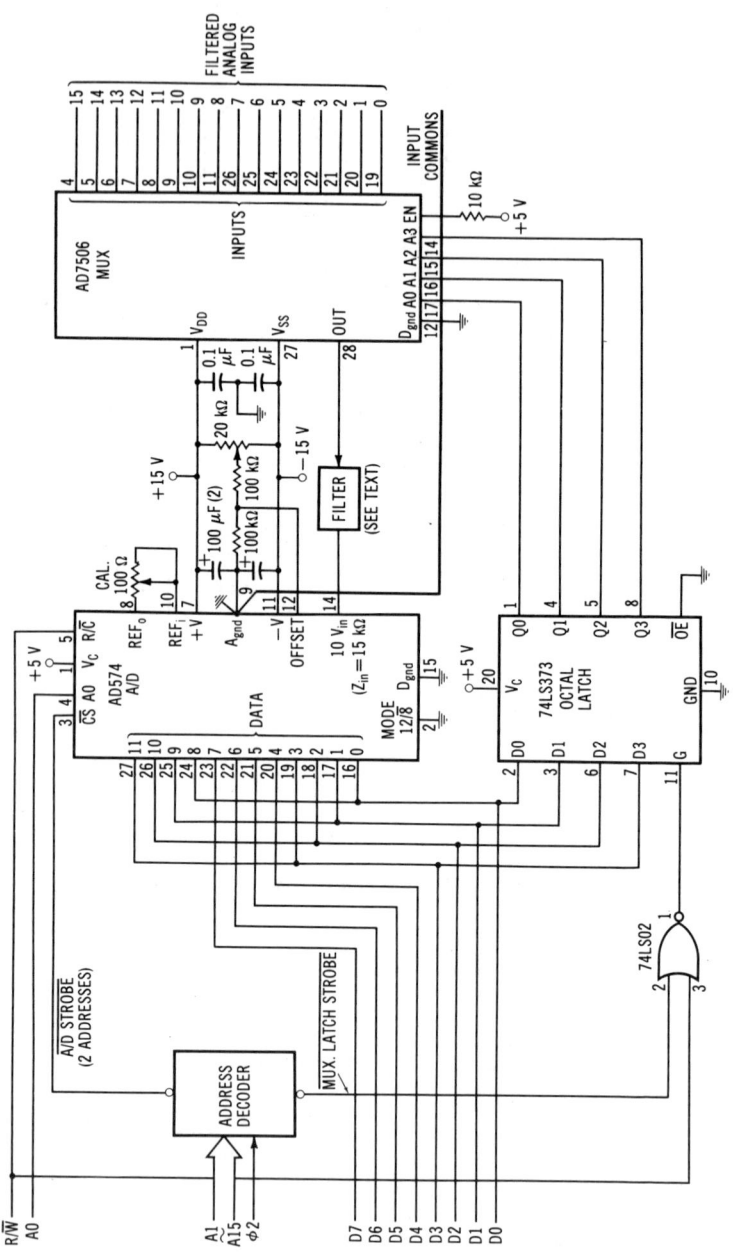

Fig. 6-5. High-speed 12-bit data acquisition system.

should be observed in this regard, as this is opposite from most conventions.

The A0 input also controls the conversion process during a write operation. If the processor writes to the base address of the device (A0 = 0), then a full 12-bit conversion (25 μs) will begin. If the processor writes to the base address +1, then a faster 8-bit conversion (16 μs) will be done. This feature makes the converter very versatile, and particularly useful in systems with critical speed problems.

The AD7506 multiplexer chip is used in this design to expand the converter for 16 inputs. The multiplexer does not contain a digital latch, so the SN74LS373 octal latch has been included to hold the digital channel select word. The desired channel is simply written to the latch address, with the top 4 bits being discarded (or used for further multiplexer expansion).

As with other converters of this type, a filter is often required to minimize input errors due to noise. This type of error is much more noticeable as the number of bits in the A/D converters increases. The exact filter design will depend on the other requirements of the application. Since the input impedance of the AD574 is 15 kΩ, very little series resistance can be tolerated.

A special note should be made of the ground (return) geometry of this design. Notice that the general ground symbol is not used in association with the analog inputs. The only connection to the general digital common is made at the analog ground terminal (A_{gnd}) of the AD574. All other input return lines converge on this point. Ground discipline is essential when there are 10 or more bits in the A/D converter. A ground plane may even be needed to obtain the specified accuracy from the converter. Normally this would consist of a solid conducting surface (except, of course, for holes for component leads) on the top of the printed circuit board, extending under all of the components of the analog section. The ground plane would be connected to the system ground at the analog ground terminal of the converter.

It is essential that each input have only the ground return path intended. If any sensor or transducer had an inherent common that could not be isolated (such as a chassis or safety ground), then a differential input amplifier would be required. Any input that could cause a significant current to flow in the return conductor may cause errors in all of the channels by inducing voltages that are effectively in series with their inputs. Many good logic designers have found themselves in trouble by treating analog signals in the same way that they treated digital signals. In fact, the discipline discussed here will often serve well in designing digital signal paths where glitches might be prone to occur.

DIFFERENTIAL INPUT AMPLIFIERS

In order to eliminate the problems just discussed, the designer may elect to turn to differential input circuitry. The differential signal may be converted to a single-ended signal (ground-referenced) before the multiplexer, or a differential multiplexer may be used with conversion to a monopolar signal occurring after the multiplexer. In industrial control applications, where reliable operation is paramount to component cost, differential input circuitry is used as a matter of course. In some cases, a differential preamplifier may even be mounted in the immediate vicinity of the transducer, thus amplifying the signal before it has been degraded by noise.

The circuits of Fig. 6-6 are two of the more common solutions to converting a differential signal to a ground-referenced signal. The simple circuit of Fig. 6-6A uses only an inexpensive op-amp and four resistors. The circuit does not offer the degree of common-mode signal rejection that a true instrument amplifier does, but it is adequate for some applications. The common-mode signal rejection of this circuit will degenerate rapidly with increased circuit gain. A typical application of this type of circuit is shown in Fig. 6-7, where a temperature signal from an LM3911 temperature sensor (that is not ground-referenced) is converted to a ground-referenced signal. The amplifier in this example has unity gain (a gain of one).

The instrument amplifier circuit of Fig. 6-6B is the most common of several types of instrument amplifiers. These devices are available in integrated form with only a few external components (such as gain-setting resistors) required. This type of amplifier is commonly used with bridge circuits, thermocouples, strain gauges, and other low-level inputs. *It is essential with all of these differential input circuits that the sum of the common-mode signal (peak-to-peak) and the desired signal (peak-to-peak) be limited to a value well less than the power supply of the circuit.* If this is not the case, an isolation amplifier may be required.

Another parameter is also important when selecting an instrument amplifier, and that is bandwidth. No matter how impressive the common-mode rejection ratio of a particular device might be, if the common-mode signal (or noise) present at the input is of a frequency that is not safely below the bandwidth of the amplifier, performance will be poor.

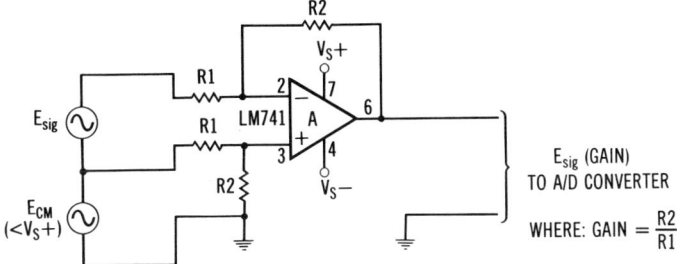

(A)   Pseudo instrument amplifier.

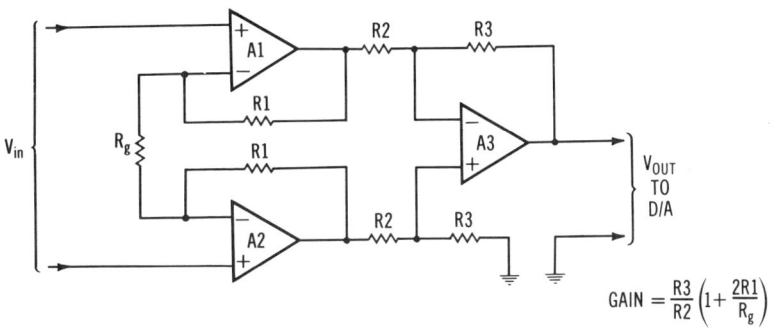

(B)   Common instrument amplifier.

Fig. 6-6.   Typical solutions to eliminating common-mode signals.

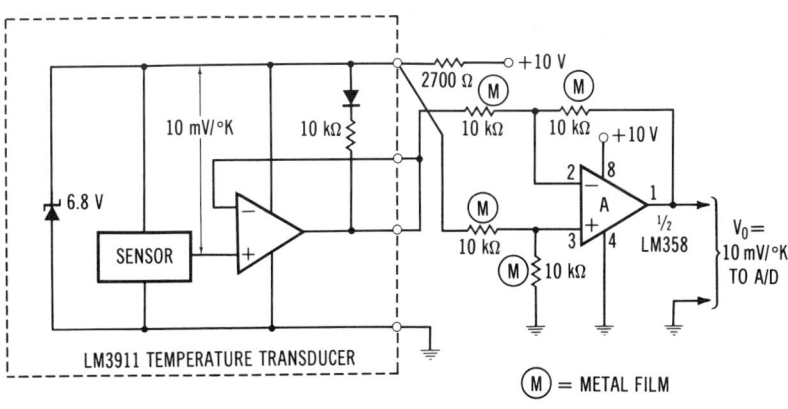

Fig. 6-7.   A simple, signal-supply temperature interface.

ISOLATION AMPLIFIERS

When a signal is present with a very high common-mode signal component, or when the frequency content of the common-mode component is unreasonably high, an isolation amplifier may offer a solution.

A simplified version of the classic "flying capacitor" circuit is shown in Fig. 6-8. The circuit simply uses a double-pole

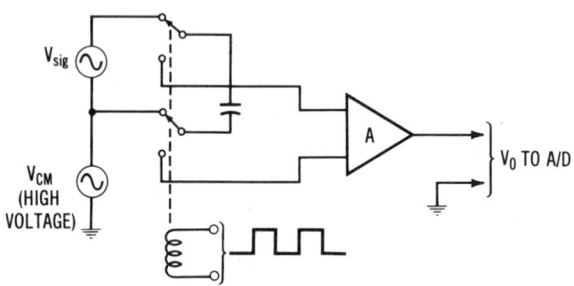

Fig. 6-8. "Flying capacitor" isolation amplifier circuit.

double-throw relay to switch a capacitor across the voltage source to be measured, and then across the input of the input amplifier. The timing will be determined by the capacitor value, the output impedance of the source, and the input impedance of the input amplifier. The input amplifier will normally have a very high impedance FET front end, to prevent the capacitor from discharging significantly while conversion is taking place. If the converter is not fast, an analog sample-and-hold circuit might be required between the input amplifier and the A/D converter.

While this circuit offers both high-voltage and high-frequency isolation, it has the distinct disadvantage of incorporating a mechanical relay. The transients generated by the relay-drive circuit complicate the design, and the reduced reliability of a mechanical movement is a negative factor also. Nevertheless, both problems can be solved to some extent by using a high-quality relay.

The Analog Devices Model 289 isolation amplifier (see Fig. 6-9) represents one of several solid-state approaches available in hybrid or modular form. In this device, the signal is converted to a proportional high-frequency signal that is then transformer-coupled to a receiving circuit, where it is converted back to a ground-referenced signal. The high-voltage isolation of this cir-

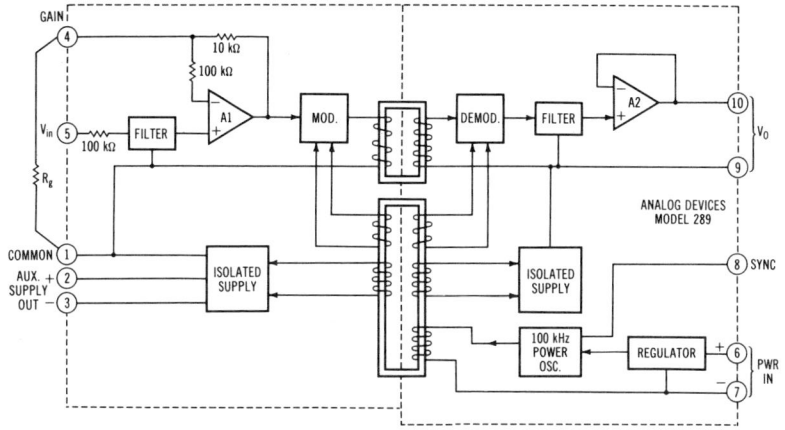

Fig. 6-9. Transformer-coupled isolation amplifier circuit.

cuit is quite good, but the high-frequency isolation is somewhat more limited than that of the "flying capacitor." Notice that the circuit does offer one distinct advantage (besides eliminating the relay), and that is that the signal is amplified before transmission and translation.

Another approach to isolation is to place the A/D converter at the site of the transducer. The digital signal can then be transmitted by either optoisolator or fiber-optical cable. The readings may be transmitted in an asynchronous format by using UARTs, thus requiring only a single path. Optical cable is becoming increasingly popular for this type of application because of its excellent isolation and electromagnetic interference immunity (i.e., lightning, nuclear radiation, etc.).

7

Digital-to-Analog Coverters and Closed-Loop Control

The microprocessor system designer is often required to generate and output an analog signal for use by peripheral equipment. Very often this equipment contains a certain amount of rudimentary power control circuitry which, in turn, provides a high-current and/or high-voltage signal to drive a heater, motor, or lighting device. Given a choice, most designers will avoid including the design of high-power circuitry in their control system design, and take the option of purchasing this "driver" equipment from another vendor. The reason for this preference is that there is a lot more to this type of circuitry than there might seem to be at first glance. Not only are there many hardware considerations, there are also government regulations that must be complied with. These regulations cover safety, and EMI (electromagnetic interference) or RFI (radio frequency interference) emissions.

The result of this division of hardware is that the microprocessor system designer is often required to supply a relatively small analog signal that is proportional to the result he wants from the power driver. Some of the common interface levels are:

0 to +5 volts dc
0 to +10 volts dc
−15 to +15 volts dc
2 to 10 mA
4 to 20 mA

Some motor speed controllers and other drivers have factory- or user-programmable options for selecting one or more of the above interface levels. The primary tool for providing this signal from the digital data that the microprocessor uses is the D/A (digital-to-analog) converter.

THE FUNDAMENTAL D/A CONVERTER

There are many ways to produce an analog signal that is proportional to a given digital value. However, only a few techniques find much popularity. The generalized block diagram of Fig. 7-1 represents the most popular approach. The reader will probably notice the R-2R ladder network as the heart of the successive approximation A/D converter discussed in the previous chapter.

A wide variety of D/A converter chips are available that contain one or more of the elements shown in the block diagram. Some of these devices contain nothing more than the ladder network, and some contain all of the elements shown. The op-

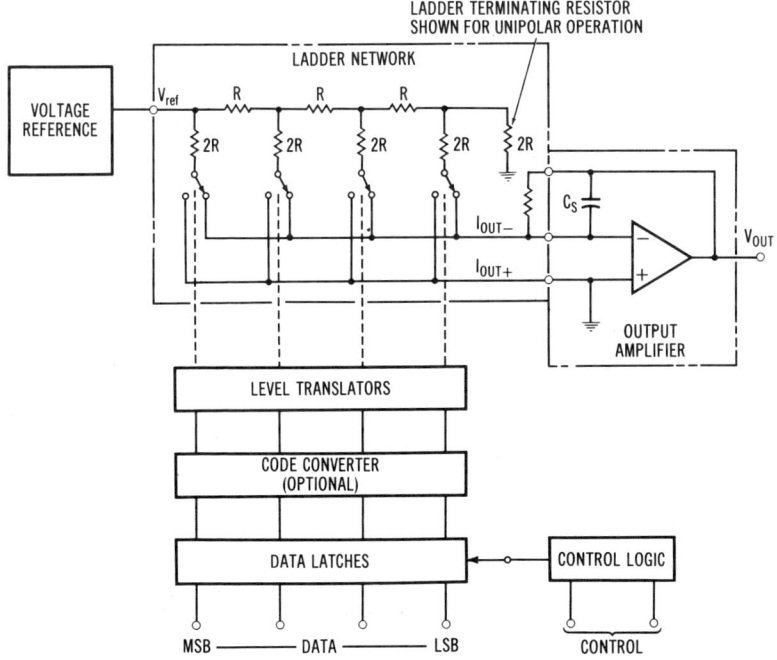

Fig. 7-1. Elements of a D/A interface.

eration of this type device is relatively simple. The control logic is used in conjunction with the data latches. In a lower resolution (8-bit) converter, this may simply be some AND gate elements used with the latch strobes. In higher resolution converters, the latches may be banked into groups of 4 bits or 8 bits, which can be controlled separately by the microprocessor through the control logic and write operations.

When separate latches are provided, a problem can arise. The problem is caused by the fact that between the time the microprocessor writes to one latch and then to the other latch, there exists an unwanted combination of words that may be grossly different from either the original or new word. For this reason, such converters are usually *double-buffered.* This is done by adding another set of latches between the level translators and the set of latches that the microprocessor is interfaced to. This set of latches holds the old setting of the converter until all of the input latches contain the new data. The second latch then gates the *entire* new word to the level translators at once, avoiding the intermediate glitch.

The data from the latches also may pass through a code converter. The purpose of this converter is to allow for data to be output to the DAC in a form other than the pure binary required by the R-2R network. Some converters translate by using a weighted ladder corresponding to the input code desired. Digital-to-analog converters are available for BCD, excess-gray, offset-binary, binary, 2s-complement, and other codes. Converters with BCD inputs are most often used with nonintelligent devices such as digital panel meters, since microprocessors usually represent numbers in a binary form. The AD7110 converter even has a logarithmic relationship between the digital input and the analog output, as is discussed later.

The digital word is applied to the ladder network switch elements through a level translator. The switch elements may be bipolar transistors (usually in faster D/As) or CMOS switching elements. The level translators used will depend on the switching elements to be driven. The two bus lines of the ladder usually are used to drive an output amplifier. Even if the output amplifier is not included in the converter, the feedback resistor will be included with the ladder, since this is used for initial calibration and temperature tracking.

If the output of the converter is to be a voltage signal, the output amplifier will be wired in a simple inverting configuration as shown in Fig. 7-1. A stabilizing capacitor (C_s) may be necessary with fast op-amps to prevent oscillation that might otherwise result from stray capacitances within the ladder.

The input voltage to the ladder may be a fixed reference or a variable signal. While the great majority of D/A converters use a fixed internal or external voltage reference, a variable signal input has many advantages in some applications. Most D/A converters that have an internal voltage reference do not connect it directly to the ladder. Instead, the signal is usually made available on an external pin which must then be connected to another pin that corresponds to the input of the ladder. This configuration allows the designer to trim, measure, or divide the reference, or to replace it with another signal. Since the output of the converter is proportional to the reference signal multiplied by the digital word, converters with an external reference input are sometimes referred to as *multiplying D/A converters.*

The circuitry of some D/A converters will generate an output signal that is proportional to the digital word, with the maximum output occurring when all bits are true. Other converters obey the binary 2s-complement convention, with the most significant bit being 0 for positive output values and 1 for negative values. The possible combinations of digital and analog input polarities are shown graphically in Fig. 7-2. A converter that can operate with both polarities of digital and analog inputs is called a *four-quadrant multiplying converter.* Such a converter should obey the algebraic laws. That is to say that a negative signal at the analog input with a negative binary word should result in a positive output. To assure that the designer understands that a converter complies with this convention, the

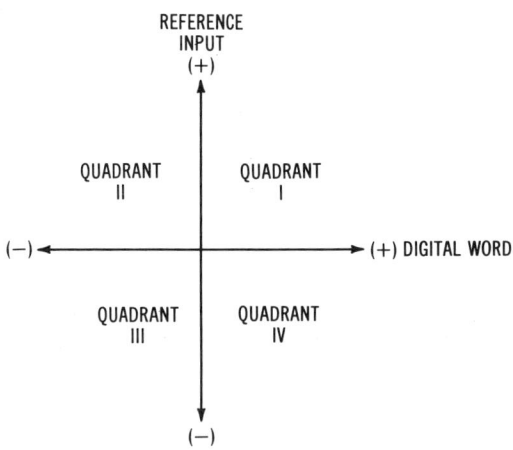

Fig. 7-2. Definition of quadrants for D/A converters.

manufacturer may refer to it as a *true four-quadrant multiplying D/A converter.*

If a D/A converter is accurate enough that an increasing digital input will always result in an increase of the output, it is said to be *monotonic.* While this might seem like something that can be taken for granted, it is important that the designer assure that the chosen D/A converter will be monotonic at the system working voltages and temperature range. One of the most common tests for monotonicity (although not conclusive in itself) is to enter a digital word with the most significant bit low and all other bits high and measure the output. All bits are then complemented, and the output is measured to determine that it increased by approximately one LSB (least significant bit) value.

A SIMPLE 8-BIT D/A CONVERTER INTERFACE

The Signetics NE5018 D/A converter (Fig. 7-3) contains all the major circuit elements required for implementing a D/A interface. With the addition of a few bypass and stabilization capacitors and a diode, the designer has a reliable D/A inter-

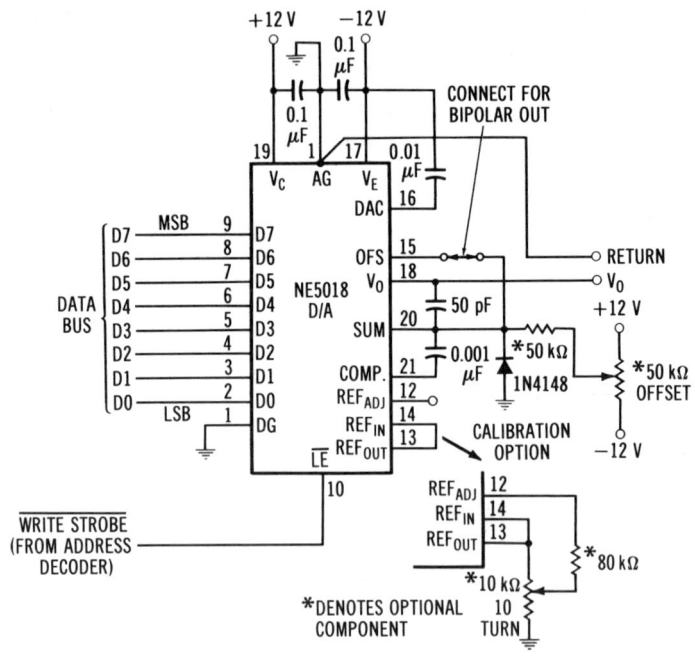

Fig. 7-3. Schematic of a single-chip D/A converter.

face. The converter can be configured as either a monopolar or a bipolar type unit with reasonably good accuracy. When the designer chooses a D/A converter with a built-in latch, it is necessary to assure that the speed of the latch is adequate with respect to the system speed. Since the 6502 cannot enter any wait states during a write cycle, a buffering latch will be necessary if the built-in latch is not sufficiently fast.

A PRECISION FOUR-QUADRANT D/A CONVERTER

When an application requires a higher resolution D/A converter, or when four-quadrant operation is required, a device such as the AD7522L shown in Figs. 7-4 and 7-5 may be used. This device is available in lower resolution (accuracy) versions at a reduced cost. The suffix letter determines the resolution.

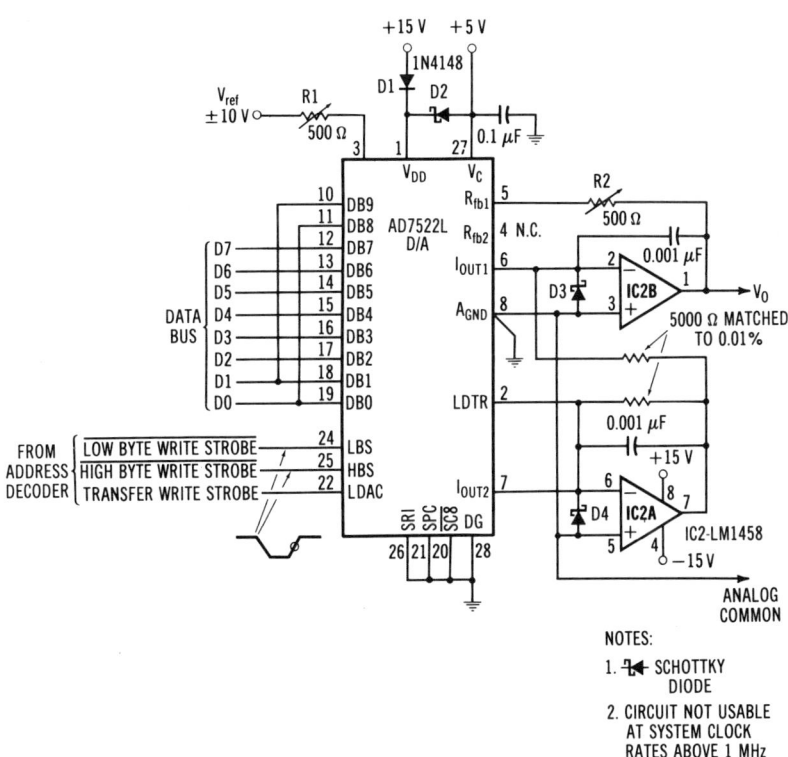

Fig. 7-4.   A four-quadrant, 10-bit D/A converter interface.

Because of some of the unique capabilities of the AD7522, it may be used for 8-bit applications, with the two lower bits unused. The control logic in the DAC allows for this type operation.

The input registers of the AD7522 are composed of D-type flip-flops that can be configured for parallel or serial loading. In the parallel loading configuration (Fig. 7-4), the input flip-flops are grouped into two registers with their positive edge-triggered clock inputs connected together within each group (LBS and HBS). The D inputs are available for connection to the system data bus.

The circuit of Fig. 7-4 also shows the output amplifier arrangement for bipolar operation. Notice that the ladder terminating resistor (LDTR) is connected in parallel with the complementary ladder current output ($I_{out\ 2}$). This current signal is inverted by op-amp IC2A, and is summed with the ladder current output ($I_{out\ 1}$) by the output amplifier IC2B. The two calibration resistors, R1 and R2, are initially set to 0 ohms. These resistors are set by loading the input latches with all 0s. If the output is greater than $+V_{ref}$, increasing R2 will allow it to be set to $+V_{ref}$. If the output is less than $+V_{ref}$, the output can be adjusted with R1. Notice that all 0s is equal to a full-scale analog output, and an analog zero output is set by having all 0s except for a 1 in the most significant bit. The output correlation of this circuit is shown in Table 7-1. Notice that the reference to "negative" in the output column assumes a positive V_{ref}.

The code represented in Table 7-1 is not any accepted representation of binary numbers, but it can be generated easily by manipulating 2s-complement numbers. The program sequence for doing this conversion with a positive reference would simply be:

1. Negate the 2s-complement number by complementing all bits and adding one to the result.
2. Complement the most significant (sign) bit.

If a negative voltage reference were used, the first step could be omitted. Notice that this conversion is only with reference to full scale, and any adjustment to provide a correlation in volts or other units of measure would have to be done separately.

AN OPTICALLY ISOLATED D/A CONVERTER

The versatility of the input register arrangement of the AD7522 is demonstrated by the circuit of Fig. 7-5. This circuit

Table 7-1. Digital-to-Analog Correlation for Fig. 7-4

Digital Input	Analog Output
1111111111	1 LSB less than full negative
1000000001	negative by 1 LSB
1000000000	0
0111111111	positive by 1 LSB
0000000001	1 LSB less than full positive
0000000000	full positive

Note: 1 LSB is equal to 2^{-9}.

allows for a precise and completely isolated analog output. Isolation is accomplished by using the converter in the serial loading mode of operation. If only 8-bit resolution were required, the SC8 pin could be tied to ground. With SC8 low, the two least-significant register flip-flops will be bypassed during serial loading.

The timing diagram of Fig. 7-5 shows the method used to transfer data to the D/A. On the negative-going edge of the clocking signal, the desired bit (inverted) is output to the optical isolator and allowed to stabilize. The positive-going edge of the clocking signal strobes the data bit into the input of the shift register. When no data is clocked into the DAC for a prescribed time interval (T_g), the missing pulse detector (IC1A & B) generates a load strobe signal that transfers the shift register data into the D/A holding register. The missing pulse detector could be replaced by a third optically isolated control signal, but the circuit shown provides for fewer control lines and less software. Time delay T_g must be considerably longer than period T_c during which the clock is in the high state between bits. The sum of T_g and T_L (load pulse width) must be much less than the minimum time between the end of one loading cycle and the beginning of the next. The designer also must consider the frequency response of the optoisolator chosen for the interface.

The output configuration of Fig. 7-5 provides a unipolar output swing. This circuit will produce a voltage proportional to the unsigned binary input, but of opposite polarity from the reference voltage. This output circuit could be interchanged with the output circuit of Fig. 7-6, depending on the application.

The designer should bear in mind the possibility of using a UART in conjunction with an optoisolator and a standard D/A converter (see the chapter on serial interfaces) as an alternative to the approach of Fig. 7-5. A UART allows for the reduction of the link to a single pair of wires, but UART circuits become more complicated with resolutions above 8 bits. As always, the decision will depend on the constraints and requirements of the

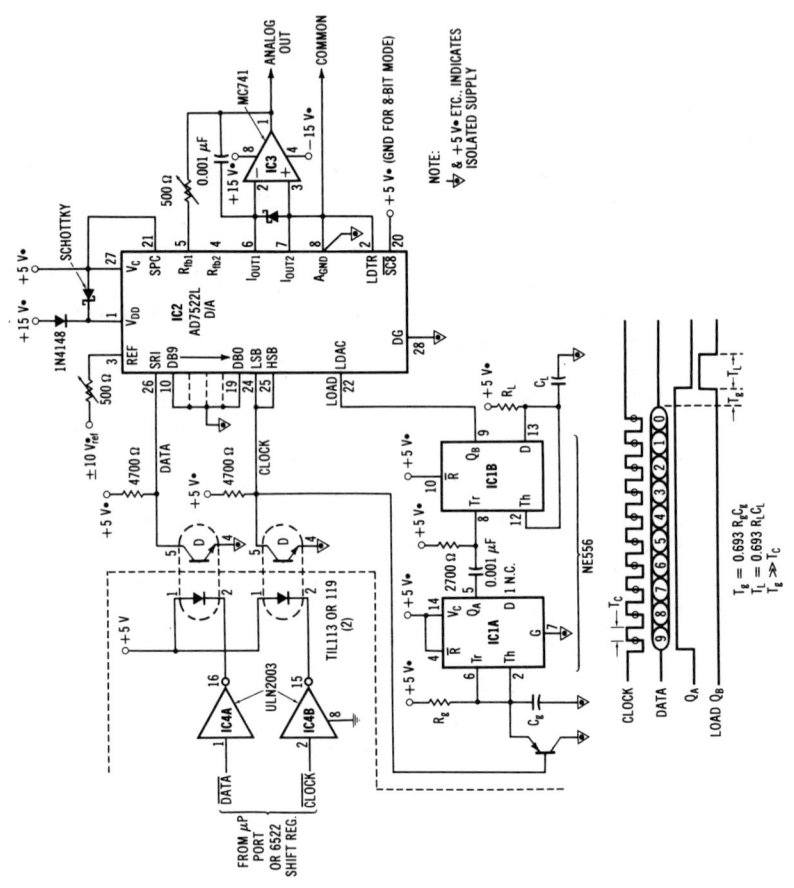

Fig. 7-5. An isolated 10-bit D/A circuit.

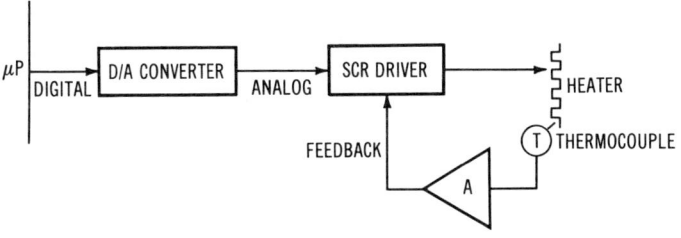

(A) Loop closed at the driver.

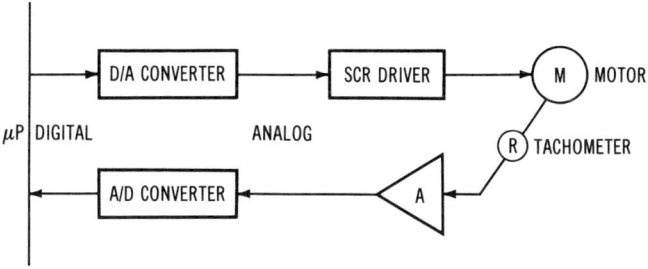

(B) Loop closed at the processor.

Fig. 7-6. Two ways of closing the feedback loop.

application. Another alternative also is explained after some system considerations have been addressed.

CLOSING THE FEEDBACK LOOP

When any process is to be controlled by automatic equipment, it is normal for some type of feedback to be used to assure accurate and safe results. For example, a simple home thermostat serves as feedback to the furnace control unit. Accurate control without feedback is very difficult and requires extensive modeling of the target system under control. Feedback is always more desirable when it can be accomplished. The two diagrams of Fig. 7-6 show the most common ways in which the loop is closed. In Fig. 7-6A the controller has a built-in feedback circuit. In this configuration, the SCR driver/temperature controller will provide a result (in this case a temperature) that is proportional to the analog signal present at its input. This configuration relieves the processor of the task of closing the loop, but it requires that the analog interface be a precise representation of the desired temperature.

The fact that a controller has built-in feedback does not exclude the possibility of closing the loop externally as is done in Fig. 7-6B. In this case, the processor commands the motor controller with an intermediate analog signal, and reads the result accomplished in response to the command by reading the feedback. While an analog (generator) type tachometer was chosen for this illustration, a digital (pulse) tachometer also could have been used. The absolute accuracy and long-term stability of the intermediate command signal (DAC and SCR driver) is not particularly important, as the processor will simply compensate for any error, provided that the feedback signal is accurate.

CONTROLLING THE CLOSED-LOOP SYSTEM

In the simplest case, the microprocessor could simply increment or decrement the intermediate command at a fixed rate in response to the polarity of the error as determined by subtracting the feedback from the desired result (set point). In other words, if the set point were higher than the feedback reading, the microprocessor would increment the intermediate command until the reading exceeded the set point. When the reading of the feedback was higher than the set point, the processor would simply decrement the intermediate command at a fixed rate. The stepping rate would have to be sufficiently slow to allow for the delay (lag) of the system. This delay might be a result of mechanical inertia, or of the time required to heat a large mass; it also will include the response limitations of the controller or driver. If the stepping rate is too fast, the loop response will be "under damped" and the result will be that the speed (or temperature, etc.) will be made to oscillate about the set point. Unfortunately, if the stepping rate is slow enough for stability, the time required to bring the system up to the set point, or to change set points, may be prohibitively long.

PROPORTIONAL CORRECTION

An improvement can be made to the control scheme just discussed by varying either the size of the correction step, or the rate of the step, or both, in response to the magnitude of the error. This would allow for fast transitions between set points, with relatively fine control around the set points. This technique is often adequate, and is usually easy to implement. If significant response variations are expected from system to system, the constant(s) that are used to calculate the step changes as a function of the error may need to be changed. If the system under design has an operator interface such as a keyboard, it can be used to make these adjustments. A password or other "key" can be used to prevent changing these values by unauthorized individuals. If this is done, it may be necessary to reenter the values after a power down, unless provision is made for nonvolatile memory. One alternative is to enter the values through a dip-switch and simple 8-bit input port as described in Chapter 2. The concept of adjusting control system response after installation becomes more important as the control algorithm becomes more complex, and as the response is optimized.

THE PID CONTROL ALGORITHM

In systems requiring optimal response, a PID (proportional, integral, differential) algorithm may offer the solution. Since this is not a book on control systems theory, PID control is not discussed in depth. The reader is encouraged to refer to one of the reference books on this subject listed at the end of the chapter, if he/she has a serious application.

Essentially, the PID algorithm generates an output command value that is the sum of the following terms:

1. P—Proportional to the error.
2. I—The integral of the error since system power up.
3. D—The derivative of the error (negated polarity).

A microprocessor system can usually do an adequate simulation of the true mathematical function of this algorithm without an elaborate floating-point math program. A simple integer-multiply routine is sufficient for this calculation. This approximation is done by setting up an evenly timed interrupt program. At each interrupt the feedback signal is read and error is calculated. The PID equation can be simply represented by:

ERROR = Set Point − Reading
INTEG = Ki(Error) + INTEG (Initialized to zero at start-up.)
DERIV (−) = Error − Last Error
OUTPUT = Kp(Error) + INTEG + Kd(DERIV)

The sequence for determining the output command is:

1. Zero the OUTPUT accumulator (one or more memory locations).

2. Determine the INTEG (integral) term:
   a. Multiply the error by the constant Ki.
   b. Do a signed add (±) of the result to the memory location INTEG and place the result in INTEG.
   c. Limit counting to prevent decrementing through zero or counting past all 1s to zero. (INTEG is always a positive value, assuming the command is always positive.)
   d. Place the INTEG result (or the higher bits of it) in the OUTPUT accumulator.
3. Determine the DERIV (derivative) term:
   a. Do a signed subtract of the error found at the last interrupt from the present error. (This gives the negative value of the unscaled derivative.)
   b. Multiply the result by the constant Kd, and do a signed add of the result to the OUTPUT accumulator.
   c. Save the present error for the next interrupt.
4. Calculate the proportional term:
   a. Multiply the error by the constant Kp.
   b. Do a signed add of the result to the output accumulator.

Truncation (division) can be done by bit and byte shifting to avoid using division. For example, the INTEG accumulator will normally consist of from 16 to 32 bits, with the multiplied error term added each time. By using only the top 8 or 10 bits in the calculation of the OUTPUT command, an automatic truncation (division) is done. This gives the fine control that is required with this term (the integral term provides the long-term accuracy of the result).

The actual program is not included in this book, as it will vary with the resolution of the OUTPUT command, the feedback input, and the general system speed. It is very helpful in such systems if the constants can be adjusted during operation. Notice that the INTEG term is scaled before accumulation rather than after. This prevents sudden jumps in the output as the operator changes constant Ki. The derivative term is normally small, as it can cause system instability rather easily.

The approximation of the above algorithm to the true PID equation is better as the interrupt rate is increased, but this may load the microprocessor down if carried to the extreme. This loading effect is one of the primary reasons for keeping the mathematical calculations simple. It might be mentioned that the designer who hopes to control such a process with an inefficient high-level language, such as an interpretive BASIC, will normally find he is unable to obtain the speed required for anything other than the simplest tasks. Such shortcuts usually amount to programming "into the wind."

AN A/P (ANALOG-TO-POTENTIOMETER) CONVERTER

Now that the reader is an expert in control systems theory, the interface of Fig. 7-7 can be explained. This interface is used only in systems where the loop is closed through the processor (Fig. 7-6B). The reason for this is that its accuracy and stability over time and temperature are rather mediocre. Since these limitations are not a problem when the circuit is within the control loop, it can be very useful in these systems.

Many of the power control modules on the market were originally designed for use with a 10-turn potentiometer as a command input. It is very common for these circuits to provide a dc voltage to the potentiometer of from +5 to +15 volts. The command input could easily be provided by a D/A converter, except that the common lead of the potentiometer input is often at line potential. This is especially true in systems operating from 220-volt lines. Connecting the output of an unisolated D/A converter to this input will cause disastrous results. While the manufacturers of these devices usually offer an isolated interface module, it often doubles the cost of the controller (typically $250 to $500 more). The isolation schemes offered earlier in this chapter could be used, except that they usually require an additional set of isolated power supplies.

The circuit of Fig. 7-7 operates from the potentiometer voltages supplied by most controllers. While the dc voltage must be positive (this is usually the case), the resourceful designer

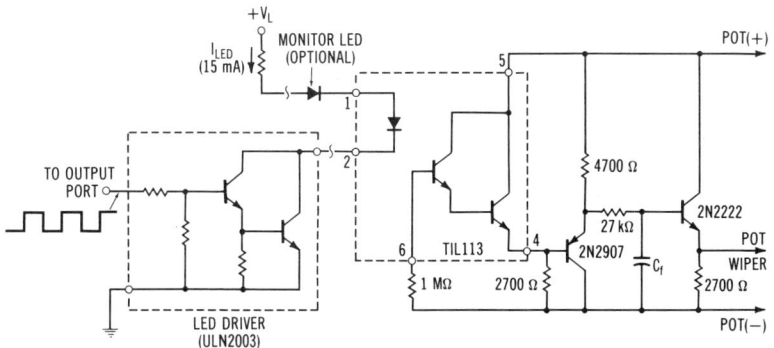

Fig. 7-7.   An analog-to-potentiometer converter circuit.

should have no problem adapting this circuit to negative dc voltages if needed. *Note: Never attempt to use this circuit where the potentiometers use ac voltages (as are found in cheap light dimmers and motor controllers).*

The operation of the circuit is simple. The microprocessor provides a square-wave signal, where the duty cycle is proportional to the percent of full-scale command desired. A resolution of 256 is usually adequate, and can be obtained by interrupting the processor at a rate 256 times as great as the square-wave frequency desired. The interrupt sequence would increment an 8-bit counter on each interrupt. At a count of zero, the output(s) would be turned on. A comparison would then be made and at each subsequent interrupt to determine if the count was equal to the value(s) to be output. When the count matched the particular output, the processor would turn off the output bit corresponding to the output(s) that matched. Output-averaging filter capacitor C_f must be sufficiently large to eliminate the square-wave frequency (in this case 256 times the interrupt rate) from the output. Since most control systems are relatively slow, usually this is not a problem, but the high interrupt rate may cause undesirable levels of system loading. If this is the case, a hardware counter could be devised to "unload" the interrupt task from the microprocessor.

CONTROLLING AUDIO VOLUME

In the D/A circuits mentioned so far, the signal voltage to the ladder network was a dc reference. The circuit of Fig. 7-8 shows that this does not have to be the case. This circuit uses an AD7110, which has a logarithmically weighted ladder, to operate like a digitally controlled audio attenuator. The chip also includes three FET switches (S1, S2, and S3) that turn on sequentially at low volume levels to provide for loudness compensation. Since the AD7110 has no input latches, this function is provided by the addition of an SN74LS373 octal latch. While bit 7 is not used, bit 6 of the latch provides the capability of turning the loudness compensation on and off from the program.

FIRING SCRS AND TRIACS

Despite the problems mentioned at the beginning of this chapter, some applications will require the designer to interface triacs and SCRs to the 6502 in such a way as to produce the effect of analog control. The two most common firing techniques are shown in Fig. 7-9.

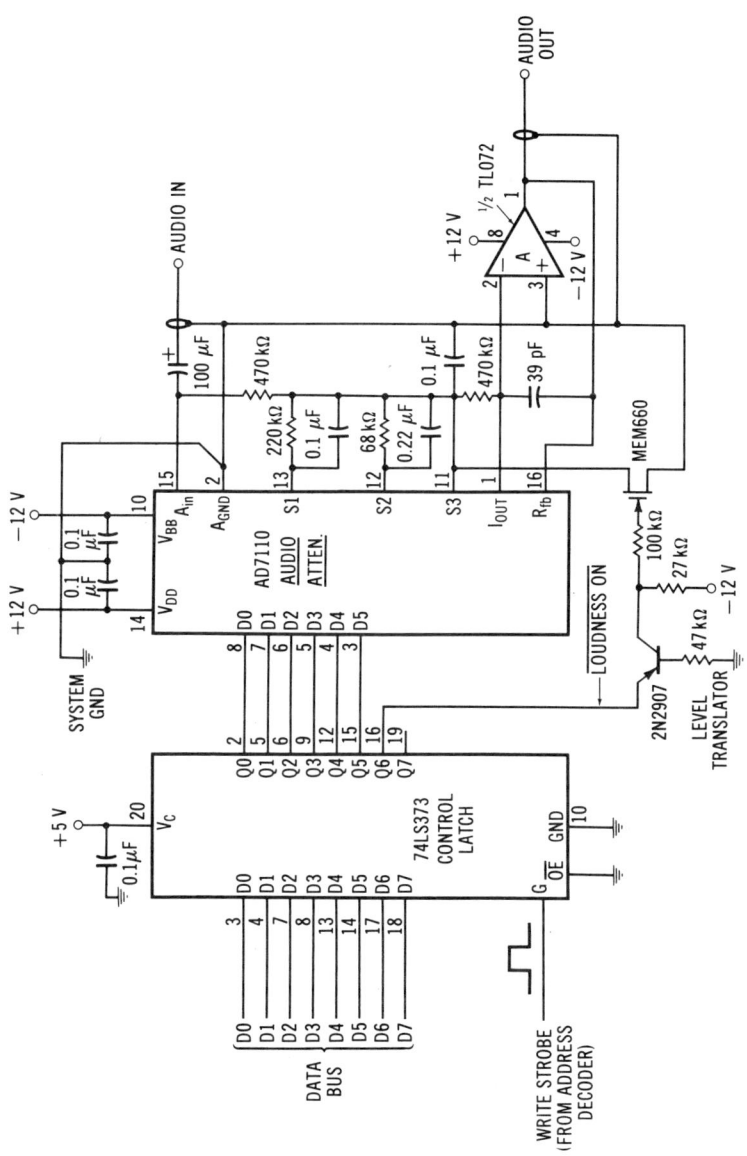

Fig. 7-8. Schematic of a volume control interface.

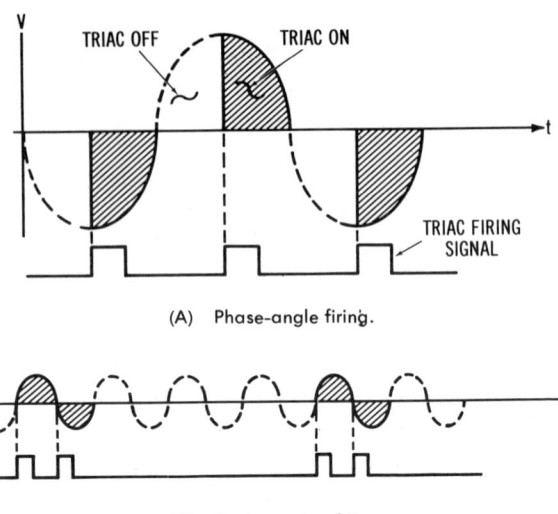

(A) Phase-angle firing.

(B) Zero-crossing firing.

Fig. 7-9. Two methods of triac firing.

When phase-angle firing is used, the processor is interrupted at, or otherwise reads, the zero crossing of the line voltage waveform. It will then produce a firing pulse at a time in the cycle that is inversely proportional to the desired output. That is to say that for a full output the firing pulse would occur at the beginning of the cycle, and for near-zero output it would occur near the end of the current cycle. The advantage of this approach is that relatively fast response rates can be accomplished. There are two major disadvantages to phase-angle firing, however. The first problem is that the output is sinusoidally related to the time delay of the firing pulse. While this problem can be overcome relatively easily by the use of a sinusoidal translation table, the second problem is somewhat more serious.

The second problem of phase-angle firing is that a large amount of EMI (electromagnetic interference) is caused by the sharp wave front when the SCR or triac fires and the line is at a significant voltage level. This sharp wave front is caused by the positive feedback effect inside the SCR and will interfere with radio and television communications. An elaborate and often expensive LC filter is usually required to reduce this interference to an acceptable level.

Because of the EMI problem, the firing scheme depicted in

Fig. 7-9B is often preferred. This approach always has the SCR or triac firing at the beginning of the cycle. The magnitude of the output is controlled by firing the device one or more cycles and then not firing it for a certain number of cycles. The simplest algorithm is simply to count the number of cycles (N_{tot}) equal to the resolution desired. The processor would simply fire the SCR for the first N_{on} cycles of each group of cycles, where N_{on}/N_{tot} is the desired output level.

Unfortunately, the major disadvantage of zero-crossing firing is that the higher the resolution required, the slower and less smooth the response. It is possible to improve the firing algorithm, and thus improve the response time if necessary. An improved firing sequence might fire the SCR for three out of ten cycles on even groups, and four out of ten cycles on odd groups to produce the effect of 35% output.

Zero-crossing firing has one additional advantage to phase-angle firing. Since the SCR or triac is never fired with the line voltage high, the stress on the device is relieved, and less powerful (and expensive) devices can be used.

One of the most popular approaches to implementing direct SCR firing outputs is to use prepackaged triacs and firing circuits contained in solid-state relays. These devices contain an optoisolator coupled to a triac through a zero-voltage firing circuit.

The possible analog output configurations are almost without limit. It is important that the designer keep an open mind when trying to determine the most effective analog output interface for a given requirement.

REFERENCES

Dorf, R. C. *Modern Control Systems*. Reading, MA: Addison-Wesley Publishing Co.

Cadzow and Martens. *Discrete Time and Computer Control Systems*. Englewood Cliffs, NJ: Prentice-Hall, Inc.

Kirk, D. *Optimal Control*. Englewood Cliffs, NJ: Prentice-Hall, Inc.

8

Bypassing and Driving High-Current Loads

A logic designer may feel that *he* is immune to the noise and interference problems that plague his counterparts in the communications and analog fields. This optimistic attitude often causes the designer to consider only the Boolean (logical) aspects of a design, and not to consider the flow of ground and supply currents that may cause improper circuit operation. The result of this oversight is often hardware that operates erratically or not at all. This situation is frequently compounded when improper operation is declared a glitch and is treated by the experimental addition of bypass capacitors and jumper wires. The result of this black-magic cure is sometimes referred to as a "kluge," and is often prone to relapses. A recurrence of the original glitch may be caused by something as simple as changing vendors on one IC. Thus, in this chapter, the proper use of bypassing and the driving of high-current and transient-producing loads is discussed.

THE NATURE OF GROUND-REFERENCED LOGIC

A typical TTL inverter circuit is shown in Fig. 8-1A. If the reader will envision this circuit as a comparator and a reference voltage supply (as shown in Fig. 8-1B), it will become obvious that all logic inputs are essentially differential in nature. While some logic families (most notably ECL) have external differential inputs, most microprocessor devices are single-ended. Thus, the second input of these devices is effectively wired to an internal reference voltage, which is, in turn, referenced to ground.

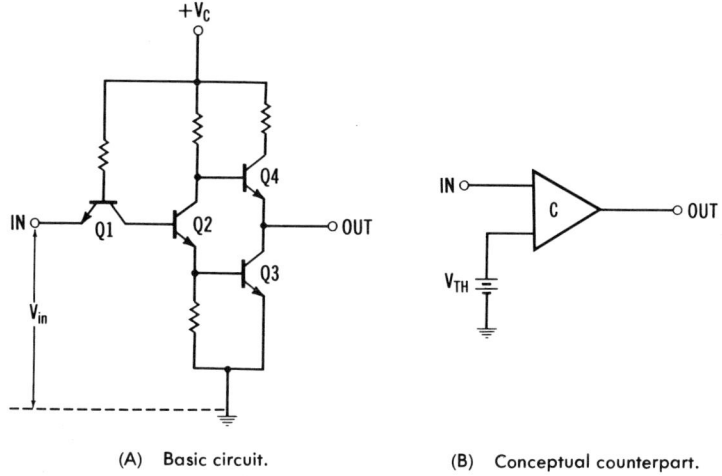

(A) Basic circuit.　　　　(B) Conceptual counterpart.

Fig. 8-1.　TTL inverters.

In the case of the circuit of Fig. 8-1A, the reference voltage is primarily the sum of the V_{BE} voltages of transistors Q2 and Q3.

Since the input to such a circuit is being compared to ground, it must be realized that the ground potential at the input may not be the same as it is at the sending device. Thus, the received signal is actually the sum of the transmitted signal and the voltage drop between the two grounds.

THE CAUSES OF GROUND NOISE

The ground line between two points has a resistive and an inductive component. The voltage drop across a ground path may be minimized in two primary ways: by reducing the current through it, and by reducing the resistive and inductive components. The resistive and inductive factors can be reduced by shortening the path length, while the resistive component also can be reduced by increasing the cross section of the ground path. In the case of printed circuit boards, these precautions might take the form of the widening of ground conductors and the use of a heavier (e.g., 2-oz) copper-board stock. A printed circuit board with a separate ground-plane layer may become necessary as system speeds and complexities are increased; but, this usually is not needed in 6502 and 6800 microprocessor systems. The voltage drop caused by the inductive component of the path also can be reduced by lowering the frequency content of the signals flowing in the conductor.

While all of the above precautions will reduce the resistive and inductive components within a ground conductor, it is essential to coordinate this with a systematic prevention of unnecessary currents in these paths. In order to prevent these currents, it is first necessary to understand their origin. The grossly simplified equivalent circuit of the power-related aspects of a typical IC is shown in Fig. 8-2. Notice that the current in the common lead of the IC can be represented as consisting of two components: a steady dc value (I_S) and a signal-related noise value (I_n). The relationship between the data input to a hypothetical IC and the resulting noise current is shown in Fig. 8-3. Notice that it is common for spikes to occur in the common

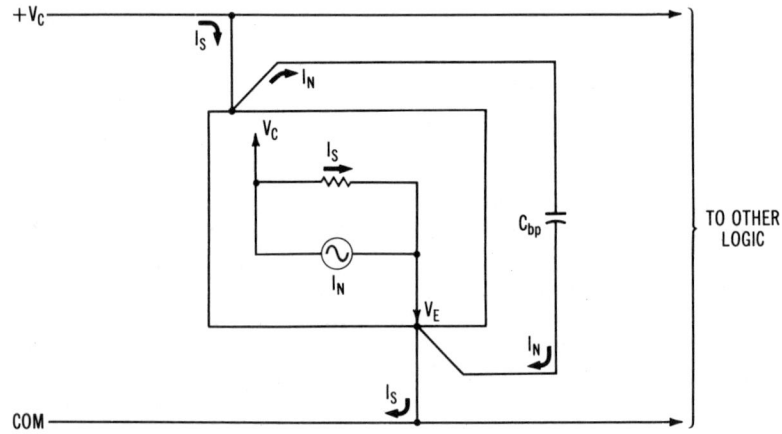

Fig. 8-2.   Circuit showing typical logic noise and supply currents.

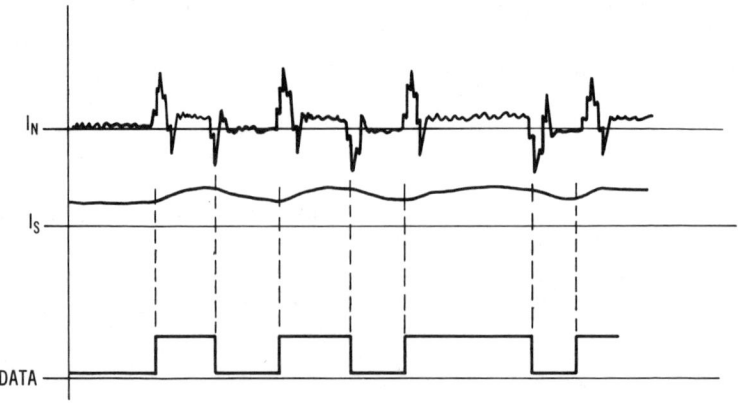

Fig. 8-3.   Waveforms showing the hypothetical correlation between data and noise signals.

pin current of an IC as its input changes state. These spikes are caused by the charging of internal and external capacitances as the input and output levels change.

In the interest of accuracy, it should be pointed out that the current through each output pin of an IC will be added to either the V_C pin current or the ground pin current of the IC, depending on whether the output is sinking or sourcing current. This current usually may be ignored in planning bypassing, unless the drive current levels become higher than normal TTL levels. In the event of higher drive levels, the precautions for driving heavy loads (covered later in this chapter) will apply.

THE PROPER USE OF BYPASS CAPACITORS

When one envisions each chip as an unwanted signal generator, the solution becomes obvious. The solution is a bypass capacitor. The bypass capacitor, C_{bp} (Fig. 8-2), shunts the higher-frequency noise signals (or switching transients) generated by the chip, and leaves only the dc and low-frequency components flowing in the ground path. Notice that the capacitor is shown connected directly between the power supply terminals of the IC, thus preventing any significant noise signal from flowing in the ground or positive supply path. This is the ideal case, but is seldom practical. However, it is important that those who are responsible for wiring or printed circuit layout understand the desirable configuration and approach it as closely as possible. As a rule, there should be one bypass capacitor for each chip. It may be tempting to reduce the number of these capacitors with the goal of cutting production costs. Unfortunately, the costs of such frugality are often far larger than the savings.

As in the circuits of the preceding chapters, bypass capacitors are often omitted from a schematic. Sometimes a note is placed on a drawing indicating that each chip is to be bypassed with a 0.1 μF disc capacitor. The resulting printed circuit layout or breadboard actually might be *worse* than if no bypass capacitors were used at all. The simplified layout of Fig. 8-4 shows some of the ways that bypassing can be misapplied. The result of such a design is that noise signals flow in diverse loops through the circuit. The malfunction that follows is often called a *ground loop* (although it is usually a combination of many loops). These mistakes are usually the result of the layout technician believing that only the total count of capacitors is important, not their placement. A correct placement of these capacitors is shown in Fig. 8-5. Once the designer begins to think of

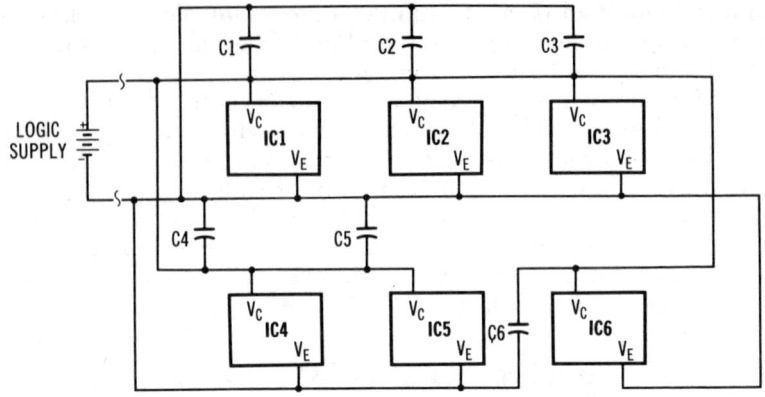

Fig. 8-4. Bypass capacitors are used *incorrectly* in this circuit.

the chips as "noise generators that must be shorted out," the proper placement strategy becomes clear.

PLANNING CURRENT PATHS

It is a common fallacy to believe that if two wires are connected together, it doesn't matter *where* they are connected together. Nothing could be further from the truth. Just as it is important to consider the flow of noise currents when placing bypass capacitors in a logic circuit, it is even more important to consider the flow of load currents.

Designers, who have not learned to consider the flow of currents within their circuits, often resort to unnecessary and expensive isolation techniques to avoid problems. In higher budget systems, these precautions may be a good investment,

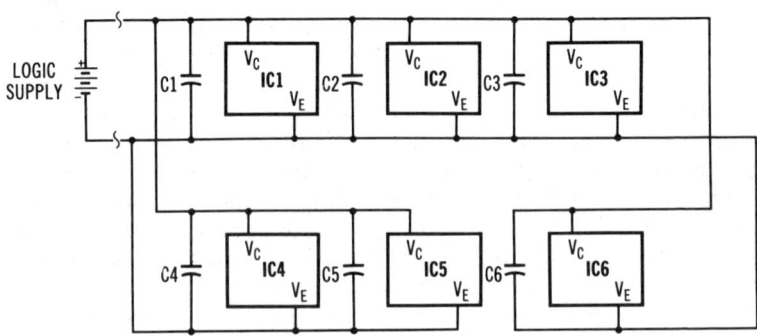

Fig. 8-5. Bypass capacitors are used *correctly* in this circuit.

but in cost-sensitive products they can mean the loss of a competitive edge.

There are any number of loads that are inherently troublesome. For example, incandescent lamps change resistance rather sharply as they heat up. When such a lamp is first turned on, a significant current surge may result.

Inductive loads are also troublesome, but in a different way. Once current is established in an inductive load, it does not like to be interrupted. When the driving current is terminated, the magnetic field in an inductor begins to collapse. This collapse generates a back-voltage that may destroy the driver transistor by reverse breakdown. The accepted practice for eliminating this danger is to provide a *snapback diode*. This diode will provide a path for the back-current, thus preventing a build up of the back-voltage. Ideally the diode should be mounted on the load, thus preventing the snapback current from flowing in any of the logic circuit supply or ground conductors.

A proper interface for several inductive loads is shown in Fig. 8-6. Notice that the base drive currents and the load currents are indicated on the schematic. While the solenoid power common and the logic common of this circuit are connected together, they are connected at only one place. This point has been designated the *ground node*. While the base drive currents flow through this node to the logic system ground, the load currents flow through the node to the solenoid power supply ground. *Ideally, none of the load currents flow through the logic ground path.*

Unfortunately, there are unplanned circuit elements that do not normally show up on the schematic. For example, there is usually a significant capacitance between any power supply and the power line ground. The result of these capacitances can be simplified to a single equivalent capacitance between the grounds of the solenoid power supply and the logic power supply. This unwanted capacitance is shown in Fig. 8-6 as C_{stray}. Stray capacitance is usually composed primarily of the capacitances of the power transformers, and secondarily of the stray capacitances in the large filter capacitors. If precautions are not taken, the high-frequency energy present in the solenoid power supply current can couple through this capacitance to the logic ground. Since this high-frequency content is produced at the drivers and loads, it can be eliminated there before it reaches the stray-capacitance path at the power supply. This is done by bypass capacitor C_{bp}. This capacitor must be much larger than the stray capacitances in the system. While Fig. 8-6 shows only one such capacitor for all of the

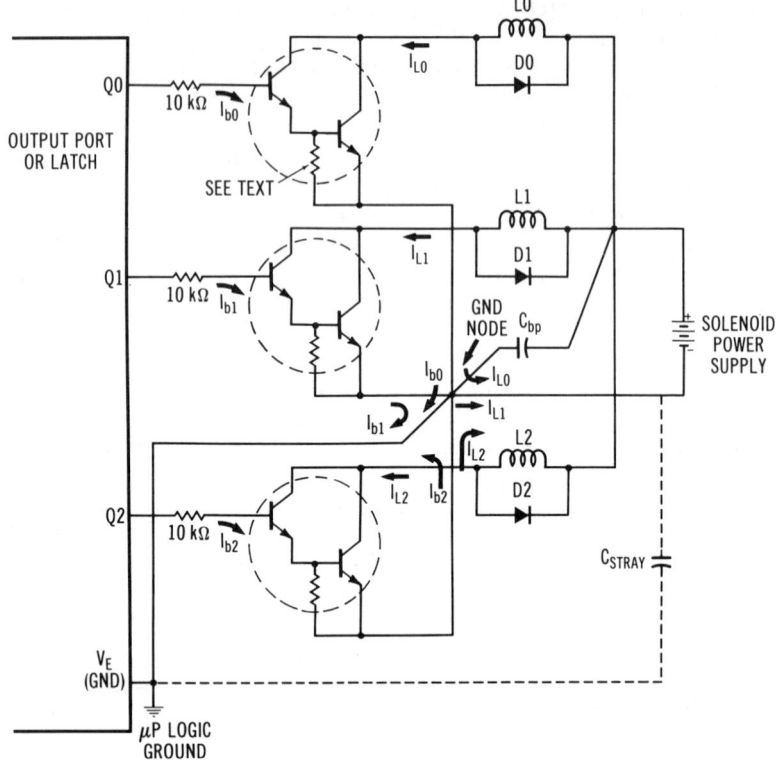

Fig. 8-6. Circuit topography for driving inductive loads.

solenoid drivers, a capacitor on each driver (between the supply side of the load and the emitter of the driving transistor) would be even more preferable.

When it is necessary to use high-value capacitors, the designer will not be able to use disc types, but will be forced to use electrolytics. Unfortunately, electrolytic capacitors may not "look like" a pure capacitance at high frequencies. This is often because the internal surfaces are spiraled, thus introducing appreciable resistive and inductive components. When such capacitors are used, they should be used in parallel with a low inductance and low ESR (equivalent series resistance) capacitor such as a ceramic disc. A 0.1-μF disc capacitor in parallel with a 100-μF tantalum capacitor is an excellent combination.

There are other practical considerations as well. For example, if the Darlington transistors of Fig. 8-6 are constructed from discrete npn transistors, a base turn-off resistor is necessary on the second (output) transistor of each Darlington. This resistor prevents the leakage currents in the first (input) transistor from causing improper operation of the output transistor.

In order to understand what *is* correct in Fig. 8-6, it will help to review an example of an improper design. Such a design is shown in Fig. 8-7. In this example, the designer has made the mistake of connecting the solenoid power supply common lead to the logic power ground. Notice that the load currents, therefore, flow in the common ground lead between points X and Y. The resulting voltage drop, V_g, will appear as if in series, voltage-wise, with the input signals to the port or latch. The result is not easily predictable.

Avoiding this pitfall may be very difficult in bus-oriented systems. Besides the logic power (+5 volts dc), there is often a +12- to 15-volt dc and a −12- to −15-volt dc power source available on the back plane of such systems. If separate commons (grounds) are provided for these supplies, the designer may still face a potential problem, and that is the placement of the *ground node*. In the event that only one board in the system will be using any appreciable current from these supplies, the ground node should be placed on this board (as in Fig. 8-6). If two or more boards are driving heavy loads from these supplies, it may be necessary to use more than one ground node (very undesirable) and to improve bypassing at each load and driver. It is likely that such systems may require additional supplies, and techniques such as optoisolation.

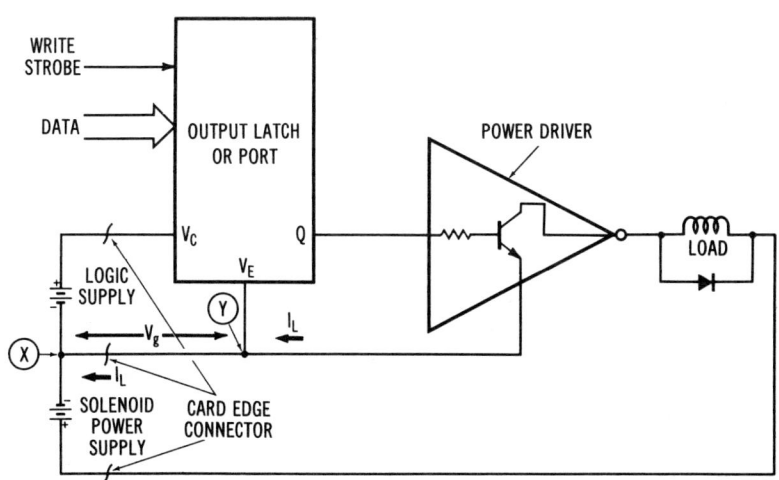

Fig. 8-7. Incorrect topography is used in this circuit.

If a bussed system has only a single ground for the logic and auxiliary supplies, the designer should still maintain separate common conductors from the logic and auxiliary supply terminals to the back-plane ground terminal. Doing this places the ground node as close to the load as possible and minimizes the crosstalk between supplies.

ISOLATION OF LOAD CURRENTS

It is often desirable to completely isolate load currents from the microprocessor system. This is absolutely essential if the load supply common is at any potential above earth ground, or if there is the danger that it may become connected to such a potential. Isolation also becomes desirable where the load is located some distance from the microprocessor system. Such long lengths of wire often have large voltage transients induced on them, especially during lightning storms. Heavy industrial equipment (especially welding equipment) also will induce dangerous or disruptive transients into long lines. Additionally, isolation may be desirable in complex systems where ground nodes cannot be separated and controlled, or where sensitive analog circuitry is present.

The circuit of Fig. 8-8 shows a typical use of optoisolators. Notice that the TIL113 and TIL119 were selected because they contain a Darlington phototransistor, and thus do not require as much LED drive current as the non-Darlington devices. Even so, the LED drive current is at the upper limit of what can be supplied by a TTL latch such as the 74LS373. Calculation of this current must take into account the worst-case current transfer ratio of the selected optocoupler.

Before calculating the resistor R_{LED} value that would provide this current, the designer must subtract the saturation voltage of the driver (approximately 1.0 volt) and the forward drop of the LED (approximately 1.8 volts) from the positive supply to which it is connected. If the 5-volt logic supply is used for powering the diode, the current through the diode will fluctuate significantly with temperature and from unit to unit. This fluctuation is due to changes in the voltage drops of the driver and LED being a large part of the total supply. A more stable drive current can be provided if a larger voltage drop is available across resistor R_{LED}. To provide this higher drop, a higher potential supply may be used. If the diode is connected to the 5-volt logic supply or to a regulated supply, bypass capacitor C_{bp2} may be included in the circuit. However, if the LED is connected to an unregulated supply (such as the supply voltage

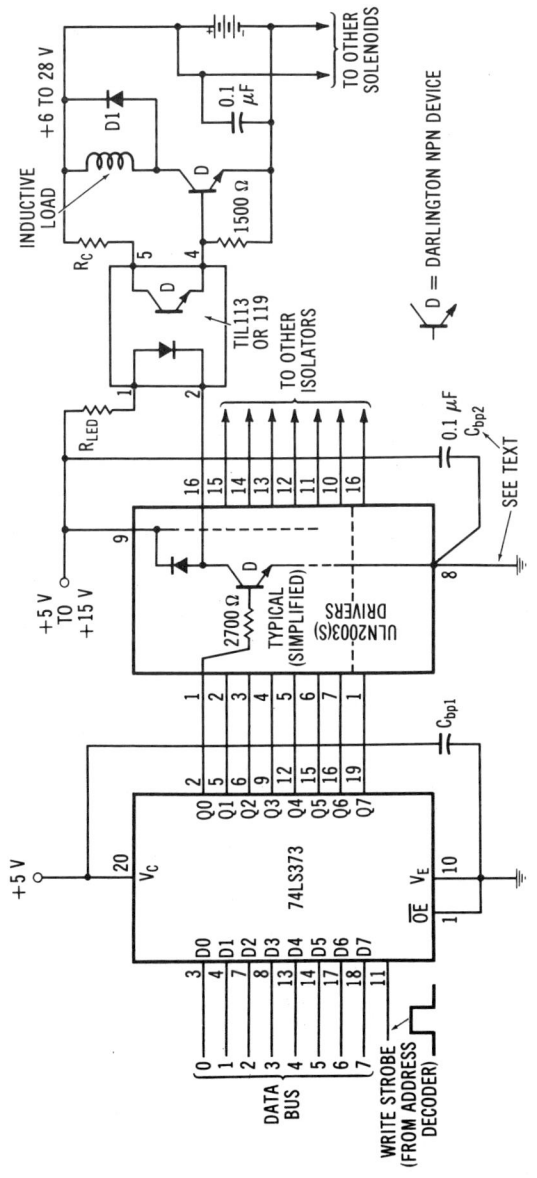

Fig. 8-8. Optical isolation of inductive and heavy loads.

present at the input to the 5-volt dc regulator), capacitor C_{bp2} should be omitted. The reason for this is that the capacitor might couple the noise of the raw supply onto the system ground. This could be worse than the load current noise that was being eliminated.

Notice that the ULN2003 contains a built-in snapback diode for each output transistor. While these diodes are not important in the circuit of Fig. 8-8, the designer may elect to use this chip to drive inductive loads directly. If this is done, some precautions are in order. The cathode line of these diodes should be connected to the positive load supply, but the designer should still provide snapback diodes at any inductive load. *If this is not done, the positive supply wire of each load must return to the immediate vicinity of pin 16 of the ULN2003.*

FIBER OPTICS AND OTHER ISOLATION TECHNIQUES

There are other isolation techniques as well. One of the techniques that is growing in popularity is the use of fiber optics. This technology has made great strides in the past few years, but is still somewhat expensive for use in systems where price is of prime importance. From the logic designer's standpoint, a fiber-optic link usually can be treated as a serial link. The considerations discussed in the earlier chapter on serial interfaces are generally applicable to fiber optics. There is one distinction worth making about fiber-optic, radio, and other communications links, and that is that it should be determined if the link is dc or dynamic (ac). Direct current links can be interfaced directly to devices such as UARTs, while alternating current links must be used with an uninterrupted stream of data (even though no information is being sent) or with a subcarrier (such as a modem). Direct current links are generally used in short interconnect applications and where isolation is the main factor. Direct current fiber-optic links usually have a shorter range than their alternating current counterparts, and are more applicable to interface designs.

With the availability of a wide variety of marvelous LSI ICs, you may have begun to hear statements like, "Anyone can design a computer system now!" The answer to this statement is, "Yes, but it still takes a trained and careful designer to develop a system that works right and reliably." While these new devices allow the designer to work at a higher (system) level than in years past, he/she still must understand the fundamentals of circuit design!

APPENDIX A

Data Sheets

FEATURES

- Operation from DC to 4.0 MHz
- Low Power - typ.<10mW @ 3.0 MHz
- 4V-11V Operation
- Programmable Word Length, Stop Bits and Parity
- Automatic Data Formatting and Status Generation
- Compatible with Industry Standard UART's
- Crystal Operation—IM6403

CMOS/LSI UNIVERSAL ASYNCHRONOUS RECEIVER TRANSMITTER (UART) IM6402/6403 IM6402A/6403A

GENERAL DESCRIPTION

The IM6402 and IM6403 are CMOS/LSI subsystems for interfacing computers or microprocessors to an asynchronous serial data channel. The receiver converts serial start, data, parity and stop bits to parallel data verifying proper code transmission, parity, and stop bits. The transmitter converts parallel data into serial form and automatically adds start, parity, and stop bits. The data word length can be 5, 6, 7 or 8 bits. Parity may be odd or even. Parity checking and generation can be inhibited. The stop bits may be one or two or one and one-half when transmitting 5 bit code.

The IM6402 and IM6403 can be used in a wide range of applications including modems, printers, peripherals and remote data aquisition systems. CMOS/LSI technology permits operating clock frequencies up to 4.0 MHz (250K Baud) an improvement of 10 to 1 over previous PMOS UART designs. Power requirements, by comparison, are reduced from 300mw to 10mw. Status logic increases flexibility and simplifies the user interface.

The IM6402 differs from the IM6403 on pins 2, 17, 19, 22, and 40 as shown in the connection diagram. The IM6403 utilizes pin 2 as a control and pins 17 and 40 for an inexpensive crystal oscillator as shown on page 5. TBREmpty and DReady are always active. All other input and output functions of the IM6402 and IM6403 are as described.

ORDERING INFORMATION

CIRCUIT MARKING AND PRODUCT CODE EXPLANATION

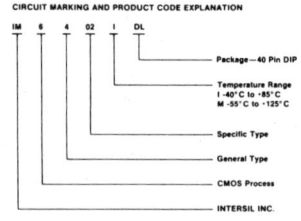

```
IM   6   4   02   I   DL
```

- Package—40 Pin DIP
- Temperature Range
  I -40°C to +85°C
  M -55°C to +125°C
- Specific Type
- General Type
- CMOS Process
- INTERSIL INC.

CONNECTION DIAGRAM

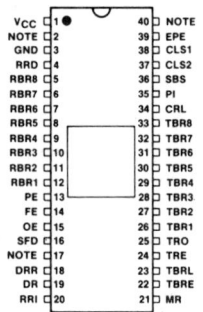

Vcc	1	40	NOTE
NOTE	2	39	EPE
GND	3	38	CLS1
RRD	4	37	CLS2
RBR8	5	36	SBS
RBR7	6	35	PI
RBR6	7	34	CRL
RBR5	8	33	TBR8
RBR4	9	32	TBR7
RBR3	10	31	TBR6
RBR2	11	30	TBR5
RBR1	12	29	TBR4
PE	13	28	TBR3
FE	14	27	TBR2
OE	15	26	TBR1
SFD	16	25	TRO
NOTE	17	24	TRE
DRR	18	23	TBRL
DR	19	22	TBRE
RRI	20	21	MR

PACKAGE DIMENSIONS

DL 40 Pin DIP

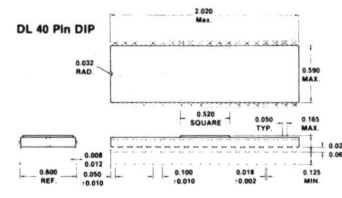

PIN	IM6402	IM6403
2	N/C	CONTROL
17	RRC	OSC IN
40	TRC	OSC OUT

NOTE:

ABSOLUTE MAXIMUM RATINGS

Supply Voltage	+12.0V
Input or Output Voltage Applied	GND − 0.3V to VCC + 0.3V
Storage Temperature Range	-65°C to 150°C
Operating Temperature Range	
Industrial IM6402A/03AI	-40°C to +85°C
Military IM6402A/03AM	-55°C to +125°C

DC CHARACTERISTICS V_{CC} = 4V to 11V, T_A = Industrial or Military

PARAMETER	SYMBOL	CONDITIONS	MIN	TYP	MAX	UNITS
Logical "1" Input Voltage	V_{IH}		70% VCC			V
Logical "0" Input Voltage	V_{IL}				20% VCC	V
Input Leakage	I_{IL}	OV VIN VCC	-1.0		1.0	μA
Logical "1" Output Voltage	V_{OH}	IOUT = 0	VCC - 0.01			V
Logical "0" Output Voltage	V_{OL}	IOUT = 0			GND + 0.01	V
Output Leakage	I_O	OV Vo VCC	-I.0		I.0	μA
Supply Current IM6402A/03A	I_{CC}	VIN = VCC		5.0	500	μA
Input Capacitance	C_{IN}			7.0	8.0	pF
Output Clearance	C_O			6.0	10.0	pF

AC CHARACTERISTICS V_{CC} = 10.0V, C_L = 50pF, T_A = 25°C

PARAMETER	SYMBOL	CONDITIONS	MIN	TYP	MAX	UNITS
Clock Frequency IM6402	f_{clock}		D.C.	6.0	4.0	MHz
Crystal Frequency IM6403	$f_{crystal}$		D.C.	8.0	6.0	MHz
Pulse Widths CRL, DRR, TBRL	t_{pw}		100	40		ns
Pulse Width MR	t_{pw}	See switching time	400	200		ns
Input Data Setup Time	t_{SET}	waveforms 1, 2, 3	30	0		ns
Input Data Hold Time	t_{HOLD}		50	30		ns
Output Propagation Delays	t_{pd}			40	70	ns

SWITCHING WAVEFORMS

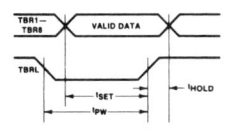

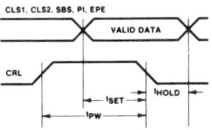

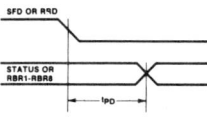

FIGURE 1.	FIGURE 2.	FIGURE 3.
DATA INPUT CYCLE	CONTROL REGISTER LOAD CYCLE	STATUS FLAG OUTPUT DELAYS OR DATA OUTPUT DELAYS

Courtesy Intersil, Inc.

ABSOLUTE MAXIMUM RATINGS

Supply Voltage	+7.0V
Input or Output Voltage Applied	GND −0.3V to V_{CC}+0.3V
Storage Temperature Range	−65°C to +150°C
Operating Temperature Range Industrial IM6402/03I	−40°C to +85°C
Military IM6402/03M	−55°C to +125°C

DC CHARACTERISTICS V_{CC} = 5.0 + − 10%. T_A = Operating Temperature Range

PARAMETER	SYMBOL	CONDITIONS	MIN	TYP	MAX	UNITS
Logical "1" Input Voltage	V_{IH}		V_{CC}− 2.0			V
Logical "0" Input Voltage	V_{IL}				0.8	V
Input Leakage	I_{IL}	$0V \leqslant V_{IN} \leqslant V_{CC}$	− 1.0		1.0	μA
Logical "1" Output Voltage	V_{OH}	I_{OH} = − 0.2 mA	2.4			V
Logical "0" Output Voltage	V_{OL}	I_{OL} = 2.0 mA			0.45	V
Output Leakage	I_O	$0V \leqslant V_O \leqslant V_{CC}$	− 1.0		1.0	μA
Supply Current	I_{CC}	V_{IN} = GND or V_{CC}; Output Open		1.0	100	μA
Input Capacitance	C_{IN}			7.0	8.0	
Output Capacitance	C_O			8.0	10.0	pF

AC CHARACTERISTICS V_{CC} = 5.0V, T_A = 25°C

PARAMETER	SYMBOL	CONDITIONS	MIN	TYP	MAX	UNITS
Clock Frequency IM6402	f_{clock}		D.C.	3.0	2.0	MHz
Crystal Frequency IM6403	$f_{crystal}$		D.C.	4.0	3.58	MHz
Pulse Widths CRL, DRR, TBRL	t_{pw}		150	50		ns
Pulse Width MR	t_{pw}	See switching time	400	200		ns
Input Data Setup Time	t_{SET}	waveforms 1, 2, 3	50	20		ns
Input Data Hold Time	t_{HOLD}		60	40		ns
Output Propagation Delays	t_{pd}			80	120	ns

IM6403 UNIVERSAL ASYNCHRONOUS RECEIVER TRANSMITTER WITH ON CHIP 4/11 STAGE DIVIDER

The IM6403 differs from the IM6402 on three inputs, TRC, RRC, and pin 2, and two outputs TBRE and DR.

Outputs DR and TBRE are not three-state, but are always active.

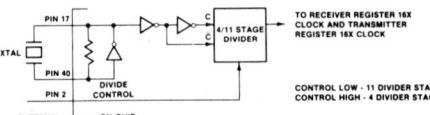

The divider chain output acts as a 16X clock to both the receiver register and transmitter register. Consequently both receiver and transmitter operate at the same frequency. The TRClock and RRClock inputs are used for a crystal oscillator while pin 2 controls the number of divider stages.

The on chip divider and oscillator allow an inexpensive crystal to be used as a timing source rather than additional circuitry such as baud rate generators. For example, a color TV crystal at 3.579545MHz results in a baud rate of 109.2 Hz for an easy teletype interface.

FUNCTIONAL BLOCK DIAGRAM

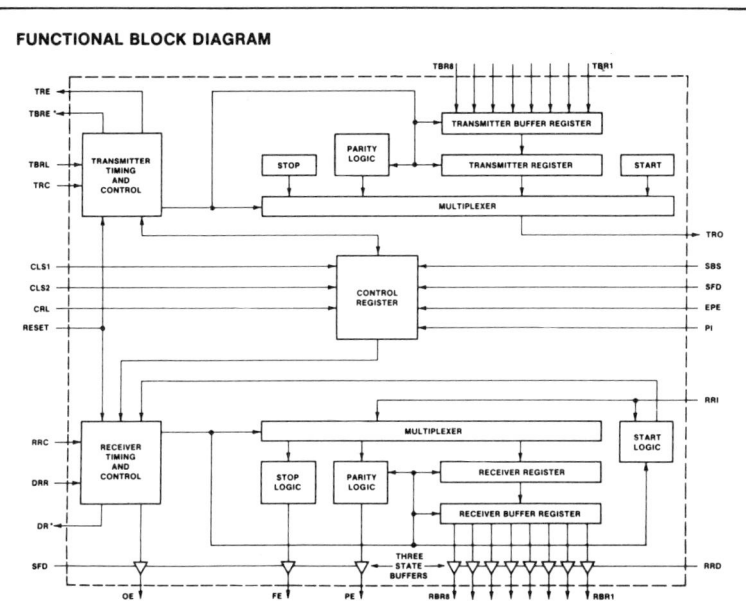

TRANSMITTER OPERATION

The transmitter section accepts parallel data, formats it and transmits it in serial form on the TROutput terminal. (A) Data is loaded into the transmitter buffer register from the inputs TR1 through TR8 by a logic low on the TBRLoad input. Valid data must be present at least t_{SET} prior to and t_{HOLD} following the rising edge of TBRL. If words less than 8 bits are used, only the least significant bits are used. The character is right justified into the least significant bit, TR1. (B) The rising edge

of TBRL clears TBREmpty. $\frac{1}{2}$ to $1\frac{1}{2}$ clock cycles later data is transferred to the transmitter register and TREmpty is cleared. $\frac{1}{2}$ cycle later transmission starts. Output data is clocked by TRClock. The clock rate is 16 times the data rate. $\frac{1}{2}$ clock cycle later TBREmpty is reset to a logic high. (C) A second pulse on TBRLoad loads data into the transmitter buffer register. Data transfer to the transmitter register is delayed until transmission of the current character is complete. (D) Data is automatically transferred to the transmitter register and transmission of that character begins one clock cycle later.

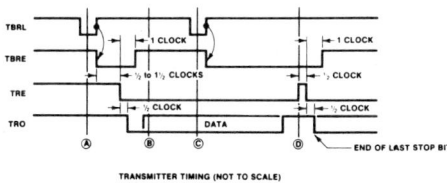

TRANSMITTER TIMING (NOT TO SCALE)

Courtesy Intersil, Inc.

139

RECEIVER OPERATION

Data is received in serial form at the RInput. When no data is being received, RInput must remain high. The data is clocked through the RRClock. The clock rate is 16 times the data rate. (A) A low level on DRReset clears the DReady line. (B) During the first stop bit data is transferred from the receiver register to the RBRegister. If the word is less than 8 bits, the unused most significant bits will be a logic low. The output character is right justified to the least significant bit RBR1. A logic high on OError indicates overruns. An overrun occurs when DReady has not been cleared before the present character was transferred to the RBRegister. A logic high on PError indicates a parity error. (C) ½ clock cycle later DReady is reset to a logic high, FError is evaluated. A logic high on FError indicates an invalid stop bit was received, a framing error.

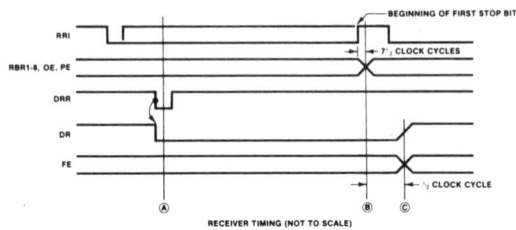

RECEIVER TIMING (NOT TO SCALE)

START BIT DETECTION

The receiver uses a 16X clock for timing. (A) the start bit could have occurred as much as one clock cycle before it was detected, as indicated by the shaded portion. The center of the start bit is defined as clock count 7½. If the receiver clock is a symetrical square wave, the center of the start bit will be located within ±½ clock cycle, ±1/32 bit or ±3.125% giving a receiver margin of 46.875%. The receiver begins searching for the next start bit at the center of the first stop bit.

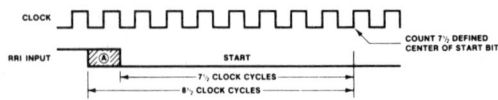

INTERFACING WITH THE IM6100 MICROPROCESSOR

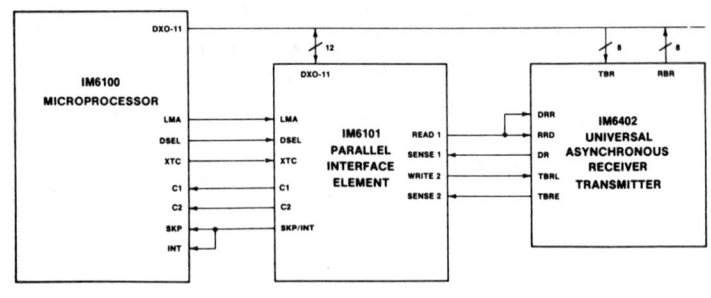

PIN ASSIGNMENT AND FUNCTIONS

PIN	SYMBOL	DESCRIPTION
1	VCC	+5 Volts Supply
2	IM6402-N/C	No Connection
	IM6403-Control	4/11 Stage Divider High: 4 Stage Low: 11 Stage
3	GND	Ground
4	RRD	A High level on RECEIVER REGISTER DISABLE forces the receiver holding register outputs RBR1-RBR8 to a high impedance state.
5	RBR8	The contents of the RECEIVER BUFFER REGISTER appear on these three-state outputs. Word formats less than 8 characters are right justified to RBR1.
6	RBR7	See Pin 5 - RBR8
7	RBR6	See Pin 5 - RBR8
8	RBR5	See Pin 5 - RBR8
9	RBR4	See Pin 5 - RBR8
10	RBR3	See Pin 5 - RBR8
11	RBR2	See Pin 5 - RBR8
12	RBR1	See Pin 5 - RBR8

PIN	SYMBOL	DESCRIPTION
13	PE	A high level on PARITY ERROR indicates received parity does not match parity programmed by control bits. When parity is inhibited this output is low.
14	FE	A high level on FRAMING ERROR indicates the first stop bit was invalid.
15	OE	A high level on OVERRUN ERROR indicates the data received flag was not cleared before the last character was transferred to the receiver buffer register.
16	SFD	A high level on STATUS FLAGS DISABLE forces the outputs PE, FE, OE, DR, TBRE to a high impedance state.
17	IM6402-RRC IM6403-OSCIN	The RECEIVER REGISTER CLOCK is 16X the receiver data rate.
18	DRR	A low level on DATA RECEIVED RESET clears the data received outputDR, to a low level.
19	DR	A high level on DATA RECEIVED indicates a character has been received and transferred to the receiver buffer register.
20	RRI	Serial data on RECEIVER REGISTER INPUT is clocked into the receiver register.

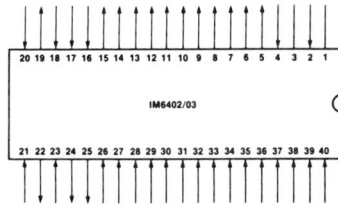

20 19 18 17 16 15 14 13 12 11 10 9 8 7 6 5 4 3 2 1

IM6402/03

21 22 23 24 25 26 27 28 29 30 31 32 33 34 35 36 37 38 39 40

PIN	SYMBOL	DESCRIPTION
21	MR	A high level on MASTER RESET clears PE, FE, OE, and DR to a low level and sets the transmitter output to a high level after 18 clock cycles.
22	TBRE	A high level on TRANSMITTER BUFFER REGISTER EMPTY indicates the transmitter buffer register has transferred its data to the transmitter register and is ready for new data.
23	TBRL	A low level on TRANSMITTER BUFFER REGISTER LOAD transfers data from inputs TBR1-TBR8 into the transmitter buffer register. A low to high transition on TBRL indicates data transfer to the transmitter register. If the transmitter register is busy, transfer is automatically delayed so that the two characters are transmitted end to end.
24	TRE 6	A high level on TRANSMITTER REGISTER EMPTY indicates completed transmission of a character including stop bits.
25	TRO	Character data, start data and stop bits appear serially at the TRANSMITTER REGISTER OUTPUT.
26	TBR1-TBR8	Character data is loaded into the TRANSMITTER BUFFER REGISTER via inputs TBR1-TBR8. For character formats less than 8 bits the TBR8, 7, and 6 inputs are ignored corresponding to the programmed word length.

PIN	SYMBOL	DESCRIPTION
27	TBR2	See Pin 26 - TBR1
28	TBR3	See Pin 26 - TBR1
29	TBR4	See Pin 26 - TBR1
30	TBR5	See Pin 26 - TBR1
31	TBR6	See Pin 26 - TBR1
32	TBR7	See Pin 26 - TBR1
33	TBR8	See Pin 26 - TBR1
34	CRL	A high level on CONTROL REGISTER LOAD loads the control register.
35	PI	A high level on PARITY INHIBIT inhibits parity generation, parity checking and forces PE output low.
36	SBS	A high level on STOP BIT SELECT selects 1.5 stop bits for 5 character format and 2 stop bits for other lengths.
37	CLS2	These inputs program the CHARACTER LENGTH SELECTED. (CLS1 low CLS2 low 5 bits) (CLS1 high CLS2 low 6 bits) (CLS1 low CLS2 high 7 bits) (CLS1 high CLS2 high 8 bits)
38	CLS1	See Pin 37 - CLS2
39	EPE	When PI is low a high level on EVEN PARITY ENABLE generates and checks even parity. A low level selects odd parity.
40	IM6402-TRC IM6403-OSCOUT	The TRANSMITTER REGISTER CLOCK is 16X the transmit data rate.

Courtesy Intersil, Inc.

 **MOTOROLA**

ADDRESSABLE ASYNCHRONOUS RECEIVER/TRANSMITTER

The MC14469 Addressable Asynchronous Receiver Transmitter is constructed with MOS P-channel and N-channel enhancement devices in a single monolithic structure (CMOS). The MC14469 receives one or two eleven-bit words in a serial data stream. The first incoming word contains the address and when the address matches, the MC14469 is enabled to transmit two data words. Each of the transmitted words contains eight data bits, even parity bit, start and stop bit, in UART compatible format.

The received word contains seven address bits and the address of the MC14469 is set on seven pins. Thus 2^7 or 128 units can be interconnected in simplex or full duplex data transmission. In addition to the address received, seven command bits may optionally be received for data or control use.

The MC14469 finds application in transmitting data from remote A-to-D converters, remote MPUs or remote digital transducers to a master computer or MPU.

- Supply Voltage Range — 4.5 Vdc to 18 Vdc
- Low Quiescent Current — 75 μAdc maximum @ 5 Vdc
- Data Rates to 4800 Baud
- Receive — Serial to Parallel
  Transmit — Parallel to Serial
- Transmit and Receive Simultaneously in Full Duplex
- Crystal or Resonator Operation for On-Chip Oscillator

CMOS LSI
(LOW-POWER COMPLEMENTARY MOS)

ADDRESSABLE ASYNCHRONOUS
RECEIVER/TRANSMITTER

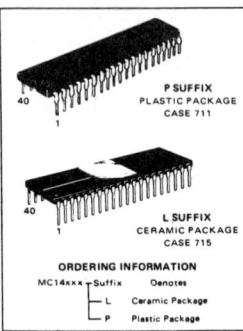

P SUFFIX
PLASTIC PACKAGE
CASE 711

L SUFFIX
CERAMIC PACKAGE
CASE 715

ORDERING INFORMATION

MC14xxx Suffix   Denotes

— L   Ceramic Package

— P   Plastic Package

BLOCK DIAGRAMS

PIN ASSIGNMENTS

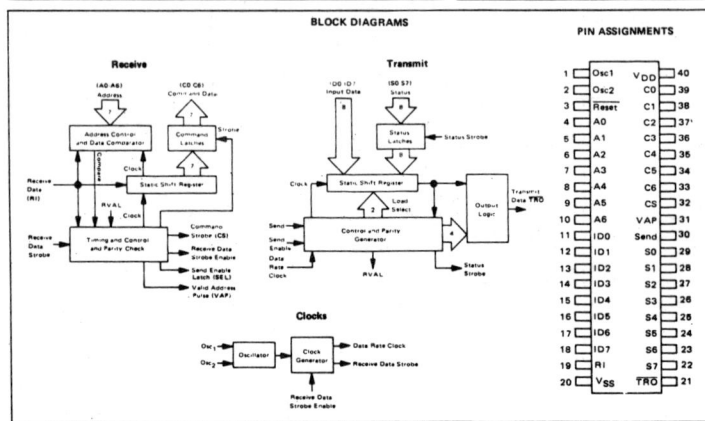

MC14469

MAXIMUM RATINGS (Voltages referenced to V_{SS}, Pin 20.

	Symbol	Value	Unit
DC Supply Voltage	V_{DD}	−0.5 to +18	Vdc
Input Voltage, All Inputs	V_{in}	−0.5 to V_{DD} + 0.5	Vdc
DC Current Drain per Pin	I	10	mAdc
Operating Temperature Range	T_A	−40 to +85	°C
Storage Temperature Range	T_{stg}	−65 to +150	°C

This device contains circuitry to protect the inputs against damage due to high static voltages or electric fields; however, it is advised that normal precautions be taken to avoid application of any voltage higher than maximum rated voltages to this high impedance circuit. For proper operation it is recommended that V_{in} and V_{out} be constrained to the range $V_{SS} \leq (V_{in}$ or $V_{out}) \leq V_{DD}$.

Unused inputs must always be tied to an appropriate logic voltage level (e.g., either V_{SS} or V_{DD}).

ELECTRICAL CHARACTERISTICS

Characteristic	Symbol	V_{DD} Vdc	−40°C Min	−40°C Max	25°C Min	25°C Typ	25°C Max	+85°C Min	+85°C Max	Unit
Output Voltage "0" Level	V_{OL}	5.0	−	0.05	−	0	0.05	−	0.05	Vdc
$V_{in} = V_{DD}$ or 0		10	−	0.05	−	0	0.05	−	0.05	
		15	−	0.05	−	0	0.05	−	0.05	
"1" Level	V_{OH}	5.0	4.95	−	4.95	5.0	−	4.95	−	Vdc
$V_{in} = 0$ or V_{DD}		10	9.95	−	9.95	10	−	9.95	−	
		15	14.95	−	14.95	15	−	14.95	−	
Input Voltage # "0" Level	V_{IL}									Vdc
(V_O = 4.5 or 0.5 Vdc)		5.0	−	1.5	−	2.25	1.5	−	1.5	
(V_O = 9.0 or 1.0 Vdc)		10	−	3.0	−	4.50	3.0	−	3.0	
(V_O = 13.5 or 1.5 Vdc)		15	−	4.0	−	6.75	4.0	−	4.0	
"1" Level	V_{IH}									Vdc
(V_O = 0.5 or 4.5 Vdc)		5.0	3.5	−	3.5	2.75	−	3.5	−	
(V_O = 1.0 or 9.0 Vdc)		10	7.0	−	7.0	5.50	−	7.0	−	
(V_O = 1.5 or 13.5 Vdc)		15	11.0	−	11.0	8.25	−	11.0	−	
Output Drive Current (Except Pin 2)	I_{OH}									mAdc
(V_{OH} = 2.5 Vdc) Source		5.0	−1.0	−	−0.8	−1.7	−	−0.6	−	
(V_{OH} = 4.6 Vdc)		5.0	−0.2	−	−0.16	−0.35	−	−0.12	−	
(V_{OH} = 9.5 Vdc)		10	−0.5	−	−0.4	−0.9	−	−0.3	−	
(V_{OH} = 13.5 Vdc)		15	−1.4	−	−1.2	−3.5	−	−1.0	−	
(V_{OL} = 0.4 Vdc) Sink	I_{OL}	5.0	0.52	−	0.44	0.88	−	0.36	−	mAdc
(V_{OL} = 0.5 Vdc)		10	1.3	−	1.1	2.25	−	0.9	−	
(V_{OL} = 1.5 Vdc)		15	3.6	−	3.0	8.8	−	2.4	−	
Output Drive Current (Pin 2 Only)	I_{OH}									mAdc
(V_{OH} = 2.5 Vdc) Source		5.0	−0.19	−	−0.16	−0.32	−	−0.13	−	
(V_{OH} = 4.6 Vdc)		5.0	−0.04	−	−0.035	−0.07	−	−0.03	−	
(V_{OH} = 9.5 Vdc)		10	−0.09	−	−0.08	−0.16	−	−0.06	−	
(V_{OH} = 13.5 Vdc)		15	−0.29	−	−0.27	−0.48	−	−0.2	−	
(V_{OL} = 0.4 Vdc) Sink	I_{OL}	5.0	0.1	−	0.085	0.17	−	0.07	−	mAdc
(V_{OL} = 0.5 Vdc)		10	0.17	−	0.14	0.28	−	0.1	−	
(V_{OL} = 1.5 Vdc)		15	0.50	−	0.42	0.84	−	0.3	−	
Maximum Frequency	f_{max}	4.5	400	−	365	550	−	310	−	kHz
Input Current	I_{in}	15	−	±0.3	−	±0.00001	±0.3	−	±1.0	µAdc
Pull-Up Current (Pins 4-18)	I_{UP}	15	12	120	10	50	100	8.0	85	µAdc
Input Capacitance (V_{in} = 0)	C_{in}	−	−	−	−	5.0	7.5	−	−	pF
Quiescent Current (Per Package)	I_{DD}	5.0	−	75	−	0.010	75	−	565	µAdc
		10	−	150	−	0.020	150	−	1125	
		15	−	300	−	0.030	300	−	2250	
Supply Voltage	V_{DD}	−	+4.5	+18.0	+4.5	−	+18.0	+4.5	+18.0	Vdc

Noise immunity specified for worst-case input combination.
Noise Margin both "1" and "0" level = 1.0 Vdc min @ V_{DD} = 5.0 Vdc
2.0 Vdc min @ V_{DD} = 10 Vdc
2.5 Vdc min @ V_{DD} = 15 Vdc

National Semiconductor

July 1979

MM58167 Microprocessor (MICROBUS™) Compatible Real Time Clock

General Description

The MM58167 is a low threshold metal-gate CMOS circuit that functions as a real time clock calendar in bus-oriented microprocessor systems. The device includes an addressable counter, addressable latch for alarm-type functions, and 2 interrupt outputs. A power-down input allows the chip to be disabled from the outside world for standby low power operation. The time base is generated from a 32,768 Hz crystal-controlled oscillator.

Features

- MICROBUS™ compatible
- Thousandths of seconds, hundredths of seconds, tenths of seconds, seconds, minutes, hours, day of the week, day of the month, and month counters with corresponding latches for alarm-type functions
- Interrupt output (maskable) with 8 possible interrupt signals:
  - Latch and counter comparison
  - Every tenth of a second
  - Every second
  - Every minute
  - Every hour
  - Every day
  - Every week
  - Every month
- Power-down mode that disables all outputs except for an interrupt output that occurs on a counter latch comparison. This is not the same as the maskable interrupt output
- Don't care states in the latches
- Status bit to indicate clock rollover during a read
- 32,768 Hz crystal reference, with only the input tuning capacitor and load capacitor needed externally
- Four year calendar

Functional Description

The MM58167 is a microprocessor oriented real time clock. The circuit includes addressable real time counters and addressable latches, each for thousandths of seconds through months. The counter and latch are divided into bytes of 4 bits each. When addressed, 2 bytes will appear on the data I/O bus. The data, in binary coded decimal, can be transferred to and from the counters via the data I/O bus so that each set of 2 bytes (1 word) can be accessed independently as grouped in Table I.

If either of the bytes in the above 8-bit counter words do not legally reach 4-bit lengths (e.g., day of the week uses only the 3 least significant bits) the unused bits will be unrecognized during a write and held at V_{SS} during a read. If any illegal data is entered into the counters during a write cycle, it may take up to 4 clocks (4 months in the case of the month counter) to restore legal BCD data to the counter. The latches will read and write all 4 bits per byte. Each of the counter and latch words can be reset with the appropriate address and data inputs. The counter reset is a write function. The latches can be programmed to compare with the counters at all times by writing 1's into the 2 most significant bits of each latch, thus establishing a don't care state in the latch. The don't care state is programmable on the byte level, i.e., tens of hours can contain a don't care state, yet unit hours can contain a valid code necessary for a comparison.

Connection Diagram

Dual-In-Line Package

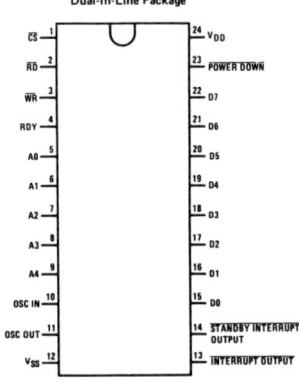

CS	1	24 V_DD
RD̄	2	23 POWER DOWN
W̄R̄	3	22 D7
RDY	4	21 D6
A0	5	20 D5
A1	6	19 D4
A2	7	18 D3
A3	8	17 D2
A4	9	16 D1
OSC IN	10	15 D0
OSC OUT	11	14 STANDBY INTERRUPT OUTPUT
V_SS	12	13 INTERRUPT OUTPUT

TOP VIEW

Courtesy National Semiconductor Corp.

Absolute Maximum Ratings

Voltage at All Inputs and Outputs	$V_{DD} + 0.3$ to $V_{SS} - 0.3$
Operating Temperature	$-25°C$ to $+85°C$
Storage Temperature	$-65°C$ to $+150°C$
$V_{DD} - V_{SS}$	6V
Lead Temperature (Soldering, 10 seconds)	$300°C$

Electrical Characteristics $T_A = -25°C$ to $+85°C$, $V_{SS} = 0V$

PARAMETER	CONDITIONS	MIN	TYP	MAX	UNITS
Supply Voltage					
V_{DD}	Outputs Enabled	4.0		5.5	V
V_{DD} (Note 1)	Power Down Mode	2.0		5.5	V
Supply Current					
I_{DD}, Static	Outputs TRI-STATE, $f_{IN} = DC$, $V_{DD} = 5.5V$			10	μA
I_{DD}, Dynamic	Outputs TRI-STATE, $f_{IN} = 32$ kHz, $V_{DD} = 5.5V$, $V_{IH} \geq V_{DD} - 0.3V$, $V_{IL} \leq V_{SS} + 0.3V$			20	μA
I_{DD}, Dynamic	Outputs TRI-STATE, $f_{IN} = 32$ kHz, $V_{DD} = 5.5V$, $V_{IH} = 2.0V$, $V_{IL} = 0.8V$			12	mA
Input Voltage					
Logical Low		0.0		0.8	V
Logical High		2.0		V_{DD}	V
Input Leakage Current	$V_{SS} \leq V_{IN} \leq V_{DD}$			1	μA
Output Impedance	(I/O and Interrupt Output)				
Logical Low	$V_{DD} = 4.75V$, $I_{OL} = 1.6$ mA			0.4	V
Logical High	$V_{DD} = 4.75V$, $I_{OH} = -400 \mu A$,	2.4			V
	$I_{OH} = -10 \mu A$	$0.8 V_{DD}$			V
TRI-STATE(π)	$V_{OUT} = 0V$,			-1	μA
	$V_{OUT} = V_{DD}$			1	μA
Output Impedance	(Ready and Standby Interrupt Output)				
Logical Low, Sink	$V_{DD} = 4.75V$, $I_{OL} = 1.6$ mA			0.4	V
Logical High, Leakage	$V_{OUT} \leq V_{DD}$			10	μA

Note 1: To insure that no illegal data is read from or written into the chip during power up, the power down input should be enabled only after all other lines (Read, Write, Chip Select, and Data Bus) are valid.

Functional Description (Continued)

TABLE I

COUNTER ADDRESSED	UNITS				MAX USED BCD CODE	TENS				MAX USED BCD CODE
	D0	D1	D2	D3		D4	D5	D6	D7	
Ten Thousandths of a Second	0	0	0	0	0	I/O	I/O	I/O	I/O	9
Tenths and Hundredths of Seconds	I/O	I/O	I/O	I/O	9	I/O	I/O	I/O	I/O	9
Seconds	I/O	I/O	I/O	I/O	9	I/O	I/O	I/O	0	5
Minutes	I/O	I/O	I/O	I/O	9	I/O	I/O	I/O	0	5
Hours	I/O	I/O	I/O	I/O	9	I/O	I/O	0	0	2
Day of the Week	I/O	I/O	I/O	0	7	0	0	0	0	0
Day of the Month	I/O	I/O	I/O	I/O	9	I/O	I/O	0	0	3
Month	I/O	I/O	I/O	I/O	9	I/O	0	0	0	1

Courtesy National Semiconductor Corp.

Functional Description (Continued)

TABLE II. ADDRESS CODES AND FUNCTIONS

A4	A3	A2	A1	A0	FUNCTION
0	0	0	0	0	Counter — Thousandths of Seconds
0	0	0	0	1	Counter — Hundredths and Tenths of Seconds
0	0	0	1	0	Counter — Seconds
0	0	0	1	1	Counter — Minutes
0	0	1	0	0	Counter — Hours
0	0	1	0	1	Counter — Day of the Week
0	0	1	1	0	Counter — Day of the Month
0	0	1	1	1	Counter — Months
0	1	0	0	0	Latches — Thousandths of Seconds
0	1	0	0	1	Latches — Hundredths and Tenths of Seconds
0	1	0	1	0	Latches — Seconds
0	1	0	1	1	Latches — Minutes
0	1	1	0	0	Latches — Hours
0	1	1	0	1	Latches — Day of the Week
0	1	1	1	0	Latches — Day of the Month
0	1	1	1	1	Latches — Months
1	0	0	0	0	Interrupt Status Register
1	0	0	0	1	Interrupt Control Register
1	0	0	1	0	Counter Reset
1	0	0	1	1	Latch Reset
1	0	1	0	0	Status Bit
1	0	1	0	1	"GO" Command
1	0	1	1	0	Standby Interrupt
1	1	1	1	1	Test Mode

All others unused.

TABLE III. COUNTER AND LATCH RESET FORMAT

D0	D1	D2	D3	D4	D5	D6	D7	COUNTER OR LATCH RESET
1	0	0	0	0	0	0	0	Thousandths of Seconds
0	1	0	0	0	0	0	0	Hundredths and Tenths of Seconds
0	0	1	0	0	0	0	0	Seconds
0	0	0	1	0	0	0	0	Minutes
0	0	0	0	1	0	0	0	Hours
0	0	0	0	0	1	0	0	Days of the Week
0	0	0	0	0	0	1	0	Days of the Month
0	0	0	0	0	0	0	1	Months

FOR COUNTER RESET A4—A0 MUST BE 10010
FOR LATCH RESET A4—A0 MUST BE 10011

Courtesy National Semiconductor Corp.

Functional Description (Continued)

Following a read of any real time counter a status bit read should be done. If during a counter read cycle the clock rolls over, the data read out could be invalid. Thus, during a read if the clock rolls over the status bit will be set. The status bit will appear on D0 when read, D1 through D7 will be zeros.

To synchronize the clock with real time a "GO" command exists which can be used to reset the thousandths of seconds, hundredths and tenths of seconds, and seconds counters. After setting the lower frequency counters (minutes through months), the appropriate address and a write pulse can be sent to reset all counters mentioned above. This allows the clock to be started at an exactly known time. It can also be used as a stopwatch function. The "GO" command is the start and a counter read is the stop point. The clock does not stop during or following a read, so each read would be a split time.

A second special command will enable the standby interrupt output. The standby interrupt output is the only input or output enabled during the power down or standby mode. Power down occurs when the power down input goes to a logical zero level. In this mode the outputs are TRI-STATED and the inputs ignored regardless of the state of the chip select. The standby interrupt is enabled by writing a 1 on the D0 line with the standby interrupt address selected. On the next counter-latch comparison the open drain output device turns on, sinking current. The output will be turned on immediately upon writing a 1 on D0 if the comparison occurred before the write, yet is still in effect. To disable the output a zero on D0 is written at the standby interrupt address. The write cycles must occur during normal operation, but the output can become active during power down. This feature can be used to turn the power back on during a power down mode (see *Figure 4* for a typical application). Refer to Tables II and III for the address input codes and functions and for the counter and latch reset format.

The interrupt output is controlled by the interrupt status register (8 bits) and the interrupt control register (8 bits). The status register contains the present state of the comparator (compares the counters and latches) and the outputs (1 bit each) of the tenths of seconds, seconds,

minutes, hours, week, day of the month, and month counters *(Figure 1)*. The interrupt status register can only be read. The interrupt control register is a mask register that regulates which of the 8 bits in the status register goes out as an interrupt. The control register cannot be read from. A 1 is written into the control register to select the appropriate interrupt output. If more than a single 1 exists in the control register each selected bit will come out as an interrupt. This will appear as an interrupt occurring at the highest frequency selected. The interrupt is acknowledged by addressing and reading the status register. Once acknowledged the interrupt output and status register are reset. The only way to disable the interrupt output is to write all 0's into the control register or to enable the power down input.

The I/O bus is controlled by the read, write, ready and chip select lines. During a read cycle ($\overline{RD}$ = 0, $\overline{WR}$ = 1, $\overline{CS}$ = 0, RDY = 0) the data on the I/O bus is the data contained in the addressed counter or latch. During a write cycle ($\overline{RD}$ = 1, $\overline{WR}$ = 0, $\overline{CS}$ = 0, RDY = 0) the data on the I/O bus is latched into the addressed counter or latch. At the start of each read or write cycle the RDY signal goes low and will remain low until the clock has placed valid data on the bus or until it has completed latching data in on a write. The chip select line is used to enable or disable the device outputs. When the chip is selected the device will drive the I/O bus for a read or use the I/O bus as an input for a write. The I/O bus will not be affected when the chip is deselected. The outputs driving the bus will go to the TRI-STATE or high impedance state. The chip will not respond to any inputs when deselected. Refer to *Figures 2 and 3* for read and write cycle timing.

The clock's time base is a 32,768 crystal controlled oscillator. Externally, the crystal, the input tuning capacitor, and the output load capacitor are required. Included internally are a high gain inverter, an RC delay, and the bias resistor. To tune the oscillator a constant read can be done on one of the higher frequency counters. For example, a constant read of the thousandths of seconds counter will place a 500 Hz signal on the D4 bus line.

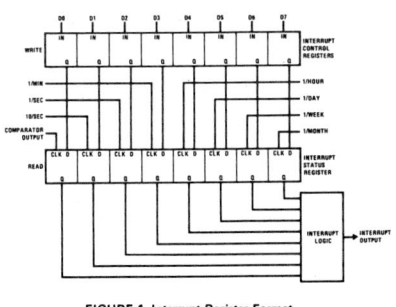

FIGURE 1. Interrupt Register Format

Courtesy National Semiconductor Corp.

Read Cycle Timing Characteristics $T_A = -25°C$ to $+85°C$, $V_{DD} = 4.0V$ to $5.5V$, $V_{SS} = 0V$

	PARAMETER	MIN	TYP	MAX	UNITS
t_{AR}	Address Bus Valid to Read Strobe	100			ns
t_{CSR}	Chip Select ON to Read Strobe	0			ns
t_{RRY}	Read Strobe to Ready Strobe			150	ns
t_{RYD}	Ready Strobe to Data Valid			800	ns
t_{AD}	Address Bus Valid to Data Valid			1050	ns
t_{RH}	Data Hold Time from Trailing Edge of Read Strobe	0			ns
t_{HZ}	Trailing Edge of Read Strobe to TRI-STATE Mode			250	ns
t_{RYH}	Read Hold Time After Ready Strobe	0			ns
t_{RA}	Address Bus Hold Time from Trailing Edge of Read Strobe	50			ns

Data bus loading is 100 pF
Ready output loading is 50 pF
Input and output AC timing levels are:
　Logical "1" = 2.0V
　Logical "0" = 0.8V

Write Cycle Timing Characteristics $T_A = -25°C$ to $+85°C$, $V_{DD} = 4.0V$ to $5.5V$, $V_{SS} = 0V$

	PARAMETER	MIN	TYP	MAX	UNITS
t_{AW}	Address Valid to Write Strobe	100			ns
t_{CSW}	Chip Select ON to Write Strobe	0			ns
t_{DN}	Data Valid Before Write Strobe	100			ns
t_{WRY}	Write Strobe to Ready Strobe			150	ns
t_{RY}	Ready Strobe Width			800	ns
t_{RYH}	Write Hold Time After Ready Strobe	0			ns
t_{WD}	Data Hold Time After Write Strobe	110			ns
t_{WA}	Address Hold Time After Write Strobe	50			ns

Data bus loading is 100 pF
Ready output loading is 50 pF
Input and output AC timing levels are:
　Logical "1" = 2.0V
　Logical "0" = 0.8V

Switching Time Waveforms

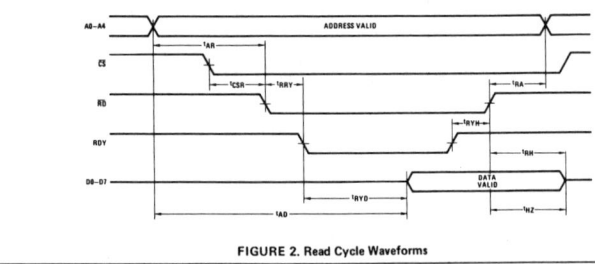

FIGURE 2. Read Cycle Waveforms

Courtesy National Semiconductor Corp.

Switching Time Waveforms (Continued)

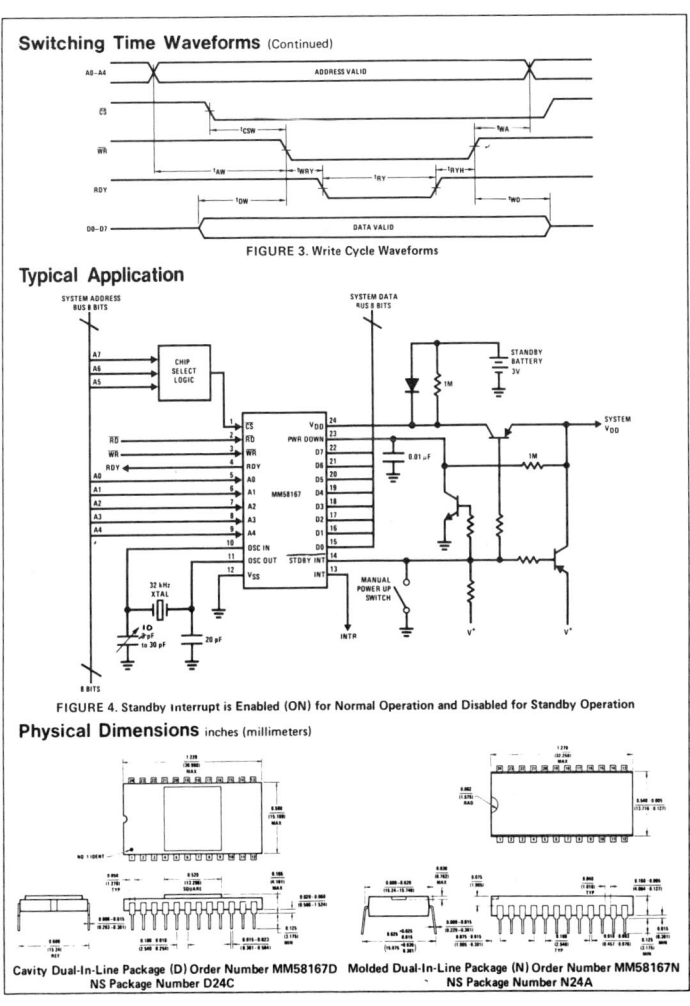

FIGURE 3. Write Cycle Waveforms

Typical Application

FIGURE 4. Standby Interrupt is Enabled (ON) for Normal Operation and Disabled for Standby Operation

Physical Dimensions inches (millimeters)

Cavity Dual-In-Line Package (D) Order Number MM58167D
NS Package Number D24C

Molded Dual-In-Line Package (N) Order Number MM58167N
NS Package Number N24A

Courtesy National Semiconductor Corp.

149

SEPTEMBER 1977

ADC0816/ADC0817 Single Chip Data Acquisition System

General Description

The ADC0816, ADC0817 (MM74C948) data acquisition components are monolithic CMOS devices with an 8-bit analog-to-digital converter, a 16-channel multiplexer and microprocessor compatible control logic. The 8-bit A/D converter uses successive approximation as the conversion technique. The converter features a high impedance chopper stabilized comparator, a 256R voltage divider with analog switch tree and a successive approximation register. The 16-channel multiplexer can directly access any one of 16 single-ended analog signals and provides the logic for additional channel expansion. Signal conditioning of any analog input signal is eased by direct access to the input of the 8-bit A/D converter.

The device eliminates the need for external zero and full-scale adjustments and features an absolute accuracy ≤ 1 LSB including quantitizing error. Easy interfacing to microprocessors is provided by the latched and decoded address inputs and latched TTL TRI-STATE® outputs.

The design of the ADC0816, ADC0817 has been optimized by incorporating the most desirable aspects of several A/D conversion techniques. The ADC0816, ADC0817 offers high speed, high accuracy, minimal temperature dependence, excellent long-term accuracy and repeatability, and consumes minimal power. These features make this device ideally suited to applications such as process control, industrial control, and machine control.

Features

- Total unadjusted error $< \pm 1/2$ LSB
- Linearity error $< \pm 1/2$ LSB
- No missing codes
- Guaranteed monotonicity
- No offset adjust required
- No scale adjust required
- Conversion time of 100 μs
- Easy microprocessor interface
- Latched TRI-STATE output
- Latched address input
- Ratiometric conversion
- Single 5V supply
- Low power consumption—15 mW

Block Diagram

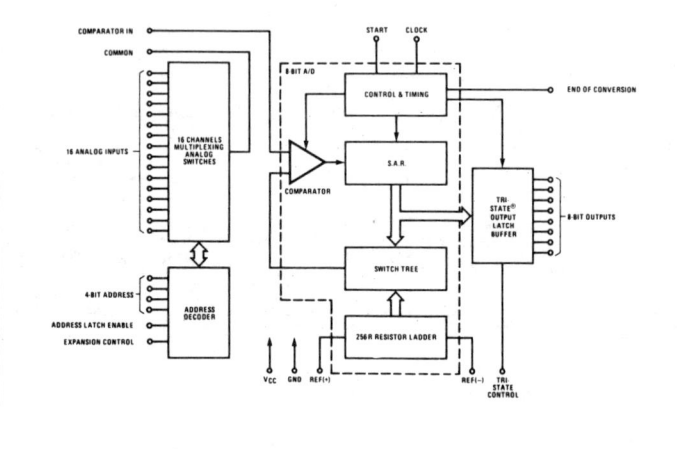

Courtesy National Semiconductor Corp.

Absolute Maximum Ratings (Notes 1 and 2)

Voltage at Any Pin Except Control Inputs	$-0.3V$ to $V_{CC} + 0.3V$
Voltage at Control Inputs	$-0.3V$ to $+15V$
(Start, TRI-STATE, Clock, ALE, ADD A,	
ADD B, ADD C, ADD D, Expansion Control)	
Operating Temperature Range	$-40°C$ to $+85°C$
Storage Temperature Range	$-65°C$ to $+150°C$
Package Dissipation (at $25°C$)	500 mW
Operating V_{CC} Range	4.5V to 6V
Absolute Maximum V_{CC}	6.5V
Lead Temperature (Soldering, 10 seconds)	$300°C$

DC Electrical Characteristics

$4.75V \leq V_{CC} \leq 5.25V$, $-40°C \leq T_A \leq +85°C$ unless otherwise noted, (Note 2)

	PARAMETER	CONDITIONS	MIN	TYP	MAX	UNITS
$V_{IN(1)}$	Logical "1" Input Voltage	$V_{CC} = 5V$	$V_{CC}-1.5$			V
$V_{IN(0)}$	Logical "0" Input Voltage	$V_{CC} = 5V$			1.5	V
$V_{OUT(1)}$	Logical "1" Output Voltage	$I_O = -360\,\mu A$	$V_{CC}-0.4$			V
$V_{OUT(0)}$	Logical "0" Output Voltage	$I_O = 1.6\,mA$			0.45	V
$V_{OUT(0)}$	Logical "0" Output Voltage EOC	$I_O = 1.2\,mA$			0.45	V
$I_{IN(1)}$	Logical "1" Input Current	$V_{IN} = 15V$			1.0	μA
	(The Control Inputs)					
$I_{IN(0)}$	Logical "0" Input Current	$V_{IN} = 0$	-1.0			μA
	(The Control Inputs)					
I_{CC}	Supply Current	Clock Frequency = 500 kHz		300	1000	μA
I_{OUT}	TRI-STATE Output Current	$V_O = 5V$			3	μA
		$V_O = 0$	-3			μA

Note 1: "Absolute Maximum Ratings" are those values beyond which the safety of the device cannot be guaranteed. Except for "Operating Temperature Range" they are not meant to imply that the devices should be operated at these limits. The table of "Electrical Characteristics" provides conditions for actual device operation.

Note 2: All voltages measured with respect to GND unless otherwise specified.

Note 3: Non-linearity error is the maximum deviation from a straight line through the end points of the A/D transfer characteristic, (Figure 2).

Note 4: Zero error is the difference between the output of an ideal and the actual A/D for zero input voltage, (Figure 2).

Note 5: Full-scale error is the difference between the output of an ideal and the actual A/D for full-scale input voltage, (Figure 2).

Note 6: Total unadjusted error is the maximum sum of non-linearity, zero and full-scale errors, (Figure 3).

Note 7: Quantization error is the ±1/2 LSB uncertainty caused by the converter's finite resolution, (Figure 3).

Note 8: Absolute Accuracy describes the difference between the actual input voltage and the full-scale weighted equivalent of the binary output code; included are quantizing and all other errors. Although rarely provided on data sheets, it is the best indication of a converter's true performance, (Figure 3).

Note 9: Supply rejection relates to the ability of an ADC to maintain accuracy as the supply voltage varies. The supply and $V_{REF(+)}$ are varied together and the change in accuracy is measured with respect to full-scale.

Note 10: Comparator input current is a bias current into or out of the chopper stabilized comparator. The bias current varies directly with clock frequency and has little temperature dependence, (Figure 5).

Courtesy National Semiconductor Corp.

LM3911 temperature controller

general description

The LM3911 is a highly accurate temperature measurement and/or control system for use over a −25°C to +85°C temperature range. Fabricated on a single monolithic chip, it includes a temperature sensor, a stable voltage reference and an operational amplifier.

The output voltage of the LM3911 is directly proportional to temperature in degrees Kelvin at 10 mV/°K. Using the internal op amp with external resistors any temperature scale factor is easily obtained. By connecting the op amp as a comparator, the output will switch as the temperature transverses the set-point making the device useful as an on-off temperature controller.

An active shunt regulator is connected across the power leads of the LM3911 to provide a stable 6.8V voltage reference for the sensing system. This allows the use of any power supply voltage with suitable external resistors.

The input bias current is low and relatively constant with temperature, ensuring high accuracy when high source impedance is used. Further, the output collector can be returned to a voltage higher than 6.8V allowing the LM3911 to drive lamps and relays up to a 35V supply.

The LM3911 uses the difference in emitter-base voltage of transistors operating at different current densities as the basic temperature sensitive element. Since this output depends only on transistor matching the same reliability and stability as present op amps can be expected.

The LM3911 is available in three package styles—a metal can 4-lead TO-5, a metal can TO-46 and an 8-lead epoxy mini-DIP. In the epoxy package all electrical connections are made on one side of the device allowing the other 4 leads to be used for attaching the LM3911 to the temperature source. The LM3911 is rated for operation over a −25°C to +85°C temperature range.

features

- Uncalibrated accuracy ±10°C
- Internal op amp with frequency compensation
- Linear output of 10 mV/°K (10 mV/°C)
- Can be calibrated in degrees Kelvin, Celsius or Fahrenheit
- Output can drive loads up to 35V
- Internal stable voltage reference
- Low cost

block diagram

typical applications

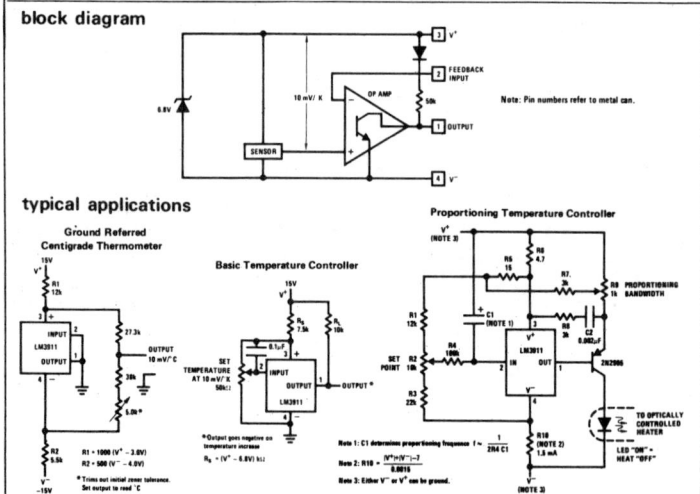

absolute maximum ratings

Supply Current (Externally Set)	10 mA	Operating Temperature Range	$-25°C$ to $+85°C$
Output Collector Voltage, V^{++}	36V	Storage Temperature Range	$-65°C$ to $+150°C$
Feedback Input Voltage Range	0V to +7.0V	Lead Temperature (Soldering, 10 seconds)	$300°C$
Output Short Circuit Duration	Indefinite		

electrical characteristics (Note 1)

PARAMETER	CONDITIONS	MIN	TYP	MAX	UNITS
SENSOR					
Output Voltage	$T_A = -25°C$, (Note 2)	2.36	2.48	2.60	V
Output Voltage	$T_A = 25°C$, (Note 2)	2.88	2.98	3.08	V
Output Voltage	$T_A = 85°C$, (Note 2)	3.46	3.58	3.70	V
Linearity	$\Delta T = 100°C$		0.5	2	%
Long-Term Stability			0.3		%
Repeatability			0.3		%
VOLTAGE REFERENCE					
Reverse Breakdown Voltage	$1\,mA \leq I_Z \leq 5\,mA$	6.55	6.85	7.25	V
Reverse Breakdown Voltage Change With Current	$1\,mA \leq I_Z \leq 5\,mA$		10	35	mV
Temperature Stability			20	85	mV
Dynamic Impedance	$I_Z = 1\,mA$		3.'		Ω
RMS Noise Voltage	$10\,Hz \leq f \leq 10\,kHz$		30		μV
Long Term Stability	$T_A = +85°C$		6.0		mV
OP AMP					
Input Bias Current	$T_A = +25°C$		35	150	nA
Input Bias Current			45	250	nA
Voltage Gain	$R_L = 36k, V^{++} = 36V$	2500	15000		V/V
Output Leakage Current	$T_A = 25°C$ (Note 3)		0.2	2	μA
Output Leakage Current	(Note 3)		1.0	8	μA
Output Source Current	$V_{OUT} \leq 3.70$	10			μA
Output Sink Current	$1V \leq V_{OUT} \leq 36V$	2.0			mA

Note 1: These specifications apply for $-25°C \leq T_A \leq +85°C$ and 0.9 mA $\leq I_{SUPPLY} \leq$ 1.1 mA unless otherwise specified; $C_L \leq 50$ pF.

Note 2: The output voltage applies to the basic thermometer configuration with the output and input terminals shorted and a load resistance of $\geq$ 1.0 MΩ. This is the feedback sense voltage and includes errors in both the sensor and op amp. This voltage is specified for the sensor in a rapidly stirred oil bath. The output is referred to V^+.

Note 3: The output leakage current is specified with $\geq$ 100 mV overdrive. Since this voltage changes with temperature, the voltage drive for turn-off changes and is defined as V_{OUT} (with output and input shorted) -100 mV. This specification applies for $V_{OUT} = 36V$.

application hints

Although the LM3911 is designed to be totally trouble-free, certain precautions should be taken to insure the best possible performance.

As with any temperature sensor, internal power dissipation will raise the sensor's temperature above ambient. Nominal suggested operating current for the shunt regulator is 1.0 mA and causes 7.0 mW of power dissipation. In free, still, air this raises the package temperature by about 1.2°K. Although the regulator will operate at higher reverse currents and the output will drive loads up to 5.0 mA, these higher currents will raise the sensor temperature to about 19°K above ambient—degrading accuracy. Therefore, the sensor should be operated at the lowest possible power level.

With moving air, liquid or surface temperature sensing, self-heating is not as great a problem since the measured media will conduct the heat from the sensor. Also, there are many small heat sinks designed for transistors which will improve heat transfer to the sensor from the surrounding medium. A small finned clip-on heat sink is quite effective in free-air. It should be mentioned that the LM3911 die is on the base of the package and therefore coupling to the base is preferrable.

The internal reference regulator provides a temperature stable voltage for offsetting the output or setting a comparison point in temperature controllers. However, since this reference is at the same temperature as the sensor temperature changes will also cause reference drift. For application where maximum accuracy is needed an external reference should be used. Of course, for fixed temperature controllers the internal reference is adequate.

Courtesy National Semiconductor Corp.

CMOS
8- and 16-Channel Analog Multiplexers

AD7506, AD7507

FEATURES
R_{ON}: 300Ω

R_{ON}: 300Ω
Power Dissipation: 1.5mW
TTL/DTL/CMOS Direct Interface
Break-Before-Make Switching
Replaces DG506/DG507

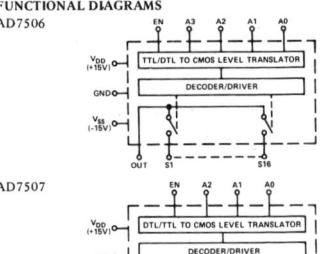

GENERAL DESCRIPTION
The AD7506 is a monolithic CMOS 16-channel analog multiplexer packaged in a 28-pin DIP. It switches a common output to one of 16 inputs, depending on the state of four address lines and an "enable". The AD7507 is identical to the
AD7506 except it has two outputs switched to two of 16
inputs depending on three binary address states and an "enable".

ABSOLUTE MAXIMUM RATINGS
(T_A = +25°C unless otherwise noted)

V_{DD} – GND . . . . +17V
V_{SS} – GND . . . . –17V
V Between Any Switch Terminals 25V
Digital Input Voltage Range . . . . V_{DD} to GND
Switch Current (I_S, Continuous) 20mA
Switch Current (I_S, Surge)
   1ms duration, 10% duty cycle 35mA
Power Dissipation (Package)
28 pin Ceramic DIP
   Up to +50°C 1000mW
   Derates above +50°C by . . . . 10mW/°C
28 pin Plastic DIP
   Up to +50°C 1200mW
   Derates above +50°C by . . . . 12mW/°C
Operating Temperature
   Plastic (J, K versions) . . . . 0 to +70°C
   Ceramic (J, K versions) . . . . –25°C to +85°C
   Ceramic (S, T versions) . . . . –55°C to +125°C
Storage Temperature . . . . –65°C to +150°C

CAUTION:
1. Do not apply voltages higher than V_{DD} and V_{SS} to any other terminal, especially
when $V_{SS} = V_{DD}$ = 0V all other pins should be at 0V.
2. The digital control inputs are zener protected; however, permanent damage may
occur on unconnected units under high energy electrostatic fields. Keep unused
units in conductive foam at all times.

FUNCTIONAL DIAGRAMS
AD7506

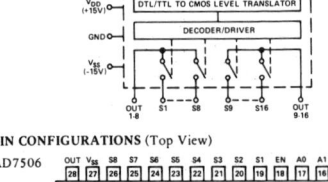

AD7507

PIN CONFIGURATIONS (Top View)
AD7506

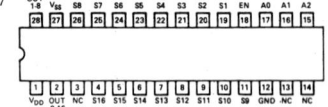

AD7507

Courtesy Analog Devices, Inc.

SPECIFICATIONS $(V_{DD} = +15V, V_{SS} = -15V$ unless otherwise noted)

PARAMETER	VERSION[1]	SWITCH CONDITION	@ +25°C	OVER SPECIFIED TEMP. RANGE	TEST CONDITIONS
ANALOG SWITCH					
R_{ON}	J, K	ON	300Ω typ, 450Ω max	550Ω max	$V_S = -10V$ to $+10V$, $I_S = 1mA$
	S, T	ON	400Ω max	500Ω max	
R_{ON} vs. V_S	All	ON	15% typ		
R_{ON} vs. Temperature	All	ON	0.5%/°C typ		
ΔR_{ON} Between Switches	All	ON	4% typ		$V_S = 0V$, $I_S = 1mA$
R_{ON} vs. Temperature Between Switches	All	ON	0.05%/°C typ		
I_S	J, K	OFF	0.05nA typ, 5nA max	50nA max	$V_S = -10V$, $V_{OUT} = +10V$
	S, T	OFF	0.05nA typ, 1nA max	50nA max	and
I_{OUT}	AD7506	J, K	OFF	0.3nA typ, 20nA max	500nA max	$V_S = +10V$, $V_{OUT} = -10V$
		S, T	OFF	0.3nA typ, 10nA max	500nA max	"Enable" Low
	AD7507	J, K	OFF	0.3nA typ, 10nA max	250nA max	
		S, T	OFF	0.3nA typ, 5nA max	250nA max	
$I_{OUT} - I_S$	AD7506	J, K	ON	0.3nA typ, 20nA max	500nA max	
		S, T	ON	0.3nA typ, 10nA max	500nA max	$V_S = 0$
	AD7507	J, K	ON	0.3nA typ, 10nA max	250nA max	
		S, T	ON	0.3nA typ, 5nA max	250nA max	
DIGITAL CONTROL					
V_{INL}				0.8V max	
V_{INH}	J, S			3.0V min	Note 2
	K, T			2.4V min	
I_{INL} or I_{INH}	All		10μA max	30μA max	
C_{IN}	All		3pF typ		
DYNAMIC CHARACTERISTICS[3]					
$t_{TRANSITION}$	J, S		700ns typ		V_{IN}: 0 to 3.0V
	K, T		700ns typ, 1000ns max		
t_{OPEN}	All		100ns typ		
t_{ON} (En)	J, S		0.8μs typ		V_{EN}: 0 to 3.0V
	K, T		1.5μs max		
t_{OFF} (En)	J, S		0.8μs typ		
	K, T		1μs max		
"OFF" Isolation	All		70dB typ		$V_{EN} = 0$, $R_L = 200Ω$, $C_L = 3.0pF$, $V_S = 3.0V$ rms, f = 50kHz
C_S	All	OFF	5pF typ		
C_{OUT}	AD7506	All	OFF	40pF typ		
	AD7507	All	OFF	20pF typ		
C_{S-OUT}	All	OFF	0.5pF typ		
C_{SS} Between Any Two Switches	All	OFF	0.5pF typ		
POWER SUPPLY					
I_{DD}	J, K	OFF	0.05mA typ, 1mA max		
	S, T	OFF	0.05mA typ, 1mA max	2mA max	All Digital Inputs Low
I_{SS}	J, K	OFF	0.05mA typ, 1mA max		
	S, T	OFF	0.05mA typ, 1mA max	2mA max	
I_{DD}	J, K	ON	0.3mA typ, 1mA max		
	S, T	ON	0.3mA typ, 1mA max	2mA max	All Digital Inputs High
I_{SS}	J, K	ON	0.05mA typ, 1mA max		
	S, T	ON	0.05mA typ, 1mA max	2mA max	

NOTES:
[1] JN, KN versions specified for 0 to +70°C; JD, KD versions for -25°C to +85°C; and SD, TD versions for -55°C to +125°C.
[2] A pullup resistor, typically 1-2kΩ is required to make the J and S versions compatible with TTL/DTL. The maximum value is determined by the output leakage current of the driver gate when in the high state.
[3] AC parameters are sample tested to ensure conformance to specifications.
Specifications subject to change without notice.

TRUTH TABLES

AD7506

A_3	A_2	A_1	A_0	E_N	"ON"
0	0	0	0	1	1
0	0	0	1	1	2
0	0	1	0	1	3
0	0	1	1	1	4
0	1	0	0	1	5
0	1	0	1	1	6
0	1	1	0	1	7
0	1	1	1	1	8
1	0	0	0	1	9
1	0	0	1	1	10
1	0	1	0	1	11
1	0	1	1	1	12
1	1	0	0	1	13
1	1	0	1	1	14
1	1	1	0	1	15
1	1	1	1	1	16
X	X	X	X	0	None

AD7507

A_2	A_1	A_0	E_N	"ON"
0	0	0	1	1 & 9
0	0	1	1	2 & 10
0	1	0	1	3 & 11
0	1	1	1	4 & 12
1	0	0	1	5 & 13
1	0	1	1	6 & 14
1	1	0	1	7 & 15
1	1	1	1	8 & 16
X	X	X	0	None

ORDERING INFORMATION

Plastic (Suffix N)	Ceramic (Suffix D)	Operating Temperature Range
AD7506JN		
AD7506KN		0 to +70°C
AD7507JN		
AD7507KN		
	AD7506JD	
	AD7506KD	-25°C to +85°C
	AD7507JD	
	AD7507KD	
	AD7506SD	
	AD7506TD	-55°C to +125°C
	AD7507SD	
	AD7507TD	

Courtesy Analog Devices, Inc.

Fast, Complete 12-Bit A/D Converter with Microprocessor Interface

AD574

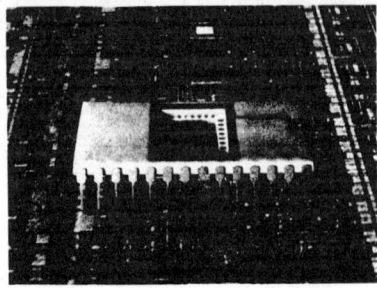

PRODUCT DESCRIPTION
The AD574 is a complete 12-bit successive-approximation analog-to-digital converter with 3-state output buffer circuitry for direct interface to an 8-, 12- or 16-bit microprocessor bus. The AD574 design is implemented with two LSI chips each containing both analog and digital circuitry, resulting in the maximum performance and flexibility at the lowest cost.

One chip is the high performance AD565 12-bit DAC and voltage reference. It contains the high speed current output switching circuitry, laser-trimmed thin film resistor network, low T.C. buried zener reference and the precision input scaling and bipolar offset resistors. This chip is laser-trimmed at the wafer stage (LWT) to adjust ladder network linearity, voltage reference tolerance and temperature coefficient, and the calibration accuracy of input scaling and bipolar offset resistors.

The second chip uses the newly-developed LCI (linear-compatible integrated logic) process to provide the low-power I^2L successive-approximation register, converter control circuitry, clock, bus interface, and the high performance latching comparator. The precision, low-drift comparator is adjusted for initial input offset error at the wafer stage by the "zener-zap" technique which trims the comparator input stage to 1/10 LSB typical error. This form of trimming, while cumbersome for complex ladder networks, is an attractive alternative to thin film resistor trimming for a simple offset adjustment and eliminates the need for thin film processing for this portion of the circuitry.

The AD574 is available in six different grades. The AD574J, K, and L grades are specified for operation over the 0 to +70°C temperature range. The AD574S, T, and U are specified for the −55°C to +125°C range. All grades are packaged in a low-profile, 0.600 inch wide, 28-pin hermetically-sealed ceramic DIP.

PRODUCT HIGHLIGHTS
1. The AD574 interfaces to most popular microprocessors with an 8-, 12-, or 16-bit bus without external buffers or peripheral interface controllers. Multiple-mode three-state output buffers connect directly to the data bus while the read and convert commands are taken from the control bus. The 12-bits of output data can be read either as one 12-bit word or as two 8-bit bytes (one with 8 data bits, the other with 4 data bits and 4 trailing zeros).

2. The AD574 will also operate equally well in a self-cycling, stand alone mode and can perform conversions and latch data into an external latch at a 40kHz sample rate.

3. The precision, laser-trimmed scaling and bipolar offset resistors provide four calibrated ranges, 0 to +10 and 0 to +20 volts unipolar, or −5 to +5 and −10 to +10 volts bipolar. Typical bipolar offset and full scale calibration of ±0.1% can be trimmed to zero with one external component each.

4. The internal buried zener reference is trimmed to 10.00 volts with a 1% maximum error and 15ppm/°C typical T.C. The reference is available externally and can drive up to 1.5mA beyond that required for the reference and bipolar offset resistors.

5. The two-chip construction renders the AD574 inherently more reliable than hybrid multi-chip designs. All three military grades have guaranteed linearity error over the full −55°C to +125°C and are especially recommended for high performance needs in harsh environments. These units are available fully processed to MIL-STD-883B, Level B.

Courtesy Analog Devices, Inc.

SPECIFICATIONS (typical @ +25°C with V_{CC} = +15, V_{LOGIC} = +5V, V_{DD} = -15V, unless otherwise specified)

DC AND TRANSFER ACCURACY SPECIFICATIONS

MODEL	AD574J	AD574K	AD574L	UNITS
RESOLUTION (max)	12	12	12	Bits
NONLINEARITY ERROR				
25°C (max)	±1	±1/2	±1/2	LSB
T_{min} to T_{max} (max)	±1	±1/2	±1/2	LSB
DIFFERENTIAL LINEARITY ERROR				
(Minimum resolution for which no				
missing codes are guaranteed)				
25°C	11	12	12	Bits
T_{min} to T_{max}	11	12	12	Bits
UNIPOLAR OFFSET (max) (Adjustable to zero)	±2	±1	±1	LSB
BIPOLAR OFFSET (max) (Adjustable to zero)	±10	±4	±4	LSB
FULL SCALE CALIBRATION ERROR				
(with fixed 50Ω resistor from REF OUT to REF IN)				
(Adjustable to zero) 25°C (max)	0.3	0.3	0.3	% of F.S.
T_{min} to T_{max} (Without Initial Adjustment)	0.5	0.4	0.35	% of F.S.
(With Initial Adjustment)	0.22	0.12	0.05	% of F.S.
TEMPERATURE RANGE		0 to +70		°C
TEMPERATURE COEFFICIENTS (Using internal reference)				
Guaranteed max change				
T_{min} to T_{max}				
Unipolar Offset	±2	±1	±1	LSB
	(10)	(5)	(5)	(ppm/°C)
Bipolar Offset	±2	±1	±1	LSB
	(10)	(5)	(5)	(ppm/°C)
Full Scale Calibration	±9	±5	±2	LSB
	(50)	(27)	(10)	(ppm/°C)
POWER SUPPLY REJECTION				
Max change in Full Scale Calibration				
+13.5V ≤ V_{CC} ≤ +16.5V	±2	±1	±1	LSB
+4.5V ≤ V_{LOGIC} ≤ +5.5V	±1/2	±1/2	±1/2	LSB
-16.5V ≤ V_{DD} ≤ -13.5V	±2	±1	±1	LSB
ANALOG INPUTS				
Input Ranges				
Bipolar		-5 to +5		Volts
		-10 to +10		Volts
Unipolar		0 to +10		Volts
		0 to +20		Volts
Input Impedance				
10 Volt Span		5k (3k min, 7k max)		Ω
20 Volt Span		10k (6k min, 14k max)		Ω
POWER SUPPLIES				
Operating Range				
V_{LOGIC}		+4.5 to +5.5		Volts
V_{CC}		+13.5 to +16.5		Volts
V_{DD}		-13.5 to -16.5		Volts
Operating Current				
V_{LOGIC}		30 typ., 40 max		mA
V_{CC}		2 typ., 5 max		mA
V_{DD}		18 typ., 30 max		mA
POWER DISSIPATION		450 typ., 725 max		mW
INTERNAL REFERENCE VOLTAGE		10.00 ±0.1 (max)		Volts
Output Current (available for external loads)		1.5 max		mA
(External load should not change during conversion)				

Specifications subject to change without notice.

Courtesy Analog Devices, Inc.

 **ANALOG
DEVICES**

CMOS 10-Bit,
Buffered Multiplying D/A Converter

AD7522

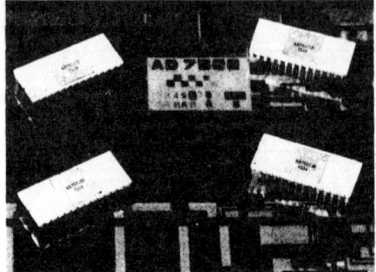

FEATURES
10-Bit Resolution
8-, 9- & 10-Bit Linearity
Microprocessor Compatible
Double Buffered Inputs
Serial or Parallel Loading
DTL/TTL/CMOS Direct Interface
Nonlinearity Tempco: 2ppm of FSR/°C
Gain Tempco: 10ppm of FSR/°C
Very Low Power Dissipation
Very Low Feedthrough

GENERAL DESCRIPTION

The AD7522 is a monolithic CMOS 10-bit multiplying D/A converter, with an input buffer and a holding register, allowing direct interface with microprocessors. Most applications require the addition of only an operational amplifier and a reference voltage.

The key to easy interface to a data bus is the AD7522's ability to load the input buffer in two bytes (an 8-bit and a 2-bit byte), and subsequently move this data to a holding register, where the digital word is converted into an analog current or voltage (with external operational amplifier). The input loading of either 8 or 10 bits can be done in a parallel or serial mode.

The AD7522 is packaged in a 28-pin DIP, and operates with a +15V main supply at 2mA max, and a logic supply of +5V for TTL interface, or +10 to +15V for CMOS interface.

A thin film on high density CMOS process, using silicon nitride passivation, ensures high reliability and excellent stability.

ORDERING INFORMATION

Nonlinearity	Temperature Range		
	0 to +70°C	–25°C to +85°C	–55°C to +125°C
0.2% (8-Bit)	AD7522JN	AD7522JD	AD7522SD
0.1% (9-Bit)	AD7522KN	AD7522KD	AD7522TD
0.05% (10-Bit)	AD7522LN	AD7522LD	AD7522UD

PACKAGE IDENTIFICATION

Suffix "D": Ceramic DIP Package
Suffix "N": Plastic DIP Package

FUNCTIONAL DIAGRAM

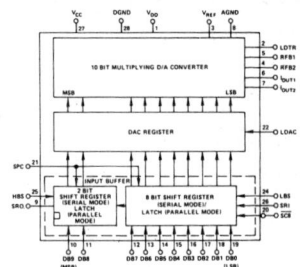

PIN CONFIGURATION

Courtesy Analog Devices, Inc.

SPECIFICATIONS (V_{DD} = +15V, V_{CC} = +5V, V_{REF} = ±10V, TA = +25°C unless otherwise noted)

PARAMETER		TA = +25°C	OVER SPECIFIED TEMP. RANGE	TEST CONDITIONS
STATIC ACCURACY				
Resolution	All	10 Bits min	10 Bits min	SC8 = "1"
Nonlinearity	AD7522J	±0.2% FSR max		
	AD7522S	±0.2% FSR max	±0.2% FSR max	
	AD7522K	±0.1% FSR max		
	AD7522T	±0.1% FSR max	±0.1% FSR max	
	AD7522L	±0.05% FSR max		
	AD7522U	±0.05% FSR max	±0.05% FSR max	$-10V \leqslant V_{REF} \leqslant +10V$
Nonlinearity Tempco[1]	AD7522J,K,L	±1ppm FSR/°C typ	±2ppm FSR/°C max	
	AD7522S,T,U		±2ppm FSR/°C max	
Gain Error	AD7522J,K,L	±0.3% Reading typ		
Gain Error Tempco[1]	AD7522J,K,L	±5ppm of Reading/°C typ	±10ppm of Reading/°C max	
	AD7522S,T,U		±10ppm of Reading/°C max	
Output Leakage Current	All		200nA max	I_{OUT1}: DB0 through DB9 = 0
at I_{OUT1} or I_{OUT2}				I_{OUT2}: DB0 through DB9 = 1
Power Supply Rejection	AD7522J,K,L	50ppm of Reading/% typ		
AC ACCURACY				
Feedthrough Error[1]	All	1mV p-p typ, 10mV p-p max		V_{REF}= 20V p-p; 10kHz
Output Current	AD7522J,K,L	500ns typ		To 0.05% of FSR for a FSR Step.
Settling Time				HBS and LBS Low to High
				LDAC = 1
REFERENCE INPUT				
Input Resistance	All	5kΩ min	20kΩ max	
ANALOG OUTPUT				
Output Capacitance				
C_{OUT1}	AD7522J,K,L	120pF typ		All Data Input High
C_{OUT2}	AD7522J,K,L	40pF typ		
C_{OUT1}	AD7522J,K,L	40pF typ		All Data Inputs Low
C_{OUT2}	AD7522J,K,L	120pF typ		
DIGITAL INPUTS				
Low State Threshold	All	0.8V max	0.8V max	V_{CC} = +5V
	All	1.5V max	1.5V max	V_{CC} = +15V
High State Threshold	All	2.4V min	2.4V min	V_{CC} = +5V
	All	13.5V min	13.5V min	V_{CC} = +15V
Input Current	AD7522J,K,L	1μA typ		
LDAC Pulse Width[1]	All	500ns min	500ns min	LDAC: 0 to +3V
HBS, LBS Pulse Width[1]	All	500ns min	500ns min	HBS, LBS: 0 to +3V
Serial Clock Frequency[1]	All	1MHz max	1MHz max	
HBS, LBS Data Set Up[2]	All	250ns min	250ns min	
Data Hold Time[3]	All	500ns min, 200ns typ	500ns min	
POWER REQUIREMENTS				
I_{DD}	All	2mA max		In Quiescent State
I_{CC}	All	2mA max		

Notes
[1] Guaranteed by design. Not tested.
[2] Data setup time is the minimum amount of time required for DB0 - DB9 to be stable prior to strobing HBS, LBS.
[3] Data hold time is the minimum amount of time required for DB0 - DB9 to be stable after strobing HBS, LBS.

Specifications subject to change without notice.

Courtesy Analog Devices, Inc.

SE/NE5018 F,N

DESCRIPTION

The NE5018 is a complete 8-bit digital to analog converter subsystem on one monolithic chip. The data inputs have input latches, controlled by a latch enable pin. The data and latch enable inputs are ultra-low loading for easy interfacing with all logic systems. The latches appear transparent when the $\overline{LE}$ input is in the low state. When $\overline{LE}$ goes high, the input data present at the moment of transition is latched and retained until $\overline{LE}$ again goes low. This feature allows easy compatibility with most micro-processors.

The chip also comprises a stable voltage reference (5V nominal) and a high slew rate buffer amplifier. The voltage reference may be externally trimmed with a potentiometer for easy adjustment of full scale, while maintaining a low temperature co-efficient.

The output of the buffer amplifier may be offset so as to provide bipolar as well as unipolar operation.

FEATURES

- 8-bit resolution
- Input latches
- Low-loading data inputs
- On-chip voltage reference
- Output buffer amplifier
- Accurate to ± 1/4 LSB (.1%)
- Monotonic to 8 bits
- Amplifier and reference both short-circuit protected
- Compatible with 2650,8080 and many other μP's

APPLICATIONS

- Precision 8-bit D/A converters
- A/D converters
- Programmable power supplies
- Test equipment
- Measuring instruments
- Analog-digital multiplication

PIN CONFIGURATION

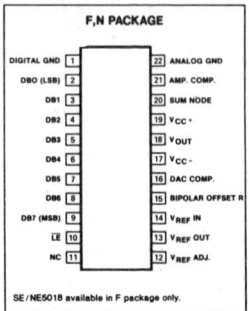

F,N PACKAGE

DIGITAL GND	1	22	ANALOG GND
DB0 (LSB)	2	21	AMP. COMP.
DB1	3	20	SUM NODE
DB2	4	19	$V_{CC}+$
DB3	5	18	V_{OUT}
DB4	6	17	$V_{CC}-$
DB5	7	16	DAC COMP.
DB6	8	15	BIPOLAR OFFSET R
DB7 (MSB)	9	14	V_{REF} IN
$\overline{LE}$	10	13	V_{REF} OUT
NC	11	12	V_{REF} ADJ.

SE/NE5018 available in F package only.

BLOCK DIAGRAM

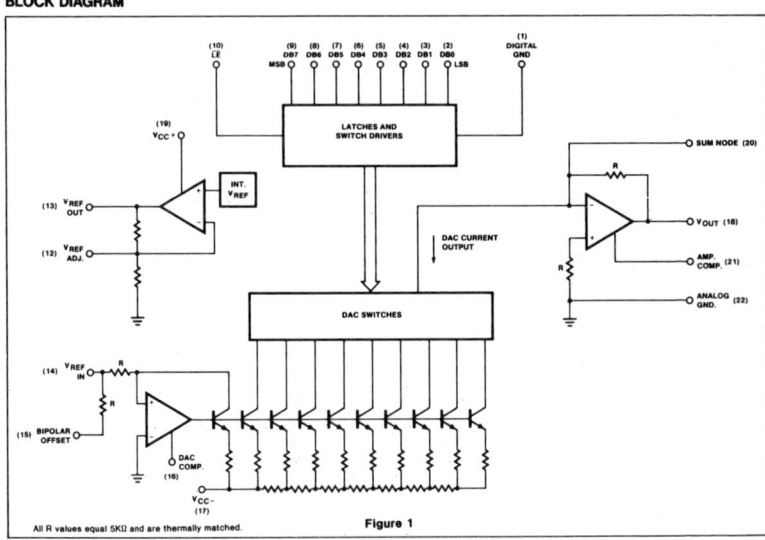

All R values equal 5KΩ and are thermally matched.

Figure 1

Courtesy Signetics Corp.

ABSOLUTE MAXIMUM RATINGS

	PARAMETER	RATING	UNIT
$V_{CC}+$	Positive supply voltage	18	V
$V_{CC}-$	Negative supply voltage	−18	V
V_{IN}	Logic input voltage	0 to 18	V
$V_{REF}IN$	Voltage at V_{REF} input	12	V
$V_{REF}ADJ$	Voltage at V_{REF} adjust	0 to V_{REF}	V
V_{SUM}	Voltage at sum node	12	V
I_{REFSC}	Short-circuit current to ground at V_{REF} OUT	Continuous	
I_{OUTSC}	Short-circuit current to ground or either supply at V_{OUT}	Continuous	
I_{REF}	Reference input current	5	mA
P_D	Power dissipation*		
	-N package	800	mW
	-F package	1000	mW
T_A	Operating temperature range		
	SE5018	−55 to +125	°C
	NE5018	0 to +70	°C
T_{STG}	Storage temperature range	−65 to +150	°C
T_{SOLD}	Lead soldering temperature (10 seconds)	300	°C

*NOTES
For N package, derate at 120°C/W above 35°C
For F package, derate at 75°C/W above 75°C

DC ELECTRICAL CHARACTERISTICS

$V_{CC}+ = +15V$, $V_{CC}- = -15V$, SE5018. $-55°C \leq T_A \leq 125°C$, NE5018. $0°C \leq T_A \leq 70°C$ unless otherwise specified! Typical values are specified at 25°C

PARAMETER		TEST CONDITIONS	SE5018			NE5018			UNIT
			Min	Typ	Max	Min	Typ	Max	
	Resolution		8	8	8	8	8	8	Bits
	Monotonicity		8	8	8	8	8	8	Bits
	Relative accuracy				±0.1			±0.1	%FS
$V_{CC}+$	Positive supply voltage		11.4	15		11.4	15		V
$V_{CC}-$	Negative supply voltage		−11.4	−15		−11.4	−15		V
$V_{IN(1)}$	Logic "1" input voltage	Pin 1 = 0V	2.0			2.0			V
$V_{IN(0)}$	Logic "0" input voltage	Pin 1 = 0V			0.8			0.8	V
$I_{IN(1)}$	Logic "1" input current	Pin 1 = 0V, $2V < V_{IN} < 18V$		0.1	10		0.1	·10	μA
$I_{IN(0)}$	Logic "0" input current	Pin 1 = 0V, $-5V < V_{IN} < 0.8V$		-2.0	−10		−2.0	−10	μA
V_{FS}	Full scale output voltage	Unipolar operation $V_{REF\ IN} = 5.000V$, $T_A = 25°C$	9.50	9.961	10.50	9.50	9.961	10.50	V
V_{FS}	Full scale output voltage	Bipolar operation $V_{REF\ IN} = 5.000V$, $T_A = 25°C$		+4.961 −5.000			+4.961 −5.000		V
V_{ZS}	Zero scale voltage			5			5		mV
I_{OS}	Output short circuit current	$T_A = 25°C$ $V_{OUT} = 0V$		15	40		15	40	mA
PSR+(out)	Output power supply rejection (+)	$V- = -15V$, $13.5V \leq V+ \leq 16.5V$, external $V_{REF\ IN} = 5.000V$		.001	.01		.001	.01	%FS/ %VS
PSR−(out)	Output power supply rejection (−)	$V+ = 15V$, $-13.5V \leq V- \leq -16.5V$, external $V_{REF\ IN} = 5.000V$		.001	.01		.001	.01	%FS/ %VS
TC_{FS}	Full scale temperature coefficient	$V_{REF\ IN} = 5.000V$		20			20		ppm/°C
TC_{ZS}	Zero scale temperature coefficient			5			5		ppm/°C

Courtesy Signetics Corp.

American Standard Code
for Information Interchange
(ASCII) Code Chart

					LEAST SIGNIFICANT BITS				
		000	001	010	011	100	101	110	111	
	00000	NUL	SOH	STX	ETX	EOT	ENQ	ACK	BEL	CONTROL
	00001	BS	HT	LF	VT	FF	CR	SO	SI	FUNC-
	00010	DLE	DC1	DC2	DC3	DC4	NAK	SYN	ETB	TIONS
	00011	CAN	EM	SUB	ESC	FS	GS	RS	US	
	00100	SP	!	"	#	$	%	&	"	
	00101	(	)	*	$	,	'	.	/	
MOST	00110	0	1	2	3	4	5	6	7	
SIGNIF-	00111	8	9	:	;	<	=	>	?	
ICANT	01000	@	A	B	C	D	E	F	G	
BITS	01001	H	I	J	K	L	M	N	O	
	01010	P	Q	R	S	T	U	V	W	
	01011	X	Y	Z	[	\	]	↑	—	
	01100	`	a	b	c	d	•	f	g	
	01101	h	i	j	k	l	m	n	o	
	01110	p	q	r	s	t	u	v	w	
	01111	x	y	z	{	:	}	~	DEL	

Control Character Functions

NUL = Null
SOH = Start of Heading
STX = Start of Text
ETX = End of Text
EOT = End of Transmission
ENQ = Enquiry
ACK = Acknowledge
BEL = Bell (ring)
BS = Backspace
HT = Horizontal Tabulation
LF = Line Feed
VT = Vertical Tabulation
FF = Form Feed
CR = Carriage Return
SO = Shift Out
SI = Shift In

DLE = Data Link Escape
DC1 = Device Control 1
DC2 = Device Control 2
DC3 = Device Control 3
DC4 = Device Control 4 (Stop)
NAK = Negative Acknowledge
SYN = Synchronous Idle
ETB = End of Transmission Block
CAN = Cancel
EM = End of Medium
SUB = Substitute
ESC = Escape
FS = File Separator
GS = Group Separator
RS = Record Separator
US = Unit Separator
DEL = Delete

Summary of the 6502 Instruction Set

The following notation applies to this summary:

A	Accumulator
X, Y	Index registers
M	Memory
P	Processor status register
S	Stack Pointer
√	Change
—	No change
+	Add
∧	Logical AND
—	Subtract
V	Logical Exclusive-OR
→, ←	Transfer to
⩲	Logical (inclusive) OR
PC	Program counter
PCH	Program counter high
PCL	Program counter low
#dd	8-bit immediate data value (2 hexadecimal digits)
aa	8-bit zero page address (2 hexadecimal digits)
aaaa	16-bit absolute address (4 hexadecimal digits)
↑	Transfer from stack (Pull)
↓	Transfer onto stack (Push)

ADC

Add to Accumulator with Carry

Operation: $A + M + C \rightarrow A, C$

N Z C I D V
√ √ √ − − √

Addressing Mode	Assembly Language Form		OP CODE	No. Bytes	No. Cycles
Immediate	ADC	#dd	69	2	2
Zero Page	ADC	aa	65	2	3
Zero Page, X	ADC	aa,X	75	2	4
Absolute	ADC	aaaa	6D	3	4
Absolute, X	ADC	aaaa,X	7D	3	4*
Absolute, Y	ADC	aaaa,Y	79	3	4*
(Indirect, X)	ADC	(aa,X)	61	2	6
(Indirect), Y	ADC	(aa),Y	71	2	5*

*Add 1 if page boundary is crossed.

AND

AND Memory with Accumulator

Logical AND to the accumulator
Operation: $A \wedge M \rightarrow A$

N Z C I D V
√ √ − − − −

Addressing Mode	Assembly Language Form		OP CODE	No. Bytes	No. Cycles
Immediate	AND	#dd	29	2	2
Zero Page	AND	aa	25	2	3
Zero Page, X	AND	aa,X	35	2	4
Absolute	AND	aaaa	2D	3	4
Absolute, X	AND	aaaa,X	3D	3	4*
Absolute, Y	AND	aaaa,Y	39	3	4*
(Indirect, X)	AND	(aa,X)	21	2	6
(Indirect), Y	AND	(aa),Y	31	2	5*

*Add 1 if page boundary is crossed.

ASL

Accumulator Shift Left

Operation: $C \leftarrow \boxed{7\,6\,5\,4\,3\,2\,1\,0} \leftarrow 0$

N Z C I D V
√ √ √ – – –

Addressing Mode	Assembly Language Form	OP CODE	No. Bytes	No. Cycles
Accumulator	ASL A	0A	1	2
Zero Page	ASL aa	06	2	5
Zero Page, X	ASL aa,X	16	2	6
Absolute	ASL aaaa	0E	3	6
Absolute, X	ASL aaaa,X	1E	3	7

BCC

Branch on Carry Clear

Operation: Branch on $C = 0$

N Z C I D V
– – – – – –

Addressing Mode	Assembly Language Form	OP CODE	No. Bytes	No. Cycles
Relative	BCC aa	90	2	2*

*Add 1 if branch occurs to same page.
 Add 2 if branch occurs to different page.
Note: AIM 65 will accept an absolute address as the operand (instruction format BCC aaaa), and convert it to a relative address.

BCS

Branch on Carry Set

Operation: Branch on $C = 1$

N Z C I D V
– – – – – –

Addressing Mode	Assembly Language Form	OP CODE	No. Bytes	No. Cycles
Relative	BCS aa	B0	2	2*

*Add 1 if branch occurs to same page.
 Add 2 if branch occurs to next page.
Note: AIM 65 will accept an absolute address as the operand (instruction format BCS aaaa), and convert it to a relative address.

BEQ

Branch on Result Equal to Zero

Operation: Branch on $Z = 1$

N Z C I D V
− − − − − −

Addressing Mode	Assembly Language Form	OP CODE	No. Bytes	No. Cycles
Relative	BEQ aa	F0	2	2*

*Add 1 if branch occurs to same page.
Add 2 if branch occurs to next page.
Note: AIM 65 will accept an absolute address as the operand (instruction format BEQ aaaa), and convert it to a relative address.

BIT

Test Bits in Memory with Accumulator

Operation: $A \wedge M, M_7 \rightarrow N, M_6 \rightarrow V$
    Bit 6 and 7 are transferred to the Status Register. If the result of $A \wedge M$ is zero then $Z = 1$, otherwise $Z = 0$

N Z C I D V
$M_7 \checkmark$ − − − M_6

Addressing Mode	Assembly Language Form	OP CODE	No. Bytes	No. Cycles
Zero Page	BIT aa	24	2	3
Absolute	BIT aaaa	2C	3	4

BMI

Branch on Result Minus

Operation: Branch on $N = 1$

N Z C I D V
− − − − − −

Addressing Mode	Assembly Language Form	OP CODE	No. Bytes	No. Cycles
Relative	BMI aa	30	2	2*

*Add 1 if branch occurs to same page.
Add 2 if branch occurs to different page.
Note: AIM 65 will accept an absolute address as the operand (instruction format BMI aaaa), and convert it to a relative address.

BNE

Branch on Result Not Equal to Zero

Operation: Branch on Z = 0

N Z C I D V
— — — — — —

Addressing Mode	Assembly Language Form	OP CODE	No. Bytes	No. Cycles
Relative	BNE aa	D0	2	2*

*Add 1 if branch occurs to same page.
Add 2 if branch occurs to different page.
Note: AIM 65 will accept an absolute address as the operand (instruction format BNE aaaa), and convert it to a relative address.

BPL

Branch on Result Plus

Operation: Branch on N = 0

N Z C I D V
— — — — — —

Addressing Mode	Assembly Language Form	OP CODE	No. Bytes	No. Cycles
Relative	BPL aa	10	2	2*

*Add 1 if branch occurs to same page.
Add 2 if branch occurs to different page.
Note: AIM 65 will accept an absolute address as the operand (instruction format BPL aaaa), and convert it to a relative address.

BRK

Force Break

Operation: Forced Interrupt PC + 2 ↓ P ↓

B N Z C I D V
1 — — — 1 — —

Addressing Mode	Assembly Language Form	OP CODE	No. Bytes	No. Cycles
Implied	BRK	00	1	7

BVC

Branch on Overflow Clear

Operation: Branch on V = 0

N Z C I D V
— — — — — —

Addressing Mode	Assembly Language Form	OP CODE	No. Bytes	No. Cycles
Relative	BVC aa	50	2	2*

*Add 1 if branch occurs to same page.
 Add 2 if branch occurs to different page.
Note: AIM 65 will accept an absolute address as the operand (instruction format BVC aaaa), and convert it to a relative address.

BVS

Branch on Overflow Set

Operation: Branch on V = 1

N Z C I D V
— — — — — —

Addressing Mode	Assembly Language Form	OP CODE	No. Bytes	No. Cycles
Relative	BVS aa	70	2	2*

*Add 1 if branch occurs to same page.
 Add 2 if branch occurs to different page.
Note: AIM 65 will accept an absolute address as the operand (instruction format BVS aaaa), and convert it to a relative address.

CLC

Clear Carry Flag

Operation: 0 → C

N Z C I D V
— — 0 — — —

Addressing Mode	Assembly Language Form	OP CODE	No Bytes	No. Cycles
Implied	CLC	18	1	2

CLD

Clear Decimal Mode

Operation: $0 \rightarrow D$

N Z C I D V
$-\ -\ -\ -\ 0\ -$

Addressing Mode	Assembly Language Form	OP CODE	No. Bytes	No. Cycles
Implied	CLD	D8	1	2

CLI

Clear Interrupt Disable Bit

Operation: $0 \rightarrow I$

N Z C I D V
$-\ -\ -\ 0\ -\ -$

Addressing Mode	Assembly Language Form	OP CODE	No. Bytes	No. Cycles
Implied	CLI	58	1	2

CLV

Clear Overflow Flag

Operation: $0 \rightarrow V$

N Z C I D V
$-\ -\ -\ -\ -\ 0$

Addressing Mode	Assembly Language Form	OP CODE	No. Bytes	No. Cycles
Implied	CLV	B8	1	2

CMP

Compare Memory and Accumulator

Operation: A − M

N Z C I D V
√ √ √ − − −

Addressing Mode	Assembly Language Form		OP CODE	No. Bytes	No. Cycles
Immediate	CMP	#dd	C9	2	2
Zero Page	CMP	aa	C5	2	3
Zero Page, X	CMP	aa,X	D5	2	4
Absolute	CMP	aaaa	CD	3	4
Absolute, X	CMP	aaaa,X	DD	3	4*
Absolute, Y	CMP	aaaa,Y	D9	3	4*
(Indirect, X)	CMP	(aa,X)	C1	2	6
(Indirect), Y	CMP	(aa),Y	D1	2	5*

*Add 1 if page boundary is crossed.

CPX

Compare Memory and Index X

Operation: X − M

N Z C I D V
√ √ √ − − −

Addressing Mode	Assembly Language Form		OP CODE	No. Bytes	No. Cycles
Immediate	CPX	#dd	E0	2	2
Zero Page	CPX	aa	E4	2	3
Absolute	CPX	aaaa	EC	3	4

CPY

Compare Memory and Index Y

Operation: Y − M

N Z C I D V
√ √ √ − − −

Addressing Mode	Assembly Language Form		OP CODE	No. Bytes	No. Cycles
Immediate	CPY	#dd	C0	2	2
Zero Page	CPY	aa	C4	2	3
Absolute	CPY	aaaa	CC	3	4

DEC

Decrement Memory by One

Operation: $M - 1 \to M$

N Z C I D V
√ √ − − − −

Addressing Mode	Assembly Language Form		OP CODE	No. Bytes	No. Cycles
Zero Page	DEC	aa	C6	2	5
Zero Page, X	DEC	aa,X	D6	2	6
Absolute	DEC	aaaa	CE	3	6
Absolute, X	DEC	aaaa,X	DE	3	7

DEX

Decrement Index X by One

Operation: $X - 1 \to X$

N Z C I D V
√ √ − − − −

Addressing Mode	Assembly Language Form	OP CODE	No. Bytes	No. Cycles
Implied	DEX	CA	1	2

DEY

Decrement Index Y by One

Operation: $Y - 1 \to Y$

N Z C I D V
√ √ − − − −

Addressing Mode	Assembly Language Form	OP CODE	No. Bytes	No. Cycles
Implied	DEY	88	1	2

EOR

Exclusive-OR Memory with Accumulator

Operation: A V M → A

NZCIDV
√ √ − − − −

Addressing Mode	Assembly Language Form		OP CODE	No. Bytes	No. Cycles
Immediate	EOR	#dd	49	2	2
Zero Page	EOR	aa	45	2	3
Zero Page, X	EOR	aa,X	55	2	4
Absolute	EOR	aaaa	4D	3	4
Absolute, X	EOR	aaaa,X	5D	3	4*
Absolute, Y	EOR	aaaa,Y	59	3	4*
(Indirect, X)	EOR	(aa,X)	41	2	6
(Indirect), Y	EOR	(aa),Y	51	2	5*

*Add 1 if page boundary is crossed.

INC

Increment Memory by One

Operation: M + 1 → M

NZCIDV
√ √ − − − −

Addressing Mode	Assembly Language Form		OP CODE	No. Bytes	No. Cycles
Zero Page	INC	aa	E6	2	5
Zero Page, X	INC	aa,X	F6	2	6
Absolute	INC	aaaa	EE	3	6
Absolute, X	INC	aaaa,X	FE	3	7

INX

Increment Index X by One

Operation: X + 1 → X

NZCIDV
√ √ − − − −

Addressing Mode	Assembly Language Form	OP CODE	No. Bytes	No. Cycles
Implied	INX	E8	1	2

INY

Increment Index Y by One

Operation: $Y + 1 \rightarrow Y$

N Z C I D V
√ √ − − − −

Addressing Mode	Assembly Language Form	OP Code	No. Bytes	No. Cycles
Implied	INY	C8	1	2

JMP

Jump

Operation: $(PC + 1) \rightarrow PCL$
$(PC + 2) \rightarrow PCH$

N Z C I D V
− − − − − −

Addressing Mode	Assembly Language Form	OP CODE	No. Bytes	No. Cycles
Absolute	JMP aaaa	4C	3	3
Indirect	JMP (aaaa)	6C	3	5

JSR

Jump to Subroutine

Operation: $PC + 2 \downarrow, (PC + 1) \rightarrow PCL$
$(PC + 2) \rightarrow PCH$

N Z C I D V
− − − − − −

Addressing Mode	Assembly Language Form	OP CODE	No. Bytes	No. Cycles
Absolute	JSR aaaa	20	3	6

LDA

Load Accumulator with Memory

Operation: M → A

N Z C I D V
√ √ − − − −

Addressing Mode	Assembly Language Form		OP CODE	No. Bytes	No. Cycles
Immediate	LDA	#dd	A9	2	2
Zero Page	LDA	aa	A5	2	3
Zero Page, X	LDA	aa,X	B5	2	4
Absolute	LDA	aaaa	AD	3	4
Absolute, X	LDA	aaaa,X	BD	3	4*
Absolute, Y	LDA	aaaa,Y	B9	3	4*
(Indirect, X)	LDA	(aa,X)	A1	2	6
(Indirect), Y	LDA	(aa),Y	B1	2	5*

*Add 1 if page boundary is crossed.

LDX

Load Index X with Memory

Operation: M → X

N Z C I D V
√ √ − − − −

Addressing Mode	Assembly Language Form		OP CODE	No. Bytes	No. Cycles
Immediate	LDX	#dd	A2	2	2
Zero Page	LDX	aa	A6	2	3
Zero Page, Y	LDX	aa,Y	B6	2	4
Absolute	LDX	aaaa	AE	3	4
Absolute, Y	LDX	aaaa,Y	BE	3	4*

*Add 1 when page boundary is crossed.

LDY

Load Index Y with Memory

Operation: M → Y

N Z C I D V
√ √ − − − −

Addressing Mode	Assembly Language Form		OP CODE	No. Bytes	No. Cycles
Immediate	LDY	#dd	A0	2	2
Zero Page	LDY	aa	A4	2	3
Zero Page, X	LDY	aea,X	B4	2	4
Absolute	LDY	aaaa	AC	3	4
Absolute, X	LDY	aaaa,X	BC	3	4*

*Add 1 when page boundary is crossed.

LSR

Logical Shift Right

Operation: 0 → | 7 | 6 | 5 | 4 | 3 | 2 | 1 | 0 | → C

N Z C I D V
0 √ √ − − −

Addressing Mode	Assembly Language Form		OP CODE	No. Bytes	No. Cycles
Accumulator	LSR	A	4A	1	2
Zero Page	LSR	aa	46	2	5
Zero Page, X	LSR	aa,X	56	2	6
Absolute	LSR	aaaa	4E	3	6
Absolute, X	LSR	aaaa,X	5E	3	7

NOP

No Operation

Operation: No Operation (2 cycles)

N Z C I D V
− − − − − −

Addressing Mode	Assembly Language Form	OP CODE	No. Bytes	No. Cycles
Implied	NOP	EA	1	2

ORA

OR Memory with Accumulator

Operation: A V M → A

N Z C I D V
√ √ – – – –

Addressing Mode	Assembly Language Form		OP CODE	No. Bytes	No. Cycles
Immediate	ORA	#dd	09	2	2
Zero Page	ORA	aa	05	2	3
Zero Page, X	ORA	aa,X	15	2	4
Absolute	ORA	aaaa	0D	3	4
Absolute, X	ORA	aaaa,X	1D	3	4*
Absolute, Y	ORA	aaaa,Y	19	3	4*
(Indirect, X)	ORA	(aa,X)	01	2	6
(Indirect), Y	ORA	(aa),Y	11	2	5*

*Add 1 on page crossing.

PHA

Push Accumulator on Stack

Operation: A ↓

N Z C I D V
– – – – – –

Addressing Mode	Assembly Language Form	OP CODE	No. Bytes	No. Cycles
Implied	PHA	48	1	3

PHP

Push Processor Status on Stack

Operation: P↓

N Z C I D V
– – – – – –

Addressing Mode	Assembly Language Form	OP CODE	No. Bytes	No. Cycles
Implied	PHP	08	1	3

PLA

Pull Accumulator from Stack

Operation: A ↑

```
N Z C I D V
√ √ — — — —
```

Addressing Mode	Assembly Language Form	OP CODE	No. Bytes	No. Cycles
Implied	PLA	68	1	4

PLP

Pull Processor Status from Stack

Operation: P ↑

```
N Z C I D V
From Stack
```

Addressing Mode	Assembly Language Form	OP CODE	No. Bytes	No. Cycles
Implied	PLP	28	1	4

ROL

Rotate Left

Operation:
```
         M or A
┌─────────────────────┐
│ 7 6 5 4 3 2 1 0 │ ← [C] ←┐
└─────────────────────┘      │
```

```
N Z C I D V
√ √ √ — — —
```

Addressing Mode	Assembly Language Form		OP CODE	No. Bytes	No. Cycles
Accumulator	ROL	A	2A	1	2
Zero Page	ROL	aa	26	2	5
Zero Page, X	ROL	aa,X	36	2	6
Absolute	ROL	aaaa	2E	3	6
Absolute, X	ROL	aaaa,X	3E	3	7

ROR

Rotate Right

Operation: $\longrightarrow \boxed{C} \rightarrow \boxed{\begin{array}{|c|c|c|c|c|c|c|c|} \hline 7 & 6 & 5 & 4 & 3 & 2 & 1 & 0 \\ \hline \end{array}}$ M or A

N Z C I D V
√ √ √ – – –

Addressing Mode	Assembly Language Form		OP CODE	No. Bytes	No. Cycles
Accumulator	ROR	A	6A	1	2
Zero Page	ROR	aa	66	2	5
Zero Page, X	ROR	aa,X	76	2	6
Absolute	ROR	aaaa	6E	3	6
Absolute, X	ROR	aaaa,X	7E	3	7

RTI

Return from Interrupt

Operation: P↑ PC↑

N Z C I D V
From Stack

Addressing Mode	Assembly Language Form	OP CODE	No. Bytes	No. Cycles
Implied	RTI	40	1	6

RTS

Return from Subroutine

Operation: PC↑, PC + 1 → PC

N Z C I D V
– – – – – –

Addressing Mode	Assembly Language Form	OP CODE	No. Bytes	No. Cycles
Implied	RTS	60	1	6

SBC

Subtract from Accumulator with Carry

Operation: $A - M - \overline{C} \rightarrow A$

Note: $\overline{C} = $ Borrow

N Z C I D V
√ √ √ − − √

Addressing Mode	Assembly Language Form		OP CODE	No. Bytes	No. Cycles
Immediate	SBC	#dd	E9	2	2
Zero Page	SBC	aa	E5	2	3
Zero Page, X	SBC	aa,X	F5	2	4
Absolute	SBC	aaaa	ED	3	4
Absolute, X	SBC	aaaa,X	FD	3	4*
Absolute, Y	SBC	aaaa,Y	F9	3	4*
(Indirect, X)	SBC	(aa,X)	E1	2	6
(Indirect), Y	SBC	(aa),Y	F1	2	5*

*Add 1 when page boundary is crossed.

SEC

Set Carry Flag

Operation: $1 \rightarrow C$

N Z C I D V
− − 1 − − −

Addressing Mode	Assembly Language Form	OP CODE	No. Bytes	No. Cycles
Implied	SEC	38	1	2

SED

Set Decimal Mode

Operation: $1 \rightarrow D$

N Z C I D V
− − − − 1 −

Addressing Mode	Assembly Language Form	OP CODE	No. Bytes	No. Cycles
Implied	SED	F8	1	2

SEI

Set Interrupt Disable Status

Operation: $1 \rightarrow I$

N Z C I D V
- - - 1 - -

Addressing Mode	Assembly Language Form	OP CODE	No. Bytes	No. Cycles
Implied	SEI	78	1	2

STA

Store Accumulator in Memory

Operation: $A \rightarrow M$

N Z C I D V
- - - - - -

Addressing Mode	Assembly Language Form	OP CODE	No. Bytes	No. Cycles
Zero Page	STA aa	85	2	3
Zero Page, X	STA aa,X	95	2	4
Absolute	STA aaaa	8D	3	4
Absolute, X	STA aaaa,X	9D	3	5
Absolute, Y	STA aaaa,Y	99	3	5
(Indirect, X)	STA (aa,X)	81	2	6
(Indirect), Y	STA (aa),Y	91	2	6

STX

Store Index X in Memory

Operation: $X \rightarrow M$

N Z C I D V
- - - - - -

Addressing Mode	Assembly Language Form	OP CODE	No. Bytes	No. Cycles
Zero Page	STX aa	86	2	3
Zero Page, Y	STX aa,Y	96	2	4
Absolute	STX aaaa	8E	3	4

STY

Store Index Y in Memory

Operation: $Y \rightarrow M$

Addressing Mode	Assembly Language Form	OP CODE	No. Bytes	No. Cycles
Zero Page	STY aa	84	2	3
Zero Page, X	STY aa,X	94	2	4
Absolute	STY aaaa	8C	3	4

TAX

Transfer Accumulator to Index X

Operation: $A \rightarrow X$

N Z C I D V
√ √ – – – –

Addressing Mode	Assembly Language Form	OP CODE	No. Bytes	No. Cycles
Implied	TAX	AA	1	2

TAY

Transfer Accumulator to Index Y

Operation: $A \rightarrow Y$

N Z C I D V
√ √ – – – –

Addressing Mode	Assembly Language Form	OP CODE	No. Bytes	No. Cycles
Implied	TAY	A8	1	2

TSX

Transfer Stack Pointer to Index X

Operation: S → X

```
N Z C I D V
√ √ — — — —
```

Addressing Mode	Assembly Language Form	OP CODE	No. Bytes	No. Cycles
Implied	TSX	BA	1	2

TXA

Transfer Index X to Accumulator

Operation: X → A

```
N Z C I D V
√ √ — — — —
```

Addressing Mode	Assembly Language Form	OP CODE	No. Bytes	No. Cycles
Implied	TXA	8A	1	2

TXS

Transfer Index X to Stack Pointer

Operation: X → S

```
N Z C I D V
— — — — — —
```

Addressing Mode	Assembly Language Form	OP CODE	No. Bytes	No. Cycles
Implied	TXS	9A	1	2

TYA

Transfer Index Y to Accumulator

Operation: Y → A

```
N Z C I D V
√ √ — — — —
```

Addressing Mode	Assembly Language Form	OP CODE	No. Bytes	No. Cycles
Implied	TYA	98	1	2

Index

Empty flag
  transmitter data buffer, 56
  transmitter register, 56
Enable register, interrupt, 31
Error
  framing, 61
  overrun, 61
  parity, 59
  time-delay, 76
  timing, 81

F

Feedback
  control, closed-loop, 116
    PID algorithm, 116
    proportional, 116
  loop, closed, 115
Fiber-optic load isolation, 134
Firing SCRs and triacs, 120
Flag
  data ready, 61
  set overflow, 15
  transmitter data buffer empty, 56
    register empty, 56
"Flying capacitor" isolation amplifier, 102
Format, paper-tape, 26
Four-quadrant D/A converter, 111
Four-quadrant multiplying D/A converter, 109
Framing error, 61
Frequency, clock, 11

G

Ground noise
  bypassing, 127
  cause, 125
Ground loops, 127
Ground node, 129
Ground-referenced logic, 124

H

Handshaking
  output, 47
  register, 48
  with interrupts, output, 49
  with mask register interrupt, 49
  with output port, 47
Handshaking logic
  input, 30
  with interrupts, 49
High-speed 12-bit data acquisition system, 99

I

Images in addresses, 20
Incandescent lamp load currents, 129
Indirect addressing, 9
Inductive load currents, 129
Input handshaking logic, 30
Input latching, 31
Input/output
  bit-mapped, 33
  fundamentals, 23-24
  page $FF, 11
Input port, 8-bit wide, 23
Input port design, advanced, 33
Input ports, 23
Instruction
  bit, 25
  load and logic, 24
  rotate, 25
  shift, 25
Instruction set, 6502, 165
Instrument amplifier, 102
Interface
  asynchronous serial, 61
  bit-mapped, 33-38
  bit-mapped output, 51
  8-bit D/A converter, 110
  inductive loads, 129
  interrupt, 27
  large-scale output, 43
  levels, 49
  levels, common, 106
  output pin-type readback, 44
  paper-tape reader, 28
  parallel output, 39
  pseudo register readback, 45
  readback register, 41
  real-time clock, 87
    software, 88
  16-channel data acquisition, 98
  temperature sensor, 102
  volume control, 120
Interface devices, asynchronous LSI, 62
Interface efficiency, output, 44
Interface software, readback, 42
Interrupt
  enable register, 31
  handshaking logic with, 49
  handshaking with mask register, 49
  interface, 27
  mask registers, 31
  multiple, 30
  nonmaskable, 18
  output handshaking, 49

Interrupt—cont
  register, 30
  request (IRQ), 16
  servicing, paper-tape reader, 29
  single, 27
Interval, stop bits, 56
Inverter, TTL, 124
I/O
  bit-mapped, 33
  fundamentals, 23-24
  page $FF, 11
IRQ signal, 16
Isolation amplifier, 104
Isolation, load current, 132-134

K

"Kluge," 124

L

Latch, octal transparent, 39
Latching, input, 31
LDA, 24
Level translater, D/A converter, 108
Load and logic instructions, 24
Load current
  isolation, 132
  optical isolation, 132
  paths, 128
Load isolation, fiber optics, 134
Logic
  arrays, programmable, 21
  ground-referenced, 124
  handshaking with interrupts, 49
  input handshaking, 30
  instructions, load, 24
Loudness compensation, audio, 120
LSI data sheets, 135
LSI devices, clock/timer, 86
LSI interface devices, asynchronous, 62

M

Mask register
  handshaking with interrupt, 49
  interrupt, 31
Measuring analog quantities, 90
Memory versus registers, 9
Modem control signals, 65
Monopolar signaling, 70
Monotonic D/A converter, 110
Multichannel A/D converter, 95
Multimode 16-bit counter/timer, 84
Multiple interrupts, 30
Multiplying D/A converters, 109

N

NMI signal, 18
Noise
  bypassing, ground, 127
  ground, cause of, 125
Noninductive load currents, 129
Noninverting buffer, 41
Nonmaskable interrupt (NMI), 18

O

Octal latch, 39
Optical isolation, load currents, 132
Optically isolated D/A converter, 112
Optoişolators, 132
Output handshaking, 47
Output handshaking with interrupts, 49
Output interface
  bit-mapped, 51
  efficiency, 44
  large-scale, 43
  parallel, 39
  pin-type readback, 44
Output ports, 39
Output port with handshaking, 47
Overflow flag, set, 15
Overrun error, 61

P

Page $FF and vectors, 10
Page $FF, I/O, 11
Page one and the stack, 10
Page zero addressing, 9
Paper-tape
  format, 26
  reader, 26
    interface, 28
    interrupt servicing, 29
Parallel output interface, 39
Parity bit, 59
Parity error, 59
Phase-angle firing, SCR, triac, 122
PID control algorithm, feedback, 117
Pin-type readback, output interface, 44
Pipelining, 12
PLAs, 21
Port
  clear address, bit-mapped, 53
  design, input, 33
  8-bit wide input, 23
  input, 23
  output, 39

READER SERVICE CARD

To better serve you, the reader, please take a moment to fill out this card, or a copy of it, for us. Not only will you be kept up to date on the Blacksburg Series books, but as an extra bonus, **we will randomly select five cards every month, from all of the cards sent to us during the previous month. The names that are drawn will win, absolutely free, a book from the Blacksburg Continuing Education Series.** Therefore, make sure to indicate your choice in the space provided below. For a complete listing of all the books to choose from, refer to the inside front cover of this book. Please, one card per person. Give everyone a chance.

In order to find out who has won a book in your area, call (703) 953-1861 anytime during the night or weekend. When you do call, an answering machine will let you know the monthly winners. Too good to be true? Just give us a call. Good luck.

If I win, please send me a copy of:

_____

I understand that this book will be sent to me absolutely free, if my card is selected.

For our information, how about telling us a little about yourself. We are interested in your occupation, how and where you normally purchase books and the books that you would like to see in the Blacksburg Series. We are also interested in finding authors for the series, so if you have a book idea, write to The Blacksburg Group, Inc., P.O. Box 242, Blacksburg, VA 24060 and ask for an Author Packet. We are also interested in TRS-80, APPLE, OSI and PET BASIC programs.

My occupation is _____
I buy books through/from _____
Would you buy books through the mail? _____
I'd like to see a book about _____
Name _____
Address _____
City _____
State _____ Zip _____

MAIL TO: BOOKS, BOX 715, BLACKSBURG, VA 24060
!!!!!PLEASE PRINT!!!!!

21836